Boston's Blues:

musicians' profiles

history

festivals

and radio listings

of blues music

in Boston

By Art Simas

ISBN: 0-7596-5271-6

This book is printed on acid free paper.

1stBooks – rev. 02/01/02

Acknowledgments

To my wife Debbie for her love and support.

Special thanks to Teo Leyasmeyer, T.J. Wheeler, Mighty Sam McClain and Ed Vadas, my blues gurus and teachers; James Montgomery and Shirley Lewis for their huge hearts; Ronnie Earl for his spirituality; J. Geils for sharing a few beers in his basement and talking about the old times; contributors Bob Margolin, Art Tipaldi, Cheryl Arena and Tom Hazeltine; and to hardworking blues people behind the scenes, such as Diana Shonk, editor and publisher of the Blues Audience newsletter, Mary Melodee Mena, who updates band listings twice a month for several publications, and Peter Cahill, secretary of the New England Blues Society to name but a few; Rosy Rosenblatt and Dave Bartlett of Tone-Cool Records; avid blues advocates Bob Montillio, Kenny Newall and Alan Muir; blues DJs Holly Harris, Mai Cramer, who gets credit for the title of the book, John Guregian, Greg Sarni, and the guys at WCUW in Worcester; and to all of the musicians who shared their stories and who continue to play the blues for us.

Thank you for technical assistance to: Cathy Cody, Kathy Diehl, "Shakey" Steve Prunier, Diana Shonk, and Debbie Simas.

On the cover:
From left to right, top row, James Montgomery, Mighty Sam McClain, Susan Tedeschi and Mike Welch. Second row, Ronnie Earl, Toni Lynn Washington, J. Geils, Luther "Guitar Junior" Johnson and Shirley Lewis.

Chapter 1:

the early scene

Dick Waterman: A true blues pioneer

What makes Greater Boston so special is its rich history of mingling generations, lifestyles and cultures. The area has always been a spawning ground for all who have a passion for music.

During the 1940s through the 1970s, Greater Boston was a required stop along the eastern seaboard, and practically the second home to many of the best musicians of the day. While the Totem Pole in Norumbega and the Cocoanut Grove on Piedmont Street in Bay Village (prior to the devastating fire in 1942) catered to the swing and dance crowd, there were many clubs that featured blues and blues-based music in Roxbury, the South End and in the former Combat Zone off Washington Street in Chinatown.

In the early to mid-1960s, Club 47, Joe's Place, The Unicorn, Paul's Mall, The Jazz Workshop, and many others featured folk, blues and roots-based music.

It wasn't unusual to see Joan Baez or Bob Dylan at one of the area's clubs one night, either performing or hanging out in the crowd, followed by Muddy Waters and Lightnin' Hopkins the next night.

"Back in those days, folk and blues were very much intertwined," according to Dick Waterman, a photojournalist and former manager of many top blues artists in the '60s and '70s.

"You cannot overemphasize the importance of the Newport Folk Festivals from '63 to '67 that drew over 50,000 people during the three-day festival -- an incredible eclectic mix. If you were great for 15 minutes you could ignite your career right there. If you used your time very well, people would leave talking about you and you could become famous overnight," Waterman said.

Teo Leyasmeyer, music director at the Cambridge House of Blues and a keyboard player, concurs with Waterman's assessment. "New England has always been fertile soil for musicians, especially blues musicians... I feel it very consistent and important for me as a way of reflecting the community since blues has influenced all kinds of music. I feel I have an obligation to honor that musical tradition."

For Waterman, that tradition began in the early 1960s. In '63-'64, Waterman was writing for Broadside Magazine, a folk magazine and also working for Manny

Boston's Blues

Greenhill for Folklore Productions. At the time, Greenhill was managing top folk stars such as Pete Seeger, Joan Baez and the Rev. Gary Davis.

Waterman was also busy cataloging the era through his photographs of the performers and places they called home for one or two weeks at a time -- places such as the Unicorn, Joe's Place, Ulysses, Jack's, Club 47, and Paul's Mall and The Jazz Workshop on Boylston Street.

In the mid-1960s, Waterman began booking acts at Club 47 in Cambridge -- Son House, Skip James and Lightnin' Hopkins. "At that time, there were no blues festivals, the market wasn't that big so you simply took what was out there.

"Most acts didn't like to play The Jazz Workshop because it was a seven-night gig with a Sunday matinee, so it was very long week," Waterman said. "Can you imagine trying to book someone today for seven straight days? But back then, that's how they did it."

A major turning point in the Greater Boston blues scene was the emergence of The Paul Butterfield Blues Band in 1965, Waterman said.

After serving as the backup group for Dylan's famous electric set at the 1965 Newport Folk Festival, the Butterfield Blues Band, minus Butterfield himself, was in an ideal position to take their Chicago style blues to a greater audience, Waterman said.

The band successfully fused the music of Elmore James, Muddy Waters, Howlin' Wolf, and others in creating a hard-driving, urban blues mix. They were a powerful force with Butterfield on harp, Elvin Bishop and Mike Bloomfield on guitars, Jerome Arnold on bass, and Sam Lay on drums.

In 1968, Waterman began his lifelong association with Bonnie Raitt, who was enrolled as a freshman at Radcliffe College. He helped her in getting gigs at Ulysses, near Porter Square and Jack's, near the Orson Welles Theater on Mass. Ave., in Cambridge. These early gigs primarily focused on blues material. She soon won a large enough following to break away from the academic world and concentrate on her newfound musical career, with Waterman at the helm. He continued to manage her career until 1986.

By 1971, Waterman was booking Joe's Place, owned by Joseph Spadafora. Joe's Place did a six-night week with no matinee on Sunday, and was closed Mondays. It became a local watering hole for George Thorogood, Raitt, Chris Smither, and dozens of other local musicians at the time, including members of the J. Geils Band.

Meanwhile, Waterman began booking more and more blues acts. "If I did anything for the Boston blues scene in a positive way, it was that I brought in acts that had not appeared in Boston for a very long time, such as T-Bone Walker, Hound Dog Taylor, Freddie King, Albert Collins, Big Mama Thornton, Otis Rush, Junior Wells, Buddy Guy, J.B. Hutto, Lowell Fulson, and Howlin' Wolf."

One particularly memorable occasion occurred when Wolf was booked for six nights. Because of the popularity of Wolf, Waterman was forced to increase the ticket price. "I kept apologizing to the people over and over because I had to raise the prices to $3 instead of $2 in order to pay Wolf," Waterman said. Despite the increase, the place was jammed every night.

The popularity of Joe's Place received interstate recognition drawing people from Worcester, southern Vermont and New Hampshire, according to Waterman. Radio station WBCN did a live, hour-long show at every Saturday night at 10 p.m. from the club.

"So the people knew of Joe's Place and were ready to party when they got there," he said.

Leyasmeyer said, "I remember when Hound Dog Taylor used to play there. There used to be lines around the block. He was one of the biggest draws ever. There was no such thing as sets for him. He'd just sit there and play with a bottle of Seagrams at his feet, playing slide -- loud -- with Ted Harvey and Brewer Phillips."

Interestingly, when George Thorogood visits the area, Leyasmeyer said, he always makes a point to go to a Korean Restaurant in Cambridge. That restaurant used to be Joe's Place.

"George says he just goes in and walks around for a while, then leaves. It's like a lighthouse for him because that was where he made the decision (after seeing Hound Dog) that this is what he was going to do for the rest of his life," Leyasmeyer said.

Behind the scenes

In addition to being associated with the blues from a business aspect, Dick Waterman continues to work behind the scenes by seeking to redress some of the wrongs administered by the recording industry. Many, many older blues artists were ripped off by record company executives. Waterman has gone to court to recoup royalties and residual payments for the estates of many of the true authors who never received the proper credit for their work.

Waterman recounts that in 1964, "I told Bukka White that several people were doing his song, 'Fixin to Die.' And he told me he hadn't gotten any money. So, in those days life was much simpler, so I just walked into Vanguard and said, "Buffy Sainte Marie has done 'Fixin to Die,' here's Bukka White's address, he's due some royalties. I walked into Electra and I said, Dave Ray (Snaker Dave Ray) has done 'Fixin to Die,' here's Bukka White's address. I walked into Columbia and said, 'Bob Dylan's done Bukka White's 'Fixin to Die' on his first album and he's due some money.'"

Waterman said, "Nowadays it's, 'My lawyer will meet your lawyer,' and they have lunch. But at that time, it was a lot simpler. 'Here's the guy's address, he's alive, send him his money.'"

In the 1990s, Waterman was able to get a sizable royalty settlement for Arthur "Big Boy" Crudup after he died for "That's All Right," which was covered by Elvis Presley and "Mean Old Frisco," which was covered by Elvis and Eric Clapton, among others.

"I've also got Sony to acknowledge a royalty debt of both artist royalties and songwriting royalties to Son House on the reissue CD that came out in '92. Although Son House died in 1988, Mrs. House was still alive, so I was able to get a very substantial financial acknowledgment from Sony on her behalf," Waterman said.

"I've also been honored to have friendships with people whom I've not had business relationships with," Waterman said. "People like Muddy, Wolf, B.B. King, Bobby Bland, Little Milton, Junior Walker, Brownie McGhee and Sonny Terry, and Robert Jr. Lockwood."

Update: Ex-Bostonian Dick Waterman is one important example of someone who was, and is, very influential in keeping this noble music alive. In the '60s, among others, he booked and managed Fred McDowell, Mississippi John Hurt,

Son House, Bonnie Raitt, Buddy Guy and Junior Wells. He found Son House living in Rochester, N.Y., and coaxed him out of retirement when no one knew what happened to him.

In 2000, Waterman was inducted into the Blues Foundation Hall of Fame for his dedication and work as an advocate for the blues.

Fred Taylor: The godfather of Boston promotions

Fred Taylor was a former mattress salesman who was between jobs in 1960.

He was known as a person who was reliable with the latest two-speed tape recording technology and he had a good ear because knew how to play piano, drums and trumpet.

After recording Joe Bucci from Malden, an extraordinary jazz B-3 organist, at Jackie's Game Bar in Lynn, Taylor sent the tape to Capitol Records -- and they signed Bucci to do a record.

"He had a great capability on the Hammond B-3 and he had feet that really played the pedals. He had a Krueger bass attachment to the pedals and he'd take bass solos with his left foot, leaving both hands free. He looked like he was playing handball because he would change stops, and he could emulate the Count Basie band because he had a set of mazzro chimes and vibes where he could throw a switch on the bottom keyboard and take a vibe solo while 'comping' on the upper board."

Taylor came up with the album concept, "Bucci Does Basie," which came out in 1961.

While he was waiting in Boston to make the trip to the recording studio in New York, Taylor walked into the Deli Bar on the corner of Stuart and Dartmouth across the street from the Back Bay station. "I saw this sign 'Dancing on the Weekends,' and asked the owner about what type of entertainment he had on the weekends. The owner, Harold Buckhalter, happened to own a string of bars in the area -- the Five O'Clock, The Sho-Bar, The Stables, practically all of the liquor joints in that area, and he decided to take a chance on Bucci, signing him to play six nights a week."

To ensure a good turnout, Taylor took out ads on WHDH radio between midnight and 2 a.m. for $6 to $8 a minute. Everyone who was into jazz was listening to that station. Bucci was a stunning success. Buckhalter was making money and Taylor forgot about going back into the mattress business.

Lenny's on the Turnpike and Wagon Wheels soon became hot spots for big band jazz greats such as Woody Herman, Stan Kenton, Harry James, Duke Ellington and Count Basie. The bands would stop over on their open dates on their way to bigger money at Lake Winnepesauke or other vacation spots further north. That started the craze, "The big bands are coming back" for an all-too-short revival. "So then I introduced the idea to some other places like the Beachcomber in Wollaston and King Phillip's in Wrentham and I had a little network going," Taylor said.

At the same time he was developing his contacts with big bands, Taylor was promoting and producing concerts. "In 1962 I got a call from George Wein's manager and we got Symphony Hall for him. And I did everything -- advertising, publicity, technical arrangement, scaled the house, and sold the damn thing out. Yet nobody even heard of this guy called Bob Dylan in 1962. He was an underground act at the time, but his manager at the time was Albert Grossman, who was a partner with George Wein, who had promoted the original Newport Folk Festivals. So that's how I started doing Peter Paul and Mary, Gordon Lightfoot and others. It all just happened, I never looked for it. We did a good job and they kept coming back."

When the Massachusetts Turnpike came through town, it devoured by eminent domain all of the bars that had been popular in the Back Bay. So Buckhalter moved his liquor licenses to Boylston Street. "So in 1963, he said he was going to open a little Jazz Workshop on Boylston Street, 'You can promote it and do the advertising for it,' Buckhalter told me. And so the first Jazz Workshop actually was in what was formerly The Stables," Taylor said.

"About a year later, Harold said he was going to build another place next door -- and that was the creation of Paul's Mall. I started doing booking and advertising for that too. Harold brought in Paul Valen, a popular piano player who was working at The Office Lounge, another place owned by Harold, and he thought Valen would be leader of the house band and general manager hence the name, Paul's Mall."

In the beginning, Paul's Mall was a comedy club -- Boston's first comedy club -- with such stars as Henny Youngman, who opened the club, Professor Irwin Corey and George Carlin.

Art Simas

After Paul Valen disappeared in 1965, Taylor was offered the chance to buy Paul's Mall. So he, Tony Moriello, who ran the Starlight Lounge in Allston (now the Wonder Bar) and a third partner acquired ownership of Paul's Mall. After that point, we turned more toward music acts, Taylor said.

Taylor was one of the first promoters to heavily use the airwaves for advertising, public relations and building relationships with the artists and the public. And the performers would do live interviews with Norm Nathan of WHDH at 2 a.m. (similar to what Mai Cramer at WGBH, Holly Harris at WBOS, John Guregian at WJUL and others do on their respective radio shows).

In 1966, Taylor and the partners acquired The Jazz Workshop. Two years later, they bought the Inner Circle restaurant. By 1969 they owned the whole complex and were also running the repertory-style Cinema 733.

Paul's Mall and the Jazz Workshop were unique in the U.S. There was no other complex that was back-to-back, and the performers raved about it to others when they went on the road.

"When you do your own little thing, you just don't know what you have here," Taylor said of the complex.

Both clubs influenced so many great local artists, and the musical spectrum was awesome -- from Miles Davis, John Coltrane and Dave Brubeck, to Bruce Springsteen (an opening act for David Bromberg in the early '70s) and Bette Midler, to Mississippi Fred McDowell, John Lee Hooker, Willie Dixon, Howlin' Wolf, Big Mama Thornton, and Muddy Waters, who played from 1967 until it closed in 1978. And so many others.

"In the early days, we played an artist for six nights," Taylor said. "So you really got to know an artist as a human being too. And the associations from those days led to a lot of the things that I do today" as music manager and talent buyer for Scullers at the Double Tree Guest Suites Hotel, 400 Soldiers Field Road, Boston. "When we first started, I was the booker, the advertising person, I did the graphics, sound and lights."

Taylor and friends also opened the first modern disco at the Braemore Hotel in Kenmore Square called The Forum, which was an "upscale disco with waitresses in Greek togas and all," he said.

"And all of this comes from Joe Bucci and Harold Buckhalter. I never planned anything," Taylor said.

Boston's Blues

Later on, Taylor was a force in promoting jazz at Great Woods (now known as the Tweeter Center off Route 140 in Mansfield, Mass.) and other venues around New England. He said he is especially proud of his association with promoting jazz tap dancers at the Opera House and at Great Woods.

"A club isn't four walls and a ceiling. A club is a person who wants to dedicate himself to a particular area of music... that's the definition of a club in this area when you talk about jazz, blues and folk. You don't get into it to get rich. That's the last thing. You want to make a living, but you can't expect much more than making a living. If you feel satisfied enough in what you're doing, then that's the extra compensation," Taylor said.

He added that musicians should always come back and hone their skills in a club atmosphere. "Don't get to the point to where you think it's beneath you. That's what I don't want to hear. Don't ever say, 'We don't play clubs.' That's like breaking off your right foot.

"The club is still the backbone of a performer's life. It's his workshop where he learns his craft and tries out his material. The experience of a performance in a club is a whole different ballgame than a concert. Not better, but a vital element," Taylor said. "You can practice till you're blue in the face, but until you play in front of an audience you don't know what's happening. The concert only happens because of the club. You feel the music, where the artist reacts to the people and the people react to the artist and a new thing is created because of it."

Web: www.scullersjazz.com

Cheryl Arena

Chapter 2:

profiles

Art Simas

Two of the most influential musicians of the Boston blues scene in the 1980s and 1990s are Matt Woodburn and Cheryl Arena.

Matt and Cheryl. Cheryl and Matt. During the course of interviewing many musicians, their names were mentioned the most because they helped others find their way within the Boston blues community.

Living and digging the blues in Boston

By Cheryl Arena

"I grew up in Belmont, Mass., and always had a passion for music.

My earliest childhood memories are of my parents' Billie Holiday and Louis Armstrong records... They also had this calypso record that I would dance around the house to, drumming on pieces of furniture.

I wanted to play drums at age 8. However my parents response was, 'Girls don't play drums.' Then I asked to play piano and they got me a "portable one" -- an accordian.

Determined to play music, I took lessons for two years, never really got the hang of it. By this time it was the mid-1960s; the Beatles were the rage and accordian was the last thing on my mind.

For the next five years I would be a listener and a dancer. I loved to dance to the Motown Sound, loved the Supremes and Little Stevie Wonder. I remember my babysitters listening to surf music like the Ventures and I really dug that kind of instrumental music too... still do.

By the time I was a teenager, the British invasion was in full swing and there were so many great bands like the Stones, Zeppelin and the Yardbirds, so at 15 when I got my first job, I bought a harmonica in the key of G and tried to play along with my records only to be totally frustrated, (not knowing you had to use different harps for each key the band's playing in), and quit after a year.

Boston's Blues

Then I saved up enough for a guitar. I wanted to play like Jeff Beck or Jimi Hendrix. Trouble was I had an acoustic guitar and it was virtually impossible to bend the strings to play like that.

A few years later I got an electric guitar and an amp and very quickly found out that the guitar had virtually little to do with my inability to play like Hendrix or Beck.

By the mid-1970s, there wasn't much on mainsteam radio that appealed to me and I started listening to jazz and fusion -- John McLaughlin, Weather Report, Chic Corea and so on. I worked at Wurlitzer's music store in Boston and went to the Jazz Workshop a lot. Little did I know that while I was listening to Mose Allison, right in the same building at Paul's Mall, Muddy Waters may have been playing and I missed out! The only blues I'd heard of and seen was B.B. King, James Cotton, Bonnie Raitt, James Montgomery and J. Geils.

I saw B.B. for $3 bucks at Harvard Stadium! I had heard Paul Butterfield and Canned Heat records and I saw Johnny Winter open for Led Zeppelin.

One rainy Sunday afternoon I heard Peter Green at a jam session at the YMCA in Cambridge (the alternate venue when the free concerts on the Cambridge Commons got rained out). I still had no idea of the vastness of the blues idiom at that point or where it came from.

In the late '70s I hooked up with an originals rock band that had a harmonica player (so they did some blues). I worked with them for seven years doing lights, sound and bookings. And they would have me up to play bass on a few tunes while the bass player played keys.

Eventually I got the courage to go off on my own and play bass in bands. Unfortunately, the bands I hooked up with were playing contemporary music of the '80s and though I was happy to be playing, I wasn't very inspired by the music.

At this point I was rapidly approaching 30 and feeling like I should give up music and get a "real job." So I started working at an electronics shop fixing amps. That didn't last long before I realized that music is a necessity for me, like food, water and air. I had to play!

That's when I started driving a limo. The hours were flexible which enabled me to pursue music again, only this time to my original instrument of choice, the harmonica. It was perfect. I had a briefcase full of harps and plenty of downtime to practice. The best thing that came from that job though was that the limo didn't have a tape deck, so I was forced to listen to the radio and that's when I discovered Mai Cramer's "Blues After Hours." I even remember the tune that made me stop and listen. It was Albert King doing "The Sky is Crying." I couldn't believe my ears. Who was this amazing singer/guitar player?

After that it was song after song of GREAT music!!! And the harp stuff...WOW! I started taping the show so I could remember all the artists' names and buy their records. I was like a little kid, so excited! I read books about the history of the blues, and it was all very fascinating to me. I could see how much the music I had always gravitated toward was influenced by the blues.

That was the beginning of a whole new world for me. I can remember being so into Janis Joplin in the late '60s and feeling like there was no other woman that could get down and dirty like her and now I was discovering all these great strong women like Big Mama Thorton, Besse Smith, Ida Cox, Memphis Minnie, Ma Rainey, Etta James, and the list goes on and on. The vastness of variety in stylings of the blues is what keeps me interested to seek more. It is utterly impossible to name all my influences but some of my favorites are Bill Broonzy, Magic Sam, Howlin' Wolf, Sonny Terry, and of course Walter Jacobs.

In 1987, I heard about the 1369 blues jam (in Cambridge) and immediately went down there with my bass and a few harps. At this point I had only been messin' with the harp for a few months. I sat in on bass and then decided to try my luck on harp. The response was overwhelming. People went nuts! What a feeling that was! That was it. After all the years of practicing so hard to play various instruments, here was an instrument that was natural for me and seemingly easy to play.

Well, it may have seemed easy at first but what I soon found out was that harmonica is one of the easiest instruments to play and one of the hardest instruments to play well. But I was ready for the challenge because it just felt so right and I could express myself so much more than I could on any other instrument.

After 13 years it's still a challenge and I still love it! I found my niche. I'm self-taught for the most part, aside from pointers here and there from various harp players and a few years ago I took about five lessons from Sonny Jr. who helped me a lot. I'm also a big advocate for Jerry Portnoy's three CD Harp Masterclass. And back in the 1369 days, I hung out with Annie Raines a lot. Obviously, we had a common bond.

Boston's Blues

I met a lot of great musicians at the jams. Gordon Beadle was one of the first people I met. He's an amazing talent and a great person, a friend for life no doubt. I learned a lot from him, from playing horn lines with him to listening to the blues tapes he's made for me.

Barbeque Bob Maglinte was also very willing to share his knowledge with me from harp licks to blues history and "tube talk." There were also some real characters like Earring George Mayweather, Silas Junior, and Mr. Cantab himself, Little Joe Cook. Just about everyone I've met to this day has been so helpful in so many ways. I have an extended family in the blues community for sure!

After going to the jams for two years, I started and ran my own jam at Wally's Café in the South End of Boston every Monday night for three years. That was great fun! Bruce Bears from Toni Lynn Washington's band played keys in the house band with me. It was packed every night!

Matt Woodburn used to come down and sit in sometimes, and I'd see him at his jam that he ran with Tim Gearan (another member of Toni Lynn's band), at Johnny D's in Somerville.

One Sunday afternoon a mutual friend of mine and Matt's kinda fixed us up. Matt eventually joined my band at Wally's, and in 1992 we decided to start our own band with Matt fronting the band. We used his nickname "the Kat in the Hat" for the band name. He got the name because he always wore a hat.

Another significant thing happened in 1992. We got married -- and what a wedding we had! There were lots of great musicians there and we played nonstop with all our friends.

We put out our first CD as Kat in 1996, and did some road trips down south to Virginia, North Carolina, Florida, Memphis, and Mississippi.

Going to the Delta gave me a feeling that is hard to describe. It felt like home and when I got the opportunity to go to Junior Kimbrough's place in Chulahoma, Miss., I thought I'd died and gone to "blues heaven." I got to play with Junior's son David and several other sons and grandsons of Junior and R.L. Burnside. The whole vibe of the place was wonderful and the people were so friendly and welcoming. It was the real deal, a real juke joint. That North Mississippi sound, that deep blues, that hypnotic drone is definitely one of my favorite styles of blues.

Art Simas

I have been very fortunate to have had the chance to sit in with some legendary blues players -- the most significant being Johnny Copeland. He was a prophetic songwriter, an amazing singer and guitar player and most of all, a very sweet person with a heart of gold.

Matt and I loved Johnny, we opened for him a few times and saw him whenever we could. He would always invite us up to play with him. The first time we opened for Johnny was at Ed Burke's in Boston, and we covered some of his tunes. Well, he loved it so much he invited me up to play with him. I was floored, he just kept eggin' me on to play a longer solo. I think he even gave me two solos in one song. I can still see him smiling. I miss him a lot. (He died July 3, 1997.) I'm happy to see his daughter Shemekia out there doin' it; she's got a great spirit just like her dad.

In '94, Matt and I went out to Chicago where I got to play on Maxwell Street before it was torn down, and I got to sit in with Junior Wells at the Checkerboard. When R.L. Burnside played at the House of Blues I showed him the pictures I had from Junior Wells' place and he invited me to sit in. I have pictures from that night too, and I don't think I've ever looked happier.

We met Honeyboy Edwards at the Boston Blues Festival and he came to our gig that night and sat in with us! And anytime we're at the Rynborn in Antrim, N.H., if Luther's (Johnson) home, he'll stop by and sit in with us. He's a lot of fun to play with.

Last year on my birthday I got to sit in with Louisiana Red at the House of Blues, and what a thrill that was!

I have been blessed with many opportunities to play with great musicians and to live in a place where there are so many awesome local musicians. So this is why when I was approached to do a jam at the Marketplace Café in Faneuil Hall in Boston, I told them I would rather do an "invite jam," so I could get to play with all my old buddies who I used to hang out with at the jams and never get to play with anymore cuz' we're all in our own bands.

Well, it's been the best learning experience to date. Every Tuesday night for the last five years I have had the opportunity to play with the best musicians in town!!! Every week is different. I put together a seven-piece band, including harp, guitar, bass, drums, keys, sax, and a singer.

With the talent we have here in Boston it's pretty easy to have a smokin' improv combo. I like to change it up and have maybe a second guitar, or two singers or

Boston's Blues

whatever strikes my fancy. It's really my baby and I have so much fun with it! The idea is to constantly mix things up and have FUN!

Some of my guest singers and players to date have been Toni Lynn Washington, Ed Scheer, Vykki Vox, Brian Templeton, Michelle Willson, Rick Russell, K.D. Bell, James Montgomery, Anita Suhanin, Scotty Shetler, Gordon Beadle, Dave Limina, Susan Tedeschi, Mike Welch, Cheryl Renee, Buck and Byrd Taylor, Dave Haley, Peter Malick, Alizon Lissance, Bruce Bears, Tom West, Marty Richards, Dean Cassell, Dave Hull, Bobby Killoran, Jesse Williams, Sandra Wright, Ed Spargo, Craig Macintyre, Tim Gearan, Paul Ahlstrand, Lou Ulrich, Kenny Gardner, Barbeque Bob, Chris Brown, Madeline Hall, John and Scott Aruda, J. Place, Shirley Lewis, Sweet Roy Jones, Amyl Justin, Teo Leyasmeyer and others I'm sure I'll think of later and kick myself eternally for forgetting to mention, for I love them all and appreciate them sharing their time and talent with me.

I feel very blessed to have so many wonderful and talented friends around me. There is truly a special group of people (musicians) in Boston and I'll tell ya that's what keeps me here, cuz' it sure ain't the weather.

In '97, we changed the name of the band to the Woodburn-Arena band. Matt stopped wearing the hat and the name didn't make sense anymore, too many people were associating us with Dr. Seuss and children's books, which had nothing to do with us.

In '99 we put out our second CD called "Juke Joint," a tribute to some of our blues heroes.

In all my musical experience, the last 13 years since I've been playing harmonica have been the most rewarding and memorable. I love to play and sing the blues. When I play, it comes from my heart and deep in my soul. The connection that I feel with the audience when they're diggin' it is hard to describe. It's an energy exchange that I thrive off of.

When I play for people who are into it, the connection is complete and when I play with musicians who are diggin' what I do, well that's the highest compliment I could ever get. That's it for me, people and music.

Recently, we did a festival in Tallahassee, Fla., at Dave's CC Club, a Blues Gathering in honor of Martin Luther King Jr. At the after-the-fest-jam, I sat in with Johnny Rawls and after I played, he said, 'Give it up for Cheryl Arena from Mississippi.'

And I said, 'I'm from Boston.'

His reply was, 'You may be from Boston but your heart's from Mississippi!'

I do believe that's true… maybe in a past life."

Matt Woodburn

Art Simas

Matt Woodburn: The former 'kat in the hat' who plays a sweet guitar

Matt Woodburn grew up in the Flatbush section of Brooklyn, N.Y. "I lived there until I was 15 and then I moved to Manhasset on Long Island and lived there for four years. Then when I was 19 I moved up here. I attended school at Berklee (College of Music) for about a year, which is where I met Gordon Beadle, one of my best friends, and he's really responsible for turning me onto the blues. I was already listening to the blues. I had been listening and playing the blues since I was about 17 and also playing rock and reggae and a lot of other things. Once I started palling around with Gordon, he was always a real explorer and he'd be out running around, finding out where places were, like the 1369, and he turned me on to that.

"The first guitar player I ever heard down there was Chris 'Stovall' Brown and I was so impressed with him. Back then he was playing a lot of Freddie King stuff and I was like super into Freddie King. So it was really cool to go into that little place and hear him and Earring George (Mayweather) and a bunch of other people.

"Chris stopped doing the jam down there for a while and I became the house guitar player with Silas Hubbard for a short period of time in mid-'80s," Woodburn said.

The 1369 was closed in the late 1980s and was transformed into "some yuppy-like chicken joint. Now it's a coffee shop," he added wryly.

"Sometimes, people that listen to the blues want to keep it this little underground society. I understand that because it's a cool kind of music and they want to keep it for themselves and they don't want to commercialize it. But at the same time, by it not being commercialized, it makes us not be able to make a living. It's kind of not there. And why not have it be available to the masses? It's not out there on the forefront and it should be because it's definitely better than a lot of the stuff that is out there now. And if more people were exposed to it, more people would be interested. More people would be buying the records," Woodburn said.

"I got into an original rock band, the Young Guns, for about a year after the 1369. And then I joined the Motor City Rhythm Kings which featured vocalist Amyl Justin. I worked with him and his band for close to four years. He's still one of my very best friends. We still play a lot of music together. Then I got in the band with Tim Gearan and Paul Ahlstrand who are in Toni Lynn

Boston's Blues

Washington's band now. So I did that for a while, probably about a year, and we also ran the jam at Johnny D's for about that length of time. That was the Renegades.

"I don't know how he (Gearan) does it, running a jam is tough work. The rule was, we'd give everybody a chance, because that's what it's about, how to play with other musicians and getting a feel for being on stage and all that. But if you're not ready to be there and you get up there, we wouldn't try to discourage them, but we let the people know you need a little more time and you can come back. You'd hear George Mayweather yell out, 'Practice at home!' That's something that's always stuck with us. He was a funny character. He was really good too. I learned a lot playing behind him at Wally's and he taught me about Chicago blues.

"After the Renegades split up Cheryl and I started to put something together. I'm not making a lot of money, but I'm able to make a living playing music in this area which I'm very grateful for and it's also exposed me to a lot of really good musicians and really fine people. And I really get the sense of family from the musicians that I know around here. We're all very close and we help each other. That's really nice. And I'm really grateful for those things. I've been to other parts of the country and stuff and it's fun to travel but I know that when I come back here that I have a lot of friends and a lot of people that I can count on."

Woodburn said that it's difficult to pinpoint The Boston Sound. "That's an interesting question, and also difficult to answer because, I mean, even Rhode Island guys have their own sound which is kind of like the Texas sound. I think the Boston sound draws more from certain regional styles than others. There seems to be a lot of people playing swing around here, a lot of jump music and stuff which you don't see in other parts of the country as much: a lot more horn-dance stuff, such as Toni Lynn's band and the Love Dogs. There's a lot of big-type of bands, but then you have the smaller bands like us and the (former) Radio Kings where we draw more from Chicago and Texas, and the West Coast sound.

"You can't really put your finger on it as to like a definite one thing because there are so many things that make the sound of this scene. I think most of the good bands are constantly evolving, not necessarily completely changing their style but incorporating different elements of music into their style. I know that's what we do. Since we made our first record ("Time Keeps Rolling") we've changed a lot in terms of the style of things that we're doing. We're kind of going more for the traditional thing now (on the second CD which was released in 1999, "Juke Joint.") It's different and it's really fun to explore the different areas and try to zero in on those sounds. It gives you more of a pallet to paint from when you're trying to come up with your own style," Woodburn said.

'Sax' Gordon Beadle

Art Simas
If it's big, bold and brassy it's gotta be 'Sax' Gordon Beadle

The big brassy sound from Gordon Beadle is a throwback to a time when honkers ruled the roost in the early rock 'n' roll world and when jazz songs were built around horn arrangements. The bigger the sound, the better Beadle loves it.

One of the most personable guys you'll ever meet, Beadle says, "I like fun music. I want to feel good, and I lean toward the older sax players who had that sound that was big and rockin', back to the days when the horn was the big thing going on in the band. I naturally like that."

Beadle, or Sax Gordon as he is known around Boston, has earned the respect of all in the business through hard work. He's a much sought-after session player here and along the East Coast. And let's not forget his excursions to Europe, where he and his brother-in-law, Leonardo Boni, regularly crisscrossed the continent, ending up back in Boni's native Italy. Beadle married Boni's sister, Marina, and they have a son.

More recently he's done stellar work with the Duke Robillard Band, which has taken him to gigs as far away as Australia, New Zealand, Brazil and Europe, and often plays with Boston's party band, The Love Dogs.

In 1996 Beadle signed with Bullseye Blues and released "Have Horn Will Travel" in 1997, a good-time, swingin' solo effort that has further propelled him toward stardom. He followed up that album with "You Knock Me Out," in 1999, also on the Bullseye Blues and Jazz label. Both efforts were produced by Duke Robillard.

He also played with the Hot Tamale Brass Band, led by percussionist Mickey Bones, and occasionally sits in with Little Red and the Riders, a swing dance group based in Worcester.

Born in Detroit, Beadle was raised in Davis, Calif., where his parents encouraged his interest in saxophone. Being in high school jazz bands taught him how to play before an audience.

"I'd do a gig for the elementary school swim party just to have an audience," he confessed.

Boston's Blues

As he got older, saxophone stars Gene Ammons, King Curtis, Ike Quebec, Illinois Jacquet, Chicago blues great J.T. Brown, Clarence Clemens and Big Jay McNeeley got his attention.

He came to Boston to attend Berklee, but only stayed a few semesters. So he went out and sought his own work. "I discovered the saxophone is fairly easy to work into a new band," he said. "The key is to focus the band while getting the audience involved in the music, even if I have to dance on the tables to do it."

Beadle sat in with many noted artists, but his four years with Grammy Award-winning guitarist Luther "Guitar Jr." Johnson established him as a top-notch player. "It's impossible to upstage an exciting performer like Luther, so you can cut loose as a musician and still contribute positively to the band's overall sound," he said.

This important relationship led to gigs and recordings with Matt "Guitar" Murphy, Charles Brown, Jimmy McCracklin with Irma Thomas, Ron Levy and Champion Jack Dupree, and many others. He even toured with Canadian rocker Colin James, opening stadium extravaganzas for The Rolling Stones' Voodoo Lounge tour. "We rode in elegant buses and ate gourmet food. It was the most luxurious tour I've ever been on," he says. "But no, we didn't actually hang with Mick."

"Boston has definitely been good to me, although the club scene isn't what it used to be. But when I was coming up, I certainly had a lot of opportunities to play with both local people and people passing through and I met a lot of people that way.

"I've thought about going to New Orleans or San Francisco," Beadle said, "but I guess I'm too broke to move for one thing. It's tough to pack up and go. Plus my wife is teaching and doing something she's always wanted to do. And, I do a lot of traveling anyway, so in some cases, it wouldn't matter where I lived."

Although Beadle's known primarily as a sideman in the U.S., he's also established himself in Europe. "I first did some major work there in 1995... and Leonardo Boni was working at home with a talented Italian blues singer, Gianna Cerchier. I came along for two months as a special guest at festivals, clubs and concerts from Sicily to Switzerland. Leo and I would use long cords to go into audiences, and they loved it, and we got great press," Beadle said.

Art Simas

In 1996, he returned to Italy after a tour with Duke Robillard and John Hammond. "Leo and I appeared on a national blues radio show and played a major concert venue in Florence.

"Personally and saxophonistically," Beadle recalls, "it was a terrific experience."

Beadle is now on his second stint as the sax man in Duke Robillard's band. "He (Robillard) and his band are such versatile musicians," Beadle said, "everyone listens to each other on a very high level. We do all kinds of blues, from jazz-oriented to rock to the sensitive, acoustic material. Duke's band explores the subtleties of volume and dimension. Every night we play, it continues my artistic education."

Beadle has played sax on two recorded songs used as soundtracks on episodes of "Homicide" and "Dark Skies" television series; recorded with piano greats Pinetop Perkins and Dave Maxwell, and Kansas City legend Jay McShann, whom Beadle describes as "the heaviest artist I've worked with -- a true original."

As he keeps piling on the credits to his musical career, he's making friends wherever he goes.

Web: harp.rounder.com

Boston's Blues
From road warrior to E-mail preacher:
The life of Bob Bell with Roomful of Blues

I don't care if they are your best friends.

When you travel around the country in an aging, arthritic Chevy Suburban hitched to a U-Haul trailer for weeks or even months at a time with 10 guys, "It's a recipe for torture," says Bob H. Bell, Roomful of Blues former road manager and now evangelist for the group, which is more popular than ever.

Bell left his native Great Britain for a "holiday" to the States in 1980. But soon the vacation turned into a land version of Gilligan's Island.

As the new publicist and driver for Roomful, Bell was along when the group found itself stranded in the middle of the Arizona desert with a broken-down shuttle bus. "This had to be the hottest day of the century," Bell said, "and here I was with 10 hungry musicians eyeing me and there's no place to go."

"You have no idea of the problems when a vehicle has a major breakdown. It was the tour to hell," Bell recalled.

Roomful eventually got a ride into Los Angeles, where they played that night.

"I had a background in the record industry in Britain, and came on board as a publicist, sound engineer and driver. I was on the road with them constantly for the better part of the '80s. I'd drive to a gig, unload the equipment, sell merchandise, break it down, get a minimum amount of sleep, get up and be on the phone the next day, then do it again later in the day. I can't believe I'm still alive," Bell says.

Today, Bell works as the group's evangelist, doing anything and everything from creative thinking to acting as the main liaison between the band, record companies, their public relations agency, the Boston-based Ted Kurland Associates, and the media.

"When we got a real sound engineer (in the early '90s) it opened up more time for me to devote a full-time career to managing the band by working out of an office in my home," Bell said.

When he first started promoting Roomful, Bell's main responsibility was educating the audience and the people who would pay their wages. "Back in the early '80s, there was no blues boom as such. So it was Roomful of Blues, more so than any other band (in this area) in the early '80s, that helped to fuel the blues revival -- along with the T-Birds and Stevie (Ray Vaughan).

"In the '70s, Roomful was one of the few bands who was out there doing this kind of blues as opposed to guitar and harmonica-based blues," Bell said.

Roomful was founded in 1968 by Michael "Duke" Robillard of Westerly, R.I.

Today, the big difference for the band is that the venues keep getting larger and Roomful is on many a promoter's list for national and international blues festivals.

Another change has come on the road trips. No longer is Bell behind the wheel muttering to himself and checking his sanity at 4 a.m. in East Cupcake. "The band is in a real bus, a vast improvement over other modes of transportation we've had over the last 20 or so years," Bell said.

"When I first started with the band, we had two Chevy Suburbans -- one of which got totaled when it was parked on the street. So we were down to one Suburban and a U-Haul trailer. We did one national tour like that -- 10 of us in the Chevy with the equipment in the U-Haul. That was horrendous.

"We realized we'd kill ourselves if we kept going like that, so we bought a Bookmobile (the once-common vehicle in the 1970s and early '80s that delivered library books in cities and towns), put in rudimentary bunks and nicknamed it, Das Book, after the movie, 'Das Bot,' because it was like a submarine on wheels. It didn't have any windows, only the windshield for the driver.

"We had that thing for about seven or eight years. We never saw any of the country -- but it did the job," Bell said.

For comfort, the most important thing is to lie down and stretch horizontally and stand and stretch. Sitting down in a car for a long period of time really sucks, he said.

After the bookmobile, the group bought a shuttle bus, which was really more of a truck with a bus body. That provided five or six years of "sterling service." Then, the Rolls Royce of the highway arrived in 1996, a 1981 MC-9 made by Motor Coach Industries, that only had 250,000 miles on it. Now, everyone has their own bunk, there are two lounge areas and a toilet on board.

Boston's Blues

Roomful has enjoyed a longtime relationship with Rounder Records, dating back to the 1980s with "Dressed Up To Get Messed Up," followed by the licensing of the "Hot Little Mama" album on Rounder's Varrick label, which came from Roomful's own Blue Flame label that was released in 1981.

"If there is any problem, I can call Marian Leighton-Levy (one of the founders of Rounder). They have a tremendous promotion department. One of the good things about Rounder is that we're (Roomful) a big fish in a small pond. We obviously command some attention. It's been a good relationship and I've been happy with them," Bell said.

Roomful released a Christmas album in 1997 and then experienced a lot of personnel changes beginning in January 1998. Lead singer Sugar Ray Norcia, trombonist Carl Querfurth, drummer John Rossi, pianist Matt McCabe, baritone saxophonist Doug James, and others left the group at various times during that year. In December 2000, only three members remained who had ties to the early 1990s -- saxophonist Rich Lataille, trumpeter Bob Enos and guitarist Chris Vachon. The trio was still with the band in May, 2001.

In creating the music, Bell says, "It's a fascinating and a frustrating process and also immensely satisfying. There's not a set template that you are applying. One of the biggest problems we have is finding enough time to let the creative juices flow. Often the reality is you're so worn out from the constant traveling or you're catching up on sleep. That sort of constant fatigue definitely works against the creative processes."

The resurgence of blues within the music industry has created an economic double-edged sword: one end tickles the consumer's fancy with a rack of new releases, while the other can kill a musician because of the severe competition within the industry.

"While there are more opportunities, there's also a vast amount of competition. There are many people that have well-known reputations who are working for very little money," Bell said.

"If this state of affairs continues, I think some of the more peripheral bands will be weeded out unless the resurgence carries on and this gets bigger and bigger, which is quite possible," he added. "The music has a lot of potential to keep going, but one of the problems in working with a large band is that one encounters a vast amount of economic problems just to keep those people out on the road."

Art Simas

"We're a big band -- a 12-headed monster that has families -- so Roomful has been responsible for the health and well-being of many, many people and we keep working all the time," Bell said. According to the Kurland agency, Roomful is on the road for about 230 days a year.

Whatever he does -- dealing with promoters, paying bills, writing press releases, supervising a promotions campaign or corresponding by e-mail -- Bell says it's his job to keep the Roomful of Blues machine well-oiled and maintained, now well beyond its 30th year.

Web: www.roomful.com

K.D. Bell

Art Simas
K.D. Bell: A man of the people

If first impressions count, then the first time you see vocalist and drummer K.D. Bell will be a memorable experience. He's likely to be wearing a bright, canary-yellow suit with matching fedora and white shoes. Even in a club lighted by a single 60-watt bulb, you'll be wanting to find your shades fast.

"I've got a matching hat for every suit that I wear, so that will make about 15 or 16. Overall, I've got 25 or 35 hats," said Bell, who changes his wardrobe after every set. "That's something I've been doing for years now. If I didn't, people would want to know what's wrong."

But K.D. (King Drummer) doesn't mind the attention or the adulation. He's a man of the people -- always willing to share a smile and a story or two. "I love the attention I get and I work hard to get it. But I just love being part of the people. I'm not a dressing-room sort of guy who will stay in the room until it's time to do the next show. I'd rather be with the people. I think more people like you for that. That's the way I've always been."

Bell sees his job as an entertainer, not just a vocalist or a member of a band. "I want to make the people feel good about themselves," he said. "Those things are so important. That's what I'm there for, I'm there to make them happy."

Getting close to the people is what pleases Bell most. "That's why I wear a cordless microphone, so I can be part of the audience. People today want to be entertained," Bell said. And that means giving the audience more than just a good sound. A lot of bands can sound very good, but there's got to be more than that, he said. "I don't think I ever do a song the same way twice. It's those extra things that come across."

Born Frederick Carver Bell, June 15, 1943, Bell learned his first musical lessons in Union Springs, Ala., as a drummer and singer when he was still in high school. He and his buddies would play at other schools, various clubs that were actually private houses which would hold weekend fish fries and in the funky juke joints in the late 1950s and early '60s. After he graduated from high school in 1962 he traveled to Miami and began his musical career in earnest, backing many of the greats in the business. He stayed in Miami for about six years; then began a four-year gig at the 4 O'Clock Club in Fort Lauderdale, a club then owned by the Mafia, he said.

Bell was good for business at the 4 O'Clock, the owners liked him, and they gave him an offer to continue playing there -- forever. When he left to come to New

Boston's Blues

England in 1968, "actually I snuck away," Bell said. One of the principals of the club relayed a message to KD's ex-wife after they had settled in Maine. She told KD, "It's a good thing he likes you because he said, 'We know where he is.'"

The reason he came to New England was because his wife wanted to visit her sister in Kittery, Maine. At the time, she was nine months pregnant with their youngest daughter.

"No, she couldn't wait till the baby was born," Bell said. "No, she had to come up here to visit her sister. And the day that I got here, that night, my daughter was born between Kittery and Portsmouth on the drawbridge. My sister-in-law was driving and all of a sudden, my daughter was being born and I had to deliver my kid in the back seat of my 1967 Chevelle."

Jennifer Morris, now in her 30s, graduated in February 1999, from nursing school in Fort Lauderdale.

After breaking up with his wife "because I got a little crazy… drinking and all the women. I wasn't a very good husband. It's that simple. I screwed up. It finally got to the point where she had all she was going to take of it, and she ended up going back to Fort Lauderdale and I stayed up here."

Bell said he's had his battles with alcohol problems. "More of us have been there than not," he said, but never drugs. "I never got hung up in that thing. I've seen people with $200 daily habits but I never did have that kind of money to do that sort of thing. I could never understand it."

Bell said he quit drinking in 1983 and smoking in 1999.

In the 1970s, Bell, on drums, formed a trio with keyboard player Bobby Brown and a female vocalist known as Pee Wee. "One time an agent booked us into a country-western joint in Salisbury. Man we were scared when we got to that place. But we managed to pull it off and people liked us." Bell also occasionally played with OJ and the Soul Beats out of Dover, N.H.

Yet, Bell is not one to dwell on the past. "What I do now is more important," he said.

"One thing musicians learn is that if you work with me, you've got to be the best." But the reward is, they'll be paid well too, he said.

Yet many bands are getting by on looks, appearances and by going through the motions. "In this business, it really doesn't depend on how good the band is. There's a lot of things involved: timing, I mean, granted, you've got to have a good package if you're going to have a ghost of a chance. But your timing's got to be right and you got to have someone there who is working for you. I'm certainly going to do my best to push myself to be the best I can short of doing anything immoral or illegal… but you gotta work for it," Bell said.

By day, Bell worked as a car salesman for seven years in the area but he's been strictly earning a living in the music business for the last five. Four or five years ago he played drums for Luther "Guitar Jr." Johnson for between four to six months. "We both knew it wasn't meant for me to stay with him," Bell said, "because at the same time I was doing my own thing."

He also played for Mighty Sam McClain for his band called The Blues Party, which had regular gigs at The Grog in Newburyport, Mass. The band also opened Morgenfields up in Portland, Maine, with K.D. on drums. Also in that show was Earl King and R.L. Burnside.

While he says he had some great times in the past, Bell is very enthusiastic about his latest project, a CD that has been a long time in the making, called "Something's Wrong." He said it's really a first-rate CD that has 12 songs with two or three originals, including the title track. Other musicians who collaborated on the project include: Scott Shetler on saxes, who also did the horn arrangements; Bobby Keyes on guitar; Keichi Hashimoto on trumpet; Tom West on keyboards; Jim Sturtevant on drums and Teddy B on bass. Harry King of Bangor, Maine is also featured on the disc and James Montgomery sits in on harp on his own "Schoolin' Them Dice" about a lesson off the streets of Philly.

"All I can say is that I hope this CD will do for me what I think it will do," Bell said. "But there is one thing I can honestly say, no CD or nobody can guarantee success. It's only within yourself and in doing the best you can do. And I do know I have a great CD."

In addition, Bell plays with the Hot Damn Band, which is based out of New York which has the Uptown Horns and other "heavy hitters" in the lineup.

You can find Bell leading the weekly jam at 5:30 p.m. every Sunday at 111 Village Square in Hampstead, N.H.

Web: bit-bet.com~neblues/kdbell

Chris 'Stovall' Brown

Art Simas
Chris "Stovall" Brown: Multitalented musician just keeps on going

"I was born in '53 and grew up in Warwick, Rhode Island. Then we moved to Massachusetts, then Rhode Island, again.

"I've lived a lot of places, New York, upstate New York, Connecticut, all over, and on the road for a number of years, then back in Boston for more than 13 years now.

"I started playing bongos at 6, drums at 8, harmonica at 11, and guitar sometime after that. Basically, what would happen was my friends and I would rehearse at my mother's house and people would leave their instruments at the house and, being the inquisitive type, I would pick them up and mess around with whatever instruments were there.

"Over the course of the years I've just picked up a lot of different instruments. I never really took any formal training on anything besides drums. Just the rudiments. I probably play 10 instruments.

"I started playing in Rhode Island and getting paid when I was 13. I was actually playing jazz and bebop then. It was at that point that I quit playing drums. I switched predominantly to harp and slide guitar when I first started to play out, but people would still call me for drum gigs. I had to turn them down because that was the only way I could make the transition.

"I had the Stovall Brown Band, blues bands starting as early as '69. At that point I was playing a lot in Misquamicut Rhode Island, alternating with Roomful of Blues at a club down there called The George.

"And this was back when Duke Robillard used to have long hair and wear overalls. I can recall the exact day when Duke discovered Buddy Johnson because they had left this gig at the club and we kind of took it over and he came down 'cause he wasn't gigging and he came down to my gig and he was jumping up and down screaming about Buddy Johnson to me. It was at that point that Roomful switched over to being a horn band with that big band sound. Before that they were just really a Chicago Blues band, doing a lot of Freddie King kind of stuff.

"They had a harp player at that point; Fran Christina was playing drums with them in those days. So I did that for a couple of years, but I always came back to my own band, but periodically I would take a break and gig with other bands.

36

Boston's Blues

"I started gigging with a band in Boston probably in 1972, a band called the Jasper Cook Band. We were being managed by T-Bone Walker's manager at the time. We did a number of gigs with T-Bone at different places including The Prism, the Jazz Workshop, places like that.

"After that I think I moved to Connecticut. I had a band pretty much out of the Connecticut area for a couple of years and working the entire New England area. It was still always the Stovall Brown Band.

"In 1973, '74 and the beginning of '75, I was working with Luther 'Georgia Boy Snake' Johnson. I guess I was playing harp with him and opening the shows. We used to do a regular gig at the Highland Tap in Roxbury, and I can recall Willie 'Big Eyes' Smith and (James) Cotton coming down one night. It was actually Cotton's birthday. He was like 38.

"Luther, well, he used to get kind of tore up and he'd be out of the picture by the second set. I was the harp player in that band, but needless to say, Cotton went on harp that night and I went on guitar, and we had Willy Smith on drums. Cotton used to sit in with us a lot. Most of the time when he was in town he'd come down -- Willie Smith was still with Muddy in those days -- and he would come down with Muddy's truck, unbeknownst to Muddy.

"So around '75, I went back and did my own thing for a while, started doing a lot of road stuff, a lot of the same circuit that Luther was doing. We were going up into Canada and upstate New York and probably down south as far as Virginia, DC, that sort of circuit.

"At this time, I wasn't the only guitarist in a band until the late '70s. Around 1976, I played with a guy named Fat Man Wilson and the Sliders. He was out of Pittsburgh originally and weighed over 400 pounds. He was kind of an East Coast legend who died in 1977.

"We were working a lot, Powerhouse was around, with George Leh and Tommy Principato and Pierre Beauregard, we pretty much worked the same circuit those guys did, the Nighthawks, they were starting to kick around then too. We did a lot of the same things. We all had pretty much the same booking agent, Harry Chickles, who brought the T-Birds up here.

"I remember their first gig up here, which was at Bunrattys, no cover. Back in those days Bunrattys was a big blues joint. Big Walter used to play there and all sorts of people. You know, doing the Speakeasy and the usual Boston haunts. So, through '77 I did gigs with Fat Man until he died.

"And then it was Stovall again doing tons and tons of road stuff. For the next three and a half to four years we were almost always on the road. Anywhere from the middle of Canada down to Florida, anywhere in that circuit. We used to do a regular Monday night in Asbury Park so no matter where we were we used to drive back down there or up there, depending where we were. We did that for six to eight months.

"We used to have Southside Johnny's horn section playing for free. They later became Springsteen's horn section. We'd hang out a lot with a lot of those guys. Johnny actually wasn't living around there very much, but Richie Labamba, who's now on the Conan O'Brien Show, was. He and I were good running buddies in those days and even had a mutual outside woman. Of course we didn't know about it at the time.

"Then, I moved to Rochester and put together another band there and did maybe two years based out of that area. In the early '80s I moved back to Providence and was gigging with different people until I put together my band again. And pretty much since then I've just been doing it and trying to make it.

"Young Neal worked for me for a while, about a year and a half to two years. I actually found him in a little bar in Bristol, R.I., I can't even remember the name of it, that's how tiny it was, when he was 19 and gave him the name Young Neal. He had a band called Neal Vitullo and the Blues Stain. That was the band that he had and then I hired him to work with me for a couple of years. Then he left to do his own thing and I continued on, and that pretty much brings us up to today.

"I did seven and a half years at Harpers Ferry on Sundays. I did the 1369 with Silas Hubbard from the beginning to the bitter end. That was around '85 I guess, '85 through '88. Yeah, George Mayweather and I used to hang out and I did George's record ('Whump It! Whump It' on Tone-Cool Records) with him. He was just one of many in the circle of people that were hanging out at the 1369 at the time -- Gordon Beadle, Madeline Hall, Eric 'Two Scoops' Moore. We'd go to the jams together and stuff, like seven nights a week. If we weren't playing we were somewhere jamming.

"Along the way I did the 'Boston Blues Blast Vol. 1' (also on Tone-Cool). I'm still waiting for Volume II to come out. I've done a few other little CDs, 'Live at the 1369,' which is probably one of the rarest Boston records of all times. It does actually exist in some form or various forms I guess. I have it. It's on SwampTone, which is the guy who used to work with Mickey Bones.

"And I'm on the one with 'Lots of Papa' and Silas, George, Juanita Jackson, Jelly Belly, Arlene Bennett, and Lady D. Most of these people aren't around anymore, or alive, as the case may be. SwampTone 6605 for the record collectors. It actually came out on cassette and then the cover was withdrawn due to protests from one person on the cover about the caricature that was on it. Everybody was caricatured on the cover and certainly this person's caricature was no worse than mine, but it was withdrawn shortly after it came out on cassette.

"Then they re-did the cover and re-did the liner notes and did it on CD. And it actually was at Tower Records for a while. I guess it's still in print. That was cut during the last couple of weeks of the 1369. They basically went in and recorded live two Sundays and everybody played three songs and then they picked just one song from each. Some other people were on it. Professor Harp was on it, Boston Baked Blues, when Rick and Hal and Chuck Morris were all playing together. The Old Dogs were on it with Watermelon Slim and Washtub Ronny and Shy Five were on it, Kenny Holiday was on it, J.B. Junior.

"I was in the house band so I'm on nine of the 14 cuts, something like that. It's a tough one to find, one for avid record collectors only," Brown said.

Brown released "Front Page Blues" on Gibraltar Records out of Brighton, Mass., in 1998. Brown is on guitar and harp and is the main vocalist; Robert Clinton on bass and background vocals; Bruce Katz on Hammond B-3 and piano; Gordon Beadle on saxes; Ed Scheer from the Love Dogs on drums, percussion and background vocals; John Abrahamson on trumpet; Ken Harris on B-3 on one song and Eric "Two Scoops" Moore does the rap on "Stole Some Love."

"I did some acoustic stuff on it, slide stuff, harp features, a little bit of everything," Brown said before the CD was available. It is one of the top CDs in the last 10 years from a Boston-based artist, featuring all original songs.

"Front Page Blues" CD is available from: Gibraltar Records, 27 Justin Road, Brighton, Mass.

Rod Carey

Boston's Blues
Rod Carey: 'My job is to stay out of the way'

People still refer to him as "Ronnie Earl's bass player" because of his stellar work with Earl and the Broadcasters for six years. While the phrase is outdated since he no longer steadily works with Earl, Rod Carey is much more than a simple bass player. He brings more than 30 years of experience to the gig, studio or jam session. That experience and the know-how -- and when -- has accorded Carey with a reputation as one of the best in the business.

For example, in January 2000, the Rhode Islander was nominated, with longtime drummer and friend, Per Hanson of Maine, for a Grammy for their work on the "Legends" CD that featured Pinetop Perkins and Hubert Sumlin.

B.B. King eventually walked away with the trophy, "but it was still an honor to be nominated for such an achievement," Carey said.

The modest Carey eloquently effuses thanks to his former boss (Earl) for giving him the opportunity to play, record and travel the world.

"I had always loved music and when I'm pretty much self-taught. I always loved blues, that raw powerful music coming from inside," Carey said. Born July 30, 1946, Carey grew up in Jersey City, N.J., and learned to play while in the service around 1965 and the early part of 1966. He then served in Vietnam during 1966-67.

Unlike most guitarists, Carey set out to be a bass player, which requires a very different mindset as opposed to a lead or rhythm guitarist.

"Bass is a supportive role," he said, "It's staying out of the way and realizing what your role is by locking in with the drums and making things happen. When you're familiar with the people and you've got this magical thing going on, you can make things happen by giving a little kick, and knocking 'em up a notch or two."

He landed a gig with Dave Howard and the High Rollers, a fine band from the Providence area in the 1980s. The band was doing a benefit gig as the opening act for Ronnie Earl and his group of Broadcasters this particular day. Something must have clicked and struck a favorable impression with Earl after hearing Carey.

"Two years later I got a phone call from Ronnie asking me to be his bass player," Carey said. "I can remember it like it was yesterday. He said, 'Are you sitting down? I want you to be my bass player.' Just an incredible call. And I was with him for six years. At the time, Dave Maxwell was on keyboards the first year and a half, then Bruce Katz came on. I got to travel, meet a lot of nice people and hang out with a lot of people... Just a wild ride."

Carey says his favorite record from his Broadcaster days is "Grateful Heart." "That record just blows my mind," he said. "Live in Europe," made in Germany in 1995, has a lot of raw energy, he added.

Looking back, Carey said, there was a very special chemistry that we had in the Broadcasters, almost an us vs. them mentality. "When you're out on the road all you have is each other. So you become sort of a family. We took care of each other."

"A lot of people were telling Ronnie, 'You can't do this, you gotta do that' as far as having a vocalist and playing instrumental blues. Many people weren't quite sure what it was, but it worked. And whenever Bruce, Per and I get together, it's sort of like the old days."

The "old days" have become more frequent as two or three of Earl's alumni have contributed to a number of albums and live gigs. For example, the trio have played on Joe Beard's 2 CDs and at a live gig at Chan's in Woonsocket, R.I.; on "Homesick For The Road" in 1999, with Debbie Davies, Kenny Neal and Tab Benoit; and at a gig in support of Michael Williams' CD, "Late Night Walk" also at Chan's; while Hanson and Carey backed Sumlin and Perkins on "Legends."

Carey, Hanson and Katz also recorded an album with Volker Klenner, a German blues guitarist/vocalist in Richenbach, near Stuttgart, Germany. They then played with Sumlin in a great show at Chan's.

Carey also teaches at the National Guitar Workshop in New Milford, Conn., during the last week of July where he meets music enthusiasts from all over the world. "Bass players are starting to get more and more respect," he said.

Right now he's not in a gigging band. "I'm picking and choosing. Fortunately people still know who I am and I'm playing locally" in the Providence and Greenville, R.I., area. "I enjoy teaching a lot and I might do more of that."

He may be teaching his son, Justin, 19, a keyboard player a few lessons in the blues -- when the time is right, of course.

Boston's Blues

Although Justin is now into a lot of "alternative stuff," his father says he's got a lot of Otis Spann records. "So there's always hope," Carey said.

Ronnie Earl

Boston's Blues
Ronnie Earl emerges triumphantly

The road to recovery has never been an easy path for Ronnie Earl Horvath. It's a struggle every day and about a year ago, it was even more of a struggle for a man who was voted the best blues guitarist by his peers. It was also the darkest hours and days for Earl, who was diagnosed with manic depression.

From Jan. 14, until Sept. 2, 2000, he set aside the business of blues and concentrated on getting back to where he felt comfortable with himself and the world.

"I was diagnosed with manic depression," Earl said, "and it got really bad in January (2000), it got to the point where I had to take a rest and take medication. I had been doing it pretty much straight out since 1977, which I was with John Nicholas, Sugar Ray (Norcia), Roomful of Blues and then Ronnie Earl and the Broadcasters. So after having a band for 14 years, it was time to stop and take a break."

During this time, Earl had got the word that he had diabetes, which didn't help matters.

"You know depression is very stigmatized. And I had to stop and take a break. All of the high-powered things that were going on in my life I pretty much had to cut loose, and reduce the stress levels. So that's what happened. I stopped because it got to be too much. And the depression was devastating," Earl said.

Earl has been a reluctant leader throughout his career when it comes to dealing with nonmusical details. "I'm really a composer playing guitar," he said in early December 2000. "I didn't want all this other stuff -- having to deal with road managers and business managers, the crew, the writers. I'm a guitar player and I tried to write, but everything started to get to be too much.

"It's one thing to own your own business and have a store in Cambridge or someplace. But having the responsibility of a band is another. I had to live with these people, and we traveled all over the place in all my various incarnations of bands. People may think that it's easy, but it's tough."

His message now is that he is making an important comeback both mentally and physically. And he's ready to get back to playing the music he loves. In February 2001, Earl began a residency at the Sit 'n' Bull Pub in Maynard, Mass., on Thursday nights. "It'll be a lot of traditional electric blues with electric guitars and some acoustic," he said.

45

Art Simas

About five years ago, Ronnie Earl and the Broadcasters used to tear the joint down week after week.

Earl said he hopes the Thursday night gig will grow into a night where young people can come in and learn the music. It's this giving spirit that drives Earl, and most blues musicians, to keep the music alive, passing the knowledge of tone, tempo and depth of emotion from one generation to another.

"I think there needs to be a place where young people can come in and see real blues. I'm just playing through my heart and soul and whatever happens I'm very grateful," Earl said.

In November 2000, Earl traveled to Woodstock, N.Y., to make "a Ronnie Earl blues album" with a few of his friends -- Irma Thomas, Kim Wilson, James Cotton, David Maxwell, Levon Helm and others.

He said the album, due out this fall, could be called, "The Triumph of the Blues Spirit" because he shook off the depression and got his life back in order.

Earl said he chose to play with the people he respects as blues players. "That's the validity of my work, the fact that all of them came to play with me on my album. That means so much more to me than if some writer somewhere likes or doesn't like the record. The important thing is the music. There are a lot of people walking around with egos. But I try not to have that. I come to play and put everything I have into it."

Often called Mr. Intensity because of his unrelenting musical ferocity, Earl said it is tough to say where the wellspring of emotions reside inside of him.

"I have a lot of feeling and I like to think that I maybe have some soul too, and it comes out in the music, I have a lot of feeling for blues and respect for all of the people who came before me -- people like Bob Margolin, Duke Robillard, Jimmy Vaughan, and Stevie Ray Vaughan. We (the Vaughans) and I played together all the time, and they were very, very nice to me.

"When I first went to Chicago when I was 19 or 20, it was like everyone was so warm. I went to Florence's on the West Side and sat in with Magic Slim. I went to the South Side and sat in with Lonnie Brooks and went somewhere else on the South Side and Son Seals let me play. And this is long before any of these people were well known. I feel very blessed that they were so warm to me," Earl said, who, at the time was just beginning to learn guitar.

Boston's Blues

"I started playing at 20. There was no one to give me blues guitar lessons and there weren't any blues videos back then. You just did it and you went to see other people. I had seen the Muddy Waters Band with Louis Myers playing guitar, and Pee Wee Madison, and Luther "Guitar Jr." Johnson and Hollywood Fats.

"When I used to sit in with Muddy Waters and Big Walter... they couldn't pronounce my last name... so that's how it got started that I used my middle name.

"And seeing Muddy, Albert King and B.B. King at the Fillmore East about 1971 -- that really got me to want to do this," Earl said.

Respecting the music and respecting the people who played the blues is very important to Earl. For him, musical creativity spawns from that respect.

"Blues is extreme creativity around a limited, chord vocabulary," Earl said. "Many times an entire song may be composed of just three chords or even one chord. Howlin' Wolf's "Smokestack Lightnin'" is one chord -- the whole song. But if you're creative and you have the soul, it's being able to make the music speak to all kinds of people, not just a limited audience.

"It's important to have a big beautiful tone and sound and to have the knowledge and wisdom and grace to know what notes to play and what not to play. I think I know all that now. I think I know what I'm doing now. I know how important it is to have tone and to have your own style and have people recognize it. I've been blessed with this way to communicate."

Earl truly has been blessed with ability and opportunities to play and record with some of the greats in the blues, past and present.

"In 1976, I started playing with John Nicholas and the Rhythm Rockers at the Speakeasy in Cambridge, then started in with Sugar Ray and the Bluetones, then from 1979-88 with Roomful of Blues and I got sober in 1988," Earl said, ticking off the historical data quicker than an adding machine. To succiently sum it up, Earl said, "I played with everybody."

Today, Earl teaches guitar at the Minor Chord in Acton. One of his students, Paul Marrochello, often accompanies Earl when they do acoustic gigs.

Earl was also a teacher at Berklee College of Music in Boston for a year in the mid-1990s.

He said his favorite jam players are local keyboard wizard David Maxwell, drummer John Rossi, formerly of Roomful of Blues, bass player Michael "Mudcat" Ward, Lucky Peterson, and the Vaughan brothers ("I played with Stevie from 1978 through the 1980s but knew Jimmy longer and played with him all through the years"), and the old crew of the Fabulous Thunderbirds.

"I'm just a guy who's playing music the way I think it should be played, and I'd say Ronnie Earl is thriving -- not retiring," he said.

"It's a good thing to take some time off. You get a different perspective when you're out of the scene for a while."

Welcome back Ronnie.

Web: telarc.com/blues

The Spirit of Ronnie Earl

By Tom L. Hazeltine Jr.

It is said the more things change, the more they stay the same. But for Boston's own Ronnie Earl, change has been constant and persistent.

While some may remember him as a different person, this is Ronnie Earl now, speaking honestly about his spiritual beliefs, his former band and their recordings, even the wild life he left behind.

One of the most enduring bands of the late 1980s and 1990s, this group of Ronnie Earl and the Broadcasters consisted of: Ronnie Earl, guitar; Bruce Katz, piano and organ; Rod Carey, bass; and Per Hanson, drums.

Note: This interview was conducted in 1995.

TH: How long with the current Broadcaster lineup?
RE: Eight years.

TH: They were with you even before your sobriety?

Boston's Blues

RE: Yes, by a year and a half.

TH: Where were you born?
RE: In New York. Rego Park, Queens.

TH: Hence, the song?
RE: Yes, Rego Park Blues.

TH: What about your time in Texas?
RE: In 1978, I lived in Austin, for two or three months, and yes, I was staying with Jimmie Vaughan and I lived with Kim Wilson and Keith Ferguson, all the Thunderbirds.

TH: Did you find that area of Texas of particular influence on you? I know certainly there is some Freddie King and T-Bone Walker in your playing.
RE: Lightnin' Hopkins, Eddie "Cleanhead" Vinson and David "Fathead" Newman are from Dallas. Illinois Jacquet was a major influence. I'm certainly influenced by Texas people. Jimmie Vaughan is my favorite guitar player.

TH: Really?
RE: Oh yeah. But I'm from New York and Boston, I'm happy to be from here. The great alto saxophone player in Duke Ellington's band, Johnny Hodges, was from Boston and the tenor saxophone player, Paul Gonzales, was from New England as well. There have been a lot of great musicians that came from Boston and New England, in general, and New York.

TH: What music do you listen to when you're at home?
RE: Right now I'm listening to a tape of the new album and trying to make peace with it.

TH: Could you talk a little about the latest recording?
RE: The new album is going to be called "Grateful Heart," and should be out in February or March. I'm a little nervous about it because it's not a straight, strict blues album. It has a lot of original compositions and… spiritual music.

TH: Did you use a different formula for this recording?
RE: Well, we used the great David "Fathead" Newman (of Ray Charles' band) on tenor sax, and he's one of my favorite musicians of all time. Sometimes when I make a new record, I sit home and I listen to it by myself and I imagine people driving to work listening to it, saying, 'This would be nice to drive to work to,' or 'This would be nice to play while you're making breakfast,' or whatever.

Art Simas

This is a record about gratitude and the gratitude is that I'm alive and sober. And, you know, that's probably the biggest thing. That's my message. Because a lot of my friends -- Hollywood Fats, John Campbell, who I produced, and Wayne Bennett are not here anymore. A lot of people have died tragically from drugs and alcohol and for some reason, seven years ago this February, I was pulled out of the fire.

TH: Seven years?
RE: Yes. My death was interrupted so that I can do God's work and play music and spread a positive message of recovery. That's what I'm trying to do. To some I'm some blues this or that but to me I'm... you know, I love blues but I just look at it as a spiritual message. I used to think that I had to be high... and all the blues guys were doing coke and drinking and wearing black leather clothes, you know. I had this image that an artist has to be suffering. The good news is, that's not true. I mean I still love to play the blues but I don't live the blues anymore. So, I hope that there's a lot of joy that comes from the music for people because I'll never stop playing the blues. I have three slow blues on this new album.

I'm not a commercially oriented musician, I just play what I feel. That's that about my message -- the younger musicians don't have to feel like they have to be cool and smoke and be bad and drink and kill themselves. I didn't know any better. I didn't know there was another way to live. Charlie Parker didn't know there was another way to live, but there is.

TH: Are you saying that if you had someone like yourself, saying, 'There's an alternative to all this, try sobriety,' things might have been different?
RE: Well, I didn't. I think I had to go through what I had to go through. We all have to go through what we have to go through -- trial and tribulations, but I'm very grateful that I'm 42 and talking about this.

TH: Do you feel that message is received well by the audience and other musicians? Do they get the gist of what you're trying to tell them?
RE: I don't know, I hope so, people seem to be awfully nice to me everywhere. You know, I've been getting a lot of gratitude reading about all these young musicians who have been mentioning me as an inspiration. I just read this "BluesWire" piece and the Radio Kings talked about seeing me play and of using me as an inspiration, and it makes me feel good. I hope I can be a spiritual inspiration as well as a musical inspiration.

TH: Not that long ago you kept to yourself after your performances. Was that related to your spirituality -- now that you're able to get up on stage with some of the people who were part of the old scene?

Boston's Blues

RE: Well, I think I had to heal from about 18 years of drinking and drugging. Also, I had to heal from 14 years straight on the road. And, for a while, I didn't want to go into clubs and I didn't want to be a part of the whole thing. Plus, I really like my privacy. But over the last few months, I've been feeling better about things, a little bit more healed inside, and I can go out and play with all these people and let them know I'm still here and still doing my thing.

I think a lot of people come to Boston and they say…'Where's Ronnie Earl, we don't see him at my gigs?' So now I'm going out more and doing that.

It's funny, and I want to be honest, I don't mind sometimes being called a local. But we do play all over the world. I love playing for the people here, and I love playing at the House of Blues. These people know me, they know my music. In a lot of ways, the rest of the country hasn't heard the lineup we have. But the people in Boston have. So, we're going out more. It's healing for me to play too; it's not only healing for other people, I need to play to heal myself.

TH: Is it the interaction with the people?
RE: Yes, just to play, it's good for me to go out and play. For a while, I mean, I was doing too much of it, 300 nights a year when I was with Roomful of Blues. But now, I can do it again in moderation.

TH: Do you have a favorite memory when you felt the audience really understood your message?
RE: They're all pretty spiritual, it just feels very healing. We're exchanging a lot of love, back and forth, that's what it feels like. As far as words and everything, I do think that music is the language of the soul, that's why that record is called that. There are no words for a lot of my songs, there are no words for a lot of these feelings that I have or that I want to express musically.

Playing with Bruce Katz, Per Hanson and Rod Carey, I mean, it's such a special thing we have, the four of us. It's funny, Bruce calls us the Beatles of the Blues. This is just a very spiritual band, we all get together and we pray before every performance, and that ain't exactly normal for blues-oriented people, you know? We give everything we have. I don't leave too much out in a show, unless the club's telling me we got to stop playing. We probably play for two and a half hours.

TH: One final question. Your life is obviously in change with your healing and your ability to travel now, is this where you see your life going in the future? More visible around town, maybe?
RE: Well, around here I'm pretty visible, I worry maybe they're going to get tired of me. I don't know what's going to happen to me, I just don't know. We just made this new album. We have another album coming out with this incredible blues guy from Rochester, N.Y., named Joe Beard. He's originally

from down South, so it's like we have two albums coming out in late winter or early spring.

TH: When is the release with Joe Beard coming out?
RE: That one is due out in February or March as well.

TH: You're really racking up the releases.
RE: Yes, well, I've been productive and that's what the future is for me. I want to keep on making quality records, trying to help people. This is another example: I went down to the House of Blues to see Joe Beard and I sat in since I hadn't seen him for awhile and I couldn't believe someone this good didn't have any records, or records that you could find.

So I went over to AudioQuest, whom I made an album for ("Still River"), and I said, 'If I played on it would you record this guy... he's great?' And they heard it and they said, 'Yeah.'

Things like that keep me going. That's what I want to do. I want to be able to help the young musicians if I can because people were nice to me -- people like Muddy Waters and B.B. King -- those guys were nice to me when I was coming up. That's what's important to me. I think that we're all here to help one another and to love one another. And all the rest of the stuff is just... stuff.

Can I say a little about the band?

TH: Sure.
RE: People are always coming up to me and saying 'You're drummer's incredible, incredible to watch.' I love to hear that because I don't think that the rhythm section gets enough credit, in life, and I don't mean just my rhythm section. Rod and Per are a great rhythm section and they work great together. And, I feel that I'm playing some of the best music of my life right now and I owe a lot of that to them because they're so supportive on and off the bandstand.

And Bruce Katz is brilliant every night. To have somebody that can play B-3 and piano, you know, I'm getting everything that I want. If it's a jazzy tune; if it's a more spiritual Coltranesque; if it's Otis Spann; and then it's Bruce. Bruce is Bruce. He has his own sound. It's very, very, very spiritually stimulating every night to play with people like that.

I'm kind of hard on myself musically and I don't want to sound like anybody else. That's my biggest thing in playing music -- to have my own voice and for people to find their own voice. When people tell me that I've found my own voice, I'm happy. That's what I wanted. It doesn't come that easy. It doesn't happen in two years. I've been playing for 20 years now. I never was able to copy other people. I just play me and that's real important, along with recognition of the musicians I'm playing with.

Boston's Blues

I'm proud of some of the young musicians here, too many to name, that are carrying on the tradition of the blues. My favorite musician is Paul Rishell. He's like a big brother to me because he came before me and I've just always been respectful of all the great musicians in town who were here before I started playing: David Maxwell and Ron Levy, people like that who have been here and saw me coming up.

There's a lot of great young musicians… It's gratifying to see.

Update on Ronnie Earl:

1998-99 - won W.C. Handy awards for best blues guitarist
late 1998 - Ronnie Earl and the Broadcasters with Katz, Hanson and Carey breaks up.
Early 2000 - suffers from depression and diabetes and decides to take some time off. Does CD in November 2000, with Irma Thomas, David Maxwell, Kim Wilson and others in Woodstock, N.Y., scheduled for September 2001, release on Telarc Records.
Returns to club scene for a Thursday "residency" in February 2001, at the Sit 'n' Bull Pub in Maynard, Mass. Sells out every show.

Chris Fitz

Boston's Blues
The high energy world of Chris Fitz

There's only one way Chris Fitz knows how to do things -- all out. That goes for any competitive situation be it sports, checkers or music. He comes at you with all he's got, and you better be ready.

Fitz has now crossed those imaginary tracks that divide the good players from the better and serious professionals with his debut CD, "Just Gettin' Started," which features nine originals of 11 songs recorded at Rivers Edge Studios in Haverhill. Fitz studiously obeyed the Stop, Look and Listen signals for the mandatory time, having sharpened his chops both on guitar and in vocal dexterity. He's served an apprenticeship with Vykki Vox's Soul Searchers in the early '90s, and has had a good five years as front man of his own group, the Chris Fitz Band.

Fitz's interest in music began in the 1970s. Of course he listened to Led Zepellin, Kiss, Aerosmith and other mega-groups of the time. But he says he was also fortunate to have two uncles who steered him toward their vinyl collections of Muddy Waters, Lightnin' Hopkins and Robert Johnson. "So from an early age I knew this was really cool stuff. And I knew right away that I identified with that style of music," Fitz said. "I picked up a guitar when I was 15 for the same reasons most teen-agers pick up a guitar -- because everyone else was doing it and they were starting rock bands. Being a competitive person, and growing up in a very athletic family I figured if they're going to start doing that, then I want to do that too."

By learning three or four chords at a time, trying to keep up with the Stones or Cream, Fitz began his evolution. At this point he didn't take the instrument seriously. There were games to be played -- players to strike out, opponents to tackle and baskets to be made, not to mention the academic drive for college -- which ranked much higher on his personal priority scale. "The guitar was a lackadaisical hobby at this point in my life," he said.

When he entered Bowdoin College in Maine in the 1980s, the instrument went with him and occupied his time in between the double-session football drills and batting practice on the baseball diamond. "I was conditioned through my family that when I got out of college I'd put a tie on and get a job, and that's what I did. I moved to San Francisco and started my career as a salesman."

While in school in 1983, Fitz happened to catch the opening act for the Moody Blues at the Worcester Centrum -- an obscure guitar player who was just getting his name out before the public, a person called Stevie Ray Vaughan.

Art Simas

"This guy comes out in bright fire-engine-red polyester pants, a kimono and a white cowboy hat and he just blew me away. After I saw him play guitar, that was it. That's what I wanted to do. I didn't stick around for the Moody Blues -- they came out and started in on "Nights In White Satin," and I said, 'I'm outta here.'"

The dream to become proficient on guitar remained dormant for a few more years until after graduation. Fitz said he still had a lot of pressure to graduate and break into the job market. So the sales job in San Fran served one particular purpose -- it allowed him to buy some equipment and get started with a fledgling music career.

"I basically locked myself in my room in San Francisco for five or six years and learned how to play guitar," Fitz said. "I spent a lot more time learning guitar and Albert King licks than on making sales calls like I was supposed to be doing. That's where the real dedication came -- in 1989 -- and I haven't looked back since."

One morning in 1991-2 Fitz woke up and said he had enough of the corporate world and quit. The music was now constantly in his brain and he couldn't wait to get back to his stringed buddy with the long neck. He sought exile in the mountains of Colorado as a ski bum for a couple of years, blowing off life.

"That didn't last, so it came time to shit or get off the pot for me and for my family. 'Hey, you got an education. Whaddya going to do? We don't care what you do -- just start doing it. If what you want to do is play music, then start doing it,'" was the message heard loud and clear after a couple of winters on the slopes.

Fitz returned home in the summer of 1993, full of confidence and ready to begin making it on his own. But he was alone in one of the most competitive music climates in the world, and especially for blues music -- Boston. "Even though I grew up on the North Shore, I didn't know a soul. I didn't know who Rick Russell was from Matt Woodburn and Cheryl Arena or anything. So I got myself a Boston Phoenix, saw where the blues jams were, and started going to them. If I was going to meet any other musicians, that was the place to go and get in the circuit.

"On one winter night I went to the 182, which was the old Bunratty's, which is now the Wonder Bar in Allston. I walked in ready to do my Stevie Ray schtick and here's this guy (Matt Woodburn) wailing on stage with the best Stevie stuff I've ever heard. And I shrunk back in the corner. I said, 'Holy shit, I got a ways to go.' But I stayed there and got on stage and did all right. Matt and Cheryl Arena were the nicest people and they gave me a lot of confidence. And I came back to the jam every Tuesday."

Within a few months, Vykki Vox, who also was at various jams around town, hooked up with Fitz and started Vykki Vox and the Soul Searchers, which was somewhat of a Stevie Ray cover band with a female singer -- nothing like the present group.

"After a year, we parted because we both knew that it was time to go in different directions," he said. But that year of playing ('94-'95) with Vykki introduced Fitz to all the clubs and gave him another education in how the business end was run. His chops also got a lot better from playing three nights a week.

"But I knew that I wanted to be the person up front, even though I never sang a lick in my life, and I wanted to do the power trio thing -- to be the Chris Fitz Band and not just be a guitar player playing for someone else," he said.

Waldo's on Boylston Street was once a regular Thursday gig for Vykki Vox and Fitz. Once they parted, though, Fitz was faced with the daunting task of assembling a band and learning to sing in four days for the next gig at Waldo's. He did it, somehow, he says, although he couldn't talk until the following week. But he kept doing it with different bass players until he found someone who was musically in synch with what he was trying to do.

Now more than five years on his own, Fitz, with Joey Sullivan on drums and Justin Meyer on bass, are "kicking butt all over the place," according to Fitz. "We're focusing on being an originals band -- and we all want the same thing, to do this for a living. We're a high energy, engaging band. I'm writing stuff that has a Keith Richards or Black Crows bent to it, to a '40s-type jump blues style."

Fitz says he thinks he's improved as a musician tenfold since he left Vykki Vox because of the challenges he's conquered in playing, singing and leading. "There's no substitute for just going out there and doing it," he says. "It's been incredible thinking back to where I was just a few years ago when I came back to Boston."

"The intensity that we carry on throughout a whole show comes from being an athlete and being aggressive. That's my approach to music, too," Fitz said. "I identify with the manic guys -- Buddy Guy, Albert Collins, even Ronnie Earl -- man the energy just knocks you out. That's where we come from as a band. It's not as much about polish as it is about real hard-core energy and playing like you mean it every minute."

Note: Fitz released his second CD, "This is My Church" in 2000, featuring a horn section, keyboards and percussion as a backdrop to his hard-driving style.

Web: chrisfitzband.com

J. Geils

J. Geils still having lots of fun

Arguably the most sustained, commercially successful blues band that came out of Boston was the J, Geils band. Through three decades, J. Geils rode the wave. Seventeen albums, national and international tours, and immediate name recognition. They were in the right place, the right time and they took advantage of it. They made it BIG.

Yet what got them there was their faith and worship of the blues masters, such as Muddy Waters, Little Walter, Howlin' Wolf, Junior Wells, James Cotton, and B.B. King. The J. Geils Band had no business plan or strategy. All they wanted to do was play with their heroes and play like their heroes. The rest of life took care of itself. This was their blues destiny.

Jay Geils walked on to the campus at Northeastern University in the fall of 1964 half-heartedly looking to make a career in engineering. Born in New York City in 1948 and growing up in New Jersey, Geils' parents, who themselves grew up as Swing Kids at the height of the Swing Era, took Jay to see the greats in jazz. "So I was a jazz guy," he said. "Actually when I got to Northeastern I played trumpet. In the third grade, I chose trumpet because I saw Louis Armstrong on TV and, after all, there were only three buttons you had to work, I figured how hard could it be?"

At this point Geils was not a big rock 'n' roll fan. Rather, he leaned toward the R&B side of Fats Domino, Little Richard and Chuck Berry -- and he hadn't heard real Chicago blues, yet. When in New Jersey, "I'd listen to radio staion WRVR in New York broadcast from the Riverside Church, and they would play a lot of jazz. And Ed Beach, the DJ, he'd sneak in a Lightnin' Hopkins or Brownie McGhee or even a Howlin' Wolf. And I remember asking myself, 'Who is this guy Howlin' Wolf?'"

Boston in 1964 was a folk coffeehouse scene. Even the musical menu for the college circuit was dominated by the national folk groups, such as the Kingston Trio or Judy Collins. In Greater Boston, there were Club 47, the Unicorn, the Sword and the Stone and a few others, which had Tom Rush, the Jim Kweskin Jug Band, and Eric von Schmidt and maybe Lightnin' Hopkins as all acoustic acts. Another coffeehouse, upstairs from the Scollay Square T stop at what is now Government Center, had John Hammond and John Lee Hooker, again, all acoustic.

Yet there was a black blues scene in clubs off of Columbus Avenue, such as the Brown Derby. "I remember B.B. King would come there and I saw Bobby Bland

Boston's Blues

there in the late 60s," Geils said. "And then in the early 1970s, there was the Sugar Shack on Boylston where I saw Wilson Pickett."

Geils was a beginning guitar player and was in dire need to learn more about the instrument. In the fall of '64, he signed up for a Folk-Blues Guitar Clinic at the local YMCA one morning. The teacher was Taj Mahal.

So moved by Taj, Geils decided to make the guitar his major instrument. He hocked his "god-awful" $25 Harmony guitar and his trumpet and traded for a Harmony 12-string. "I eventually took six strings off, but it looked like a Martin, and if you didn't have a Martin, you looked like shit. Well, I couldn't afford a Martin."

As others have documented, the defining moment for Boston's blues history was the "electric" Dylan performance with some members of the Paul Butterfield Blues Band at the Newport Folk Festival in July 1965. Everything stopped and people knew it was a big deal.

"To me, that changed everything," Geils said. "It changed it for popular music, which would have its repercussions down the road, but it definitely changed it for the Boston blues scene because this was the first time many of us heard the Butterfield Blues Band. The music was in sort of a jazz framework. There'd be a couple of vocals then somebody would blow a solo. And the marriage of some of those guys playing with Dylan changed everyone's outlook. 'What's that? I like that.'"

Later in '65 and into '66, the clubs started to book blues players. Junior Wells, Howlin' Wolf, Buddy Guy, Muddy Waters and they all came with amplifiers and drums. "That was really the start of the availability of that kind of music to college kids," Geils said.

By this time, school wasn't really a priority for Geils. Needless to say, his parents weren't too pleased either when he told them he wasn't going back in the fall of 1966. "I remember my parents and I had a big talk."

"Well Jay you know you're not doing too well at engineering school."

"Well, no shit."

"So, you can either a) Go in the Army."

"NOOOOO"

61

Art Simas

"or b) you can go to music school"

"MMMMM not bad, but I wasn't that confident about my music talents. You see, in 1961, I had been to a Stan Kenton band camp clinic in the Midwest for two weeks. And I was definitely at the bottom. I was about 15, a trumpet player and a drummer. It seemed like everyone was better than me. Keith Jarrett was there, too, and he was better than half the staff.

"It was exactly what my parents wanted me to do. They agreed to go for it, but they knew it would be an eye-opener for me because these kids could play their asses off. And I really couldn't, yet," he said.

One other option was to transfer to a smaller engineering school, such as Worcester Polytechnic Institute, now known as WPI, to start in the fall of 1966.

"Well, I was only there about a month when I met (Magic) Dick Salwicz and Danny Klein. Danny was a junior and Dick was a senior, and they started to hang out together and we started a little acoustic blues band. Danny played washtub bass, I played guitar and Dick played harmonica and kazoo. He was pretty much into the Sonny Terry thing. There was another guitar player, too, Al Couchon, so it was an acoustic blues jug band. And we even played a couple of gigs. But it was the beginning of the end. We had all heard Butterfield and it was like .. ohhhhh, yeah, we like that."

The trio tried to learn as much as they could. They pooled money to buy "The Best of Little Walter" or "The Best of Muddy Waters," and then they'd swap and try to play it. "And that was really the beginning of the J. Geils Blues Band. We felt, not only does this music really communicate with us, we can play it!!! It's not that hard, it's not like trying to play a Charlie Parker song. We were BB King blues junkies. We were up all night listening to the same cuts 10 times in a row. We just couldn't get enough.

"I only lasted one semester. At that time, you were required to go to an Army ROTC course, and I couldn't stand that. I went the first day and I never went back. So I knew I was in trouble right then," Geils said.

"After I dropped out in 1966, I moved in with Danny who had an apartment over a pizza joint on Highland Avenue in Worcester and went to work for the Polar Soda Bottling Company, which was pretty grim that winter because it would be 20 degrees outside and only 40 degrees inside the bottling company. But one amazing thing happened... we put a band together with keyboard player and a drummer."

Boston's Blues

The keyboard player, Harold, was wealthy and had a big fancy red Dodge car, Geils recalled. And it came in handy for extended road trips, such as the one to New York City to see B.B. King at the Cafe au Go Go in March 1967. "The opening act, I think, was the Colwell-Winfield Band, who was from Boston and whom we had heard about, but hadn't seen.

"So B.B.'s band comes out and they play their two or three numbers and then B comes out and he plays that first B-flat. And I'm like 'HOLY SHIT' I was transfixed. It was like 'Oh, man, I gotta do this -- real bad.' We drove back to Worcester that same night. And the first thing I decided was to get a red guitar.

"B.B. was playing a red ES 355 that night, which was the fanciest, thin hollow body I had ever seen."

Two months later, Geils sold his car to get a good guitar, an ES 345 Gibson from Eddie Bell's Guitar Center in New York. "I made a deal with a friend of mine in New Jersey. I drove my car to NJ, sold it to this guy for $700 - $800 cash; he took me to a bus station in New York where I bought the guitar and an Ampeg amp because it had wheels, put the guitar in the case on the amp, and wheeled this thing down Eighth Avenue to the Port Authority, then took a bus back to Worcester.

"At this point, we had all dropped out of WPI. I think Dick dropped out with one semester to go, but he was already a pretty good harp player. And in those days, he was the only one. And Al had dropped out and was going in the Navy.

"So we moved to Somerville and we all got factory jobs -- and we went to an open jam night at the Unicorn. And George Papadopolous, who owned the place, liked us and hired us as the house band for the whole summer, which was great. And believe me, we were not very good."

At first, it seemed a classic story -- struggling musicians working in factories during the day and playing at night. But that didn't last long. "At first I wouldn't go in on Mondays, then I'd call in sick on Monday and Tuesday. And then I wouldn't show up till Thursday. Finally the boss said, 'Do you really want this job?'

"I guess not."

And the same thing happened to everyone else. Ever since those factory jobs, Geils said he has made his living playing music.

"At one point Dick and I had considered going to Chicago," Geils said. "but the music actually came to Boston." And longtime friendships were born during this time.

For Geils, "the best times happened when you get to play or talk with these guys one-on-one -- these legendary masters. To sit in a dressing room with Muddy Waters with his shirt off... and he had this amazing physique and this bronze color to his body. He was almost like a Buddha, a mind-boggling experience. Same thing with B.B. King. You felt like you're in the presence of royalty."

Often, the heroes would teach the young guns a thing or two. Geils recalls, "One night during the summer of 1967, which was the second most amazing night for Boston blues for me, Buddy Guy and Junior Wells were at Club 47. We were playing at the Unicorn. At midnight, at the Unicorn, in walks Buddy Guy and Junior Wells and we had a jam till 3 in the morning. It was unbelievable... It was one of those nights while no one was actually teaching anyone else, you got to stand next to Buddy or Junior and you learned so much more from that than if you'd listen to a record for 10 hours.

"I was on stage with Buddy, and Junior Wells had my girlfriend cornered in either the men's room or the ladies' room, trying to put the make on her... And then I remember Junior came up with this long, slow blues... the best shit you ever heard. We were beside ourselves, the best night. And that was probably the last time that Junior came to Boston with Buddy. The next time he came to Boston, he had other guitar players with him... Lefty Dizz, Louis Myers, and others.

"We were fortunate to be there when the Boston blues scene was happening, from '66 to '68. One night at the Club 47, I was watching Junior, and in walks Paul Butterfield... and the place went fucking beserk.... and I mean literally because there was no booze being sold. It was the music and it was so good. We were standing on our chairs... we couldn't believe it.

"Soon thereafter, the Boston Tea Party opened on Berkeley Street, which was THE Boston ballroom that featured acts like Led Zeppelin, Jeff Beck Group with Rod Stewart as lead singer. And we quickly became the house band."

Ray Regan, a Kansas City lawyer, came to Boston as a fan of the underground youth culture. He wanted to be the king of the Boston underground culture in the worst way. "He proceeded to buy the radio station -- WBCN -- and made Peter Wolf his the first DJ, and it became the premiere underground FM station. He bought the underground paper, The Phoenix, and he turned a little giveaway rag paper into what it is today. And he had the club, the Boston Tea Party. He also hired Don Law to manage it -- and sweep the floor. And he decided that he had to have the hottest band in town, which happened to be my band. So he and Don managed the J. Geils Blues Band." In addition, all the top blues acts were booked there, so if the band wasn't playing on the bill, we were watching and learning.

"By '68, Dick, Danny and I had joined forces with Peter Wolf and Steven Bladd. They had a band called the Hallucinations, which had disbanded around this time. They were sort of a blues-rock band: two guitars, bass, drums, and Peter played a little harp. And we were looking for a front man and singer and a drummer."

Soon, the music was everywhere in new clubs that sprouted at the end of Boylston Street and at Paul's Mall and the Jazz Workshop. The music business was dynamic and the promotion business was blossoming, everyone following Bill Graham's lead in San Francisco.

One of the clubs was the Catacombs, a labyrinth three stories below street level. "We played there a lot. It was run by a Greek, John Kostinaras, a character. And there were no guarantees. But we were so successful, and packed the place, we changed the original deal to where we took 60 percent and he took 40. "He used to drink a lot of vodka and he'd tell me at the end of the night, 'You come drink vodka with me and count money.'

"In 1969, the Tea Party moved to Lansdowne Street and eventually became the Ark. And it was at the Tea Party where the promo man, Mario Medias, from Atlantic Records saw us. He had been in town to see another act, and he called back to his office and said there was a hot little blues band in Boston. And that's how we got on Atlantic," Geils said.

For the next decade, the J. Geils Band would be a bonafide national act.

So in a four-year period, Boston went from have no blues presence at all in 1965 to, by '69, it was everywhere, a blues explosion.

"That real first burst of Chicago blues invading Boston had tapered off a fair amount by '71-'72, plus we just weren't here that much. On our first tour, we were opening for Black Sabbath for a month. I mean, we hadn't even been out of New England. Holy shit... what is this?

Art Simas

"Another time, we got to Detroit and were playing there for two nights, and Muddy was playing at the Checkmate or the Chessmate and we went down and jammed with him," Geils said.

"But the whole music industry was evolving and looking for original material. You clearly weren't going to be a big success by being another Paul Butterfield or Mike Bloomfield. Record companies wanted a lot of original material because they wanted to own half of it. In fact our first (and only) contract with Atlantic Records, they owned half the publishing rights, and that was a deal-breaker. But that was the norm then. Nowadays, no one would give up their publishing. Plus, we were moving into a burgeoning pop-rock scene. And we wanted to have hit records," Geils said.

As the '70s moved on, the kind of blues scene that was so vibrant went into the doldrums. "Many of the people who had gotten into it, like we did, wanted to move forward and play their own songs.

"And then blues came back," Geils said. "It'll always come back. It's the basis of all American music."

(Note: For the past three years or so, Geils, Duke Robillard and Gerry Beaudoin have been been perfoming as the New Guitar Summit, a guitar meeting of jazz and blues with accompanying drums and bass. In 2000, the group released "Retrospective" which is available from Francesca Records, 14 Hammond St., Waltham, Mass.)

J. Geils and Magic Dick still play local clubs and festival gigs as Bluestime, combining some of their old songs with new material.

Dave Haley

Art Simas

Groovacious, diverse tones and moods drive Dave Haley of Two Bones and a Pick

Blame it on the Smothers Brothers. They were the instigators who woke the beast within Dave Haley when he was 12.

Right after he saw John Kay and Steppenwolf do "Magic Carpet Ride" featuring that signature Les Paul feedback, Haley had to have a guitar.

"So I started pestering my folks for one. It took them about a year or so before they finally gave me a Sears Silvertone with speakers and Silvertone amps - great amps by the way. They have a really nice distortion sound and you could feedback forever with it. From there, I became a real Hendrix freak and began listening to Clapton, Jimmy Page and John Mayall. It was all this stuff I was getting kind of second generation blues from the English invasion (perspective). It wasn't until later that I went right to the sources."

It was blues-oriented material that first inspired Haley, born in December 1955 in Dayton, Ohio. He moved to the Boston area about 18 years ago after living in Cincinnati. But after Hendrix died, he faded out of the blues-rock and headed toward jazz with Kenny Burrell and Wes Montgomery as his newfound, long-distance mentors.

"I hooked up with this organ trio but I ended up kind of scuffling to hold up my end because the organ player, Greg Thompson, played a killer Hammond B-3. This had to be around 1971-72, and it was a really nice feeling because he'd be laying down these cords down, it was so groovacious, it's like you were riding on a tidal wave. I've always been like partial to organ and that sound and that's how I got turned on to guys like Jimmy Smith, and from that I kind of got into that forum.

"After that I ended up playing fusion bands, went into the Army where I ended up in an R&B band overseas in NCO (non-commissioned officers) clubs and in a lot of disco bands. Well, that was the era then," he said.

The type of music didn't really matter as much as the substance of what the guitarist was saying musically. "I still would kind of listen to pretty much anything from guitar players that had a craft to it, or to players that had pretty good feeling," Haley said. Slowly, he found himself back into the blues while not really looking for a certain musical direction or goal.

Boston's Blues

Then a friend of Haley's who owned a vintage guitar store in the Midwest called Fretwear was always calling him to listen to check out one group or another, such as the T-Birds, and giving him tips on what who and what was hot. "He had a blues band called Shakin' Dave and the Centers, and he was always going down to these guitar shows in Austin, Texas.

"One time he said, 'Hey check this out, have you heard that Jimmy Vaughan's little brother plays guitar? I was at this club in Austin and I ended up recording it .. he's getting pretty hot.'"

Haley said this conversation took place in the late '70s, well before fame found SRV. "When I put this tape on, I remember it struck me the same as it did when I heard Hendrix. All of a sudden it was like, 'Oh my God, I can't believe it. Who is this? Listen to the tone, who is this guy?' And that just got me back full force listening to blues… into my old records, trying to learn it, pick up a little bit from different styles, how they did turnarounds and intros and all.

"Even now, it's an ongoing thing. I started seeing how people like Snooks Eaglin and others from New Orleans were mixing it up, how Bobby Radcliff was mixing it up. Funk tunes and blues -- it could be done, and it sounded great. And then, you know, you're not too far from that Magic Sam kind of thing. What's cool is the versatility and mix of all these diverse styles of blues from a straight boogie to a Chicago blues to West Coast jump to straight-ahead jazz-blues, like Kenny Burrell would play or Wes Montgomery. And you can go in and out of those different styles.

"So I started dabbling into these styles and ways of playing and the approach -- but always keeping the blues line through everything. Today, I consider us a blues band but we cover a lot of ranges of that sound," Haley said.

And that sound comes across in Two Bones and a Pick's "Butter Up 'n Go," a title taken from a Seinfeld episode where Kramer wanted to go sun tanning using just butter as lotion.

The New Orleans scene really got to Haley and his brother John, who played bass and drummer Mike Dunford.

"If you go down there, you notice that all these cats are jumping around with different styles. They're all great musicians. And any one of them can go straight into a deep blues and play it right. But then they'll jump off into like a funk tune or something else. The main thing is that they're trying to go after the audience -- peg what they're (the audience) into at that moment. It's such a diverse musical thing down there from the brass bands to the traditional stuff to the blues bands. That kind of impressed too me a lot. So that's our kind of approach now.

"Also we're really knocking our volume down lately, which is kind of nice. I must be getting old or something. I had an old 55 Gibson Explorer amp, 12 watts, that I had in my basement. My brother had spilled a drink in it years ago so it hadn't got much use. But I finally got it repaired and started playing through that and thought, 'Man this is great.' You can play with the dynamics a lot more, too.

"If you listen to a lot of the early blues bands, those guys were using very low power amps. Even like the '40s and '50s swing players they're using the amps of the day and were like 12 watts maybe 8 watts.

"The idea was to try to get a sound on this, these recordings like a lot of those old records from the '40s and '50s. Everything was miked kind of at room ambience so you got the real sound. Even the guitar amps were all in this one central room playing at the same time and everything was bleeding into the other mikes. So that was the idea when we recorded this at Rear Window Studios in Brookline, Mass. Man, I've never been more happy with the product," he said.

Two Bones and a Pick have two other recordings. The first, a self-titled calling card done in 1992 that was mainly used as a vehicle to get gigs by putting it in front of club managers and bookers. The other, "Right Here and Now," featured layered tracks, which didn't sit right with Haley after he objectively listened to it.

Compared to the first two ventures, Haley said Two Bones and a Pick is a completely different band now, which is a good thing. "You can track yourself and look back and see real growth."

"We've been around since '92. We're all good friends," Haley said. "I look more for people that we all get along with and we have fun playing with. We have a lot of fun, especially when everything is going well, it's like nothing can stop us on a good night."

Update: Two Bones and a Pick released "Juicy" in 1999. The CD exudes a West Coast swing vibe and gets your body moving in all directions.

Yet while the disc has a happy and upbeat feel to it, producing the album was a chore for the band. John Haley, David's brother, died in November 1998, and two other close friends, Randy Richardson, a one-time bassist with the band, and

Boston's Blues

Mary Francis Georges, mother of Leah Hart who is the voice of "Juicy" on the title track, also died while the band was in the process of making the CD.

Web: twobones.com

Tommy Hambridge

Boston's Blues
Tommy Hambridge: "It's a crazy friggin' world"

While Tom Hambridge may have moved a few years ago from Boston to the country capital of the world, Nashville, Tenn., his heart is still in the blues and R&B.

He was the producer and writer of many of the songs on Susan Tedeschi's "Just Won't Burn" blockbuster album and played drums, too.

He now has a record deal with a new CD out called "Balderdash" which is being distributed worldwide on Artemis Records. His label mates include Jimmy Vaughan, whom he has played with, Warren Zevon, and Steve Earle, to name a few.

A much sought-after sideman, Hambridge has played with hundreds of R&B, blues and rock musicians from Chuck Berry to The Drifters to Leslie Gore to Roy Buchanan. His versatility comes from being able to adapt himself to any music.

"I grew up in Buffalo, N.Y., and I just was playing drums like crazy and soaking up everything from Herb Albert to Tony Bennett. I think that's kind of how I came to be able to play a lot of different styles -- mainly because I didn't know any better. I'd put on 'Beggars Banquet' by the Stones and then 'Lonely Bull' by Herb Albert, then Ray Charles, then Englebert Humperdink.

"I did my first professional gig when I was in the third grade, a bar mitzvah. I always would play with kids in high school and a lot of times my parents had to drive me around to gigs. Then I started playing jazz, lots of Miles Davis, then I played a Sunday night blues jam at a club in Buffalo when I was in 10th grade and I remember opening for James Cotton with Matt Murphy on guitar."

And the blues world started to creep into his varied repertoire. People like Roy Buchanan, Muddy Waters, Johnny Winter and The Paul Butterfield Blues Band. "I got a partial scholarship to go to Berklee and immediately got a gig after an audition for John Lincoln Wright and the Sour Mash Boys. I remember when I auditioned they told me I had to be versed in all kinds of country music, from country swing to the two-step to Merle Haggard, to whatever. And I knew nothing about country music."

But he learned fast. He also learned that his newfound band was pretty popular, the musicians drew decent salaries and played all over the Northeast. "Actually, country music encompasses everything, swing, to western swing, to Chicago shuffles, to rock 'n' roll. So we played all over -- New York City to Bangor, Maine, and I played all through college."

He graduated from Berklee in 1983 and started a blues band, playing in places like the Berklee Pub on Mass. Ave. in Boston. "I would literally just walk my drums down the street to this club. I mean hookers and drug dealers were all over the place, and we would play, trying to play the blues," he said.

Right after graduation, Hambridge got a gig with Roy Buchanan. "That was incredible, 'cause I remember growing up listening to my brother's Roy Buchanan records and thinking what a serious guitar player he is, and so I remember when I got the audition for him I had my brother FedEx me all the albums so I could listen. I auditioned, got the gig on the spot, and our first show was at Jonathan Swifts, two sold-out shows; we got into a mobile home and took off on the road and I played with him for about three years.

"And during that time I was playing with Roy Buchanan, I got called to play with other people like Bo Diddly, The Drifters, a lot of Motown acts, The Marvelettes, and my name just kind of got around as the guy to call in Boston.

"Then I got a call from Chuck Berry. And I did my first show with him in about '85 and I've been playing with him pretty much at least once or twice a year since. That's amazing because I know a lot of people who have played with him and had bad experiences. But I've had nothing but great experiences with him.

"I started my own band in like '86 called T.H. and the Wreckage and we won all kinds of awards and accolades. We had like five number one songs on WBCN in Boston, and we won five Boston Music Awards. I won songwriter of the year in '91; most outstanding drummer in '91; and we won album of the year in '92, so things were really going good," he said.

The first record was called "Born to Rock," the second was "Greeting From Nowhere USA," followed by "Keep It Burning," which won album of the year, then "Pop, Rock And Twang."

Hambridge also has a solo album called "Still Running." The first two were on Black Rose Records and "Keep It Burning" was on Fast Track Records. The first

Boston's Blues

two were distributed by Rounder. The fourth ended up being on the band's own label called Bad Mood Records.

(Note: Al Cocorochio, president of Black Rose Records of Saugus, Mass., is still very much involved in following and supporting Hambridge's career. In June 2000, the label celebrated its 20-year anniversary of promoting New England-based musicians.)

Because of his background in all genres, Hambridge doesn't restrict himself to one style. "I don't just write rock or just write blues, it's kind of all over the board," he said.

"Basically, the only thing I kept doing was the gigs with Roy Buchanan. He ended up calling me for what happened to be his last show ever."

Hambridge recalled the bizarre scene. "After playing at Nightstage in Cambridge, I remember he called me on a Thursday to do an outdoor show over the weekend at the Guilford Fairgrounds in Guilford, Conn. But I was going to be in Maine on Saturday and Sunday. So I flew between the gigs in a little puddle jumper and then we drove to the fairgrounds where we did an amazing show. And that's the last time I saw him.

"He asked me if I'd do the next weekend jam in Poughkeepsie with Johnny Winter and I said, 'Okay great,' and then the road manager called me two days later from the morgue and told me that Roy had died.

"After that, I got calls from all different people to play drums for them and do records for them so I just started saying okay. I love playing with everybody and that's kind of how I was able to make a living all these years -- touring with a band called Rubber Rodeo from Rhode Island; Gary Puckett; shows with Del Shannon before he died; a bunch of gigs with Martha Reeves and the Vandellas; Leslie Gore; a tour of Europe with Barrence Whitfield and the Savages, Jonatha Brooke and Sherman Robertson; tours of Japan, China and Hong Kong with the Drifters; The Crystals, The Shirelles, and I did some gigs with Brook Benton; Patty Larkin; Cub Coda; Peaches and Herb; Tracy Nelson; and the Taylor family and Carly Simon from Martha's Vineyard, and on and on, I even did gigs with Tiny Tim.

"And I had a ball with Peter Noone of Herman's Hermits. I played the first show and he asked me, 'How the hell do you know my music so well?' And I said,

75

'Peter, it just so happens that my older sister had one of your records and I used to play, 'Can't You Feel My Heart Beat' and 'Henry The Eighth.' I would play along to the whole damn record.

"It just takes me back, you know. It's fun in a way, playing with Tommy Roe, too. I couldn't believe I remembered those old singles that had these really cool drum beats that I would practice. So it was fun and kind of surreal because I can't believe I'm actually playing 'Dizzy' with the guy… That's kind of how it worked out."

Hambridge also got into the production side for a number of artists too, producing many blues, rock and pop records. Locally, he's been a fill-in for Ronnie Earl and was a steady sideman for Sha-Na-Na.

"The thing I love about this is that there are so many opportunities, so many things. For example, last night I was with the guys from Orleans, playing 'Still The One' until 2 in the morning. And then there's odd, crazy stuff, like playing as the understudy drummer in the Broadway play 'Rent.'

"And tonight I'm supposed to meet up with Ben Orr (formerly of the Cars) and we're going to discuss some stuff about his record which could lead to nothing or could lead to who knows? Those guys sold 10 million records.

"And tomorrow I'm doing a Christmas party at the Bay Tower Room with Toni Lynn Washington. Sunday, I'm playing at The Grog with Mike Welch on guitar, David Maxwell on piano, Marty Ballou on bass and Jimmy Biggins is going to play sax at Parker Wheeler and Dennis 'Fly' Amero's weekly Sunday night jam."

Hambridge had been a staple of that session for about six years.

"The other day I got a call from someone who told me that the song that I had played on and sang is going to be on TV tomorrow," Hambridge said.

"I said, 'What do you mean, local?' He goes, 'No, a soap opera.'

"It turns out that it was on Sunset Beach. So I got up at 11:30, turned the TV on to this show and there are all of these beautiful gals on the soap opera. They go into a bar and somebody's says, 'Hey, let's everybody dance. There's a great new record out and we'll put it on.' And that was the song," he said.

Boston's Blues

Hambridge has had two of his songs reach the Top 20 at Rock Radio, has had many of his songs on many different TV shows and in major motion pictures and soundtracks. He has one of his songs on Leslie West's (Mountain) new CD and a song on Bernard Allison's latest CD, "Across the Water."

"I just finished a 50-city tour with Susan Tedeschi, opening for B.B. King and Buddy Guy, came home and wrote some songs with Jonny Lang, sat in on drums with Ringo Starr and his All Star Band, and, during the same week, welcomed my new daughter, Sarah, into the world.

"And I'm saying to myself, this is a crazy world. You know what I mean? It's just a crazy friggin' world. So you never ever know... I love this business."

Web: tomhambridge.com

Per Hanson

Boston's Blues
Per Hanson: Have sticks, will travel

There's always something that jumpstarts a budding musician. In Per Hanson's case, it was hearing the incessant beat of Gene Krupa on "Sing Sing Sing." "That really stuck in my mind. I thought it was the most exciting drumming at the time. That's the sound I remember when I grew up in the south side of New York City," said Hanson who was born in 1952.

"I wasn't really into music until I got my own set of drums when I was 12 or 13, around 1964. I was in a couple of rock 'n' roll bands that played all the standards of the day, "Louie Louie," "Wipe Out," Dave Clark Five stuff and of course, The Beatles and The Stones.

"I got into blues through my sister, who had Ricky Nelson, Elvis, Buddy Holly, and I leaned toward Buddy… and the Stones and Animals. I thought the Stones invented the blues. It took me a heck of a long time to figure out who Slim Harpo, Chester Burnett (Howlin' Wolf) were, and what they played," he said.

With the record companies pushing the British Invasion, Hanson said he was more in tune with the English drummers, Mick Fleetwood, Jon Bonham, Ginger Baker, and Keith Moon than he was with American blues artists.

"I headed more in the direction of the simpler guys like Charlie Watts and Ringo. I got to see these guys when I was about 11 or 12 -- Easter Holiday Show at the Fox Theater in New York -- Cream's first New York appearance in America; Leslie West with the Vagrants; Mitch Ryder was with his big band; Wilson Pickett was there. And they all played about 20 minutes in a review. And when it was over I got up to leave, and my brother said, 'Sit down,' and a few minutes later we got to see it all over again.

"So we saw The Who wreck their equipment twice that day. That was the most unbelievable thing I ever saw.

"I was playing in a band from Connecticut around 1970-71 and playing some blues, but not the blues that I know today. My first real exposure to the blues was opening up for James Cotton at Salisbury Beach -- for $50 and some food. But I paid close attention to the drummer there, and that's when I found out about the shuffle beat because he was doing things I wasn't doing. I guess I was playing it backwards.

"From there I was in a few different blues bands and moved up to Maine and started listening to Ronnie Earl and Sugar Ray (Norcia) and Little Anthony

(Geraci) and Mudcat Ward, Neil Gouvin, John Rossi, Duke Robillard, and Greg Piccolo."

A few years later Hanson attended a concert at Great Woods and got to meet Ronnie Earl after the show. "The call came from Ronnie in the middle of the night – three or four in the morning. We had hung out all night and I even helped him pack since he was going to Europe the next day. So he said he'd call me when he came back.

"So he called me at three or four in the morning and he sounded serious. He said he was starting a band and that he wanted me to be his drummer. 'Well you haven't heard me yet,' I said. And he said, 'Your sister said you like Fred Below. Well, that's good enough for me.'

"From there, it went from listening to a lot of people to actually playing shows with them. It's been like blues heaven ever since.

"Hubert Sumlin is one of my favorite guitar players. The first time I saw him I told him that, and I said, 'You don't know how many times I've listened to you down in my cellar. You are the heart of the guitar. You are the sparkplug that makes it go.' He was with Eddie Shaw and the Wolf Gang at the time.

"Teaming up with Ronnie was probably the best thing that ever happened to me. But I guess I was preparing for it. But I never thought it'd happen. It was a big step for me and I never looked back. I thought about my friends back home, but I was having too much fun. It's like a blues dream, Who would you like to play with tonight? How about Earl King? How about Hubert Sumlin? I can just go on and on. Unbelievable the people I've played with, like Thunderbird Davis, wonderful people and we always had a great band. And people liked it. We kept moving on, but with every new member we'd explore new territory.

"The most challenging thing was when we decided to go all instrumental about four years into the Broadcasters with David Maxwell on keyboards. That to me was like trying to fly without wings. But Ronnie had a lot of insight and he had a lot of faith in this idea. I don't know if I had the faith he had, but if he thought that we could do it, then we could do it.

"After we got out in front of the people and got some of the bugs out and got some confidence, we were almost unstoppable. Once we got over that the guitar was the vocalist, we all rallied around that.

Boston's Blues

"When I first started with Ronnie -- I knew he needed a drummer who was listening to what he was doing, like talking back and forth. Ronnie would always tell me to listen to John Rossi of Roomful of Blues.

"So I'd take what John was doing and put a little bit of me into it and it just grew. But we had years where we were working on that -- the give and take. You learned when it was room for me to take a step and you knew when there wasn't any room, you don't go anywhere. You just hold your ground and make it solid. Once you learn that, you've pretty much got it.

"We worked on the communication between us every time we were on stage. Some guys may not be told what to do, but in situations like that you have to be able to know where you're going to go. It's really important for that person to know what they want. You've got to take that feedback and not take it personally.

"Of course Ronnie had a lot of experience and he taught me so much -- how to be a performer and hold yourself up.

"It's easy to do when you walk out onto a stage with him. Because he meant business, I figured if he's going to be about that, I better be right behind him and backing him up. And that's what I set out to do. I was going to make sure this guy is happy. If I can make him happy, I'm probably going to make those people happy too, and that will make me happy.

"Ronnie was so intense himself and no nonsense. He took it very seriously and it's gotta be a certain way. I had some big shoes to fill -- John Rossi -- he was my Gene Krupa. These guys were our heroes, and Ronnie Earl Horvath was in a category by himself. I cannot compare him to anyone else as far as guitar players go. The back and forth rapport that we had -- that might be a once in a lifetime thing -- something that inspires you and places a fire under you.

"I had never sweat so much in my life as when I played with Ronnie. That was one thing, Ronnie and I always got wet. If I'd see him break a sweat, I'd be right behind him.

"It was a very special time with all the versions of the band. And the hardest time was without the vocals. Once we went to Europe and did that CD, 'Live in Europe.' Once I heard that, I knew I could relax because that was a good record. It was a great recording, great engineers. But I was in another world... I was inspired and also afraid that everything wouldn't come out right. It makes you do funny things. I listen to that now and there's some stuff that I never did before.

"I get a lot of compliments on my drumming on that album and I say, 'Well that wasn't really me.'

"To be up there with the guys was just great. And when Bruce joined the band, we started a good collaboration with those guys too. It was exciting. We're a very close unit.

"Usually, there's not a day that goes by when I think about the music that I played with Ronnie.

"Whenever I hear a guitar player, somewhere inside of me I'm always comparing them with Ronnie… and how am I sweating.

"Some come close, but I've never met a guitar player who would cut your head off right above the eyes with the blues. It's all in how you choose the notes and in how you ring them out. I guess I'll always be comparing."

Pete Henderson

Pete Henderson: Leader of The Bobby Watson Band

Pete Henderson, lead guitarist of Fatwall Jack, a group that stays close to its blues and R&B roots, was born in Natick in 1951 and learned the instrument in his twenties.

"For my twenty-first birthday I bought myself an acoustic guitar because I needed a hobby. Mostly I just liked strumming little folk songs and I've always been able to sing.

"Earlier, when I was in grammar school, I was always the one in the school plays who had the singing parts. The teachers always made me stand out front because I was the loud mouth in the class," said Henderson, who is really very soft-spoken and an overall nice guy.

Little did he know that his roles in the school plays would help him earn a living.

"A few friends of mine had moved from New York to Massachusetts, and we worked at the Fernald School, a mental health facility in Waltham. We used to jam up there every Sunday night, moving the beds around to set up and play. And the patients there loved it. I kind of struggled with the guitar at first and I wasn't real comfortable singing either, but at least I had done it. And I could definitely sing better than the other guys. They couldn't sing a note.

"Besides the residents, the administration liked it because we weren't too abusive," Henderson said. "We'd only bring in a few beers every now and then.

"Then in the spring and summer, we used to play outside on Sunday afternoons and they'd bring all the residents out, and there'd be a thousand people out on the hill listening and dancing. So that's really where I got started playing.

"That is also when the Bobby Watson Band came together. One of the patients was reading a play called 'The False Soprano' and in it there's a mention of Bobby Watson. But Bobby Watson was everybody. In the play, when people had a conversation they were saying Bobby Watson my aunt, Bobby Watson my mother, Bobby Watson my brother -- so the conversation became all about Bobby Watson.

"In the band, we'd introduce people as Aunt B on bass, Bobby Watson on drums, Bobby Watson on vocals and Bobby Watson on guitar. We had this skeleton that we used to dress up, and it became Bobby Watson. We'd carry him around with us, and we had a rocking chair, a lamp and a little rug, and we'd stick a pipe in his mouth. Sometimes he had a tuxedo on and other times he'd have on summer apparel, dressed in shorts and sunglasses.

"Somewhere, someone took a picture of him. Then we decided to make T-shirts, and we put Bobby Watson on the T-shirt. I probably sold about 10,000 of those shirts over the years," Henderson said.

In the mid- to late-1970s, The Bobby Watson Band played a lot of gigs in little clubs around the Framingham-Natick area and at a large club called The Cricket.

But the best gig to get at that time was at the Speakeasy in Cambridge. After jamming with the regulars a few times, Henderson and Bobby Watson were able to snag a few dates during the week, then it was weekend gigs. "Somehow we worked our way up and Speakeasy Pete was giving us one weekend a month and that one gig is really what got us going because Pete was probably one of the only blues clubs in the city that advertised in the Boston Phoenix with a big ad. And the ad for the weekend would read, Eddie Shaw and the Wolf Gang, Sugar Ray and the Bluetones, The James Cotton Cotton Band, and The Bobby Watson Band.

"So, with that kind of publicity, it was the best thing that could have happened to get us over the hump," Henderson said. "After that, it was easier to get around and we played all over New England, and played lots of colleges. At that time the colleges would spend lots of money to have bands come in and they'd throw these big parties, like a toga party.

"I did that until the early '90s. It kind of wound down a little bit because it was hard to replace key people because of situational things. It just got to be a huge chore and I got a little tired of it and I started doing another band on the side.

"Jack Bialka, one of the founding members (along with guitarist George McCann) and current bass player of the Blue Hornets, and I started this little band called Secret Weapons. We played on odd nights here or there. The group consisted of drummer Steve Barbuta, who was also playing with James Montgomery, and a keyboard player named Sandy Mac who also used to play with James Montgomery years ago.

"We did that for a little while and then those people were working too much, so Jack and I decided to try something else," Henderson said. "So we got Ron Sloan, a Worcester-based harmonica player, and another drummer and changed the name of the band to Little Ronnie and the Sloan Sharks.

Art Simas

"We did that for about two years. Then Ronnie went off to do something else (called Evening Sun, and became another musical mentor to rising guitarist Troy Gonyea), so I changed the name, instead of just being the Sloan Sharks, I changed it to the Loan Sharks and did that for a little while," Henderson said.

One of the original players in Fatwall Jack, Kerry Blount, was also the original sax player for Bobby Watson years ago.

"He was one of the guys that used to work at the Fernald School, so I've known him for 27 years," Henderson said. "When we started Fatwall Jack with Erica Rodney, we were thinking of another instrument and the different possibilities of what it would be and I knew Kerry played in another band but he wasn't real busy so I called him up. He lives way out in Shelburne Falls. So he's a trooper, man.

"He played with in a band called Swallow in the early 1970s which had George 'Rockin' Shoes' Leh and Parker Wheeler (who hosts a Sunday night all star jam, now in its 10th year, with Dennis 'Fly' Amero at the Grog in Newburyport, Mass.) as lead singers. They were on Atlantic Records and put out three or four LPs. They were really big for about three or four years.

"So it's just been working out with…Erica singing. She was never really into a blues thing. She had a little rock 'n' roll band, and when I first met her I made her some tapes," Henderson said. "At the time, she was happy doing her rock 'n' roll thing, but little by little I kept scratching at her, 'Hey come up to the jam, y'know.' And she got into it. I'd give her tapes and she'd learn the material, so we've tried different things.

"We do a little R&B, some swing, some West Side blues. We've been trying duets and we have maybe seven or eight but I don't want to make a whole night of that. She's lots of fun and energetic and people pick up on that.

"The name Fatwall Jack doesn't mean a thing," Henderson said. "That was a name actually that I thought of years ago for another band but the other guys didn't like it. We were like trying to think of names, looking at the back of record covers and I mentioned that, and everyone agreed, and that was it."

Fatwall Jack released its debut CD, "The Girl Next Door," in 1999. The disc received very favorable reviews in local and national press.

Web: fatwalljack.com

Professor Harp (Hugh Holmes)

Art Simas
Professor Harp: The undaunted one

There is one question that keeps nagging Professor Harp (Hugh Holmes) like a lost, hungry dog that follows you down the street. Why, after nearly three decades of exhaling his soul into his namesake instrument and establishing himself in New England, is he still not further along than many of his contemporaries?

Though his perseverance has earned the respect of many of his peers, that respect has not carried equal weight with some booking managers. Maybe it has to do with bad luck, bad timing, bad politics, any number of things. But it's there.

He's had to endure more than his share of double-bookings and last-minute cancellations. Why? That's the big question.

"I've been kept on the periphery and it's affected my career. One thing I don't like is the politics. Sometimes I feel like it's a closed circle. Why I don't know. But it shouldn't be like that. There's room for everyone on the scene," Harp said.

But the past is definitely not prologue. Harp wants to leave the past in the history books, but he also wants more than lip service.

"I'll do Memphis-type R&B, Detroit R&B, uptown blues, jump, roots rock and roll -- basically whatever moves me at the time. On the harp, I like the Texas approach. You've got to be good to do it because you've got to move a lot of air," he said.

In attempting to create a big band sound with a quartet, similar to what he first heard with the original Fabulous Thunderbirds, Harp will experiment with a 100-watt Mesa Boogie amp for his various harps and switch from diatonic to chromatic, often evoking a B-3 effect on the mouth organ.

Born in the Back Bay section of Boston, Nov. 4, 1951, Harp began toning his chops as a teenage drummer in Bridgewater. During this time in the mid-1960s, he was only interested in covering rock standards. But he couldn't find the right players and didn't have a car.

"It was terrible. It really sucked," he said. "And then when I started playing more roots music, I became more frustrated because I couldn't find players who even knew what that was.

Boston's Blues

"One night I went to the Boston Tea Party in 1969 and Rod Piazza and George Smith were there (Bacon Fat). Before that, I had never heard what a harmonica could really do. "But when I saw Rod, then George Smith, I was hooked. I've got a lot of George Smith in me. And I can't forget Muddy Waters, too."

In 1975 Muddy invited him up on stage at Pall's Mall and Harp ended up playing with him learning those "sharecropper changes" that Muddy used in his timing the hard way. "Muddy used to take a 12-bar, hold it for 15 or 16, and I had all I could do just to catch up. I learned a lot from the old man."

A few years ago, he met Solomon Burke, who also asked him to sit in with him on one of his sets. After hearing Holmes, Burke told him, "You're the Professor of the Harmonica." So Holmes decided to shorten his new moniker to Professor Harp.

Harp played with several bands over the years, but he decided to strike out on his own with his own name. After leaving The Motivators in 1992, a band he formed and nurtured, Harp created Undaunted: Professor Harp. "No matter all the trials and tribulations I go through I'm going to come back for more," he says.

"I don't feel like I'm really growing yet unless I'm getting out there more," he said. "I've always had an affinity for the blues, it fits in with who I am. And it teaches you that you have to persevere."

Luther "Guitar Junior" Johnson

Boston's Blues
Luther "Guitar Junior" Johnson: Just doing what comes natural

Luther "Guitar Junior" Johnson's dream came true on a Monday night at 9:30 in 1972. That was the time Luther had to make a telephone call to his longtime idol and fellow Chicagoan Muddy Waters, and tell him he'd be ready to play with the band that Friday night in East Lansing, Mich.

At the time, Luther was working in a steel mill in Bellwood, Ill., so he had to get permission to leave work early to make the four-hour trip to East Lansing.

"Hell, I got off work at 10 that morning. I took my time and stopped along the way and went to visit some of my wife's cousins. Muddy went on at 10, and I got there at 7. Big club, place called the White Stable. And I mean it was packed. I had been playing a lot of small clubs before, but you know wherever you go, somebody's gonna know you. So as soon as I walked in the door, people were yelling and clapping, 'Guitar Junior, Guitar Junior, yeah, yeah, it's going to be a good time tonight.' So I went up to Muddy's dressing room and he says, 'Man, you got a hand just by walking in. That's good.' And I'm saying to myself, 'Well now, I guess I put something in his mind now, I'm glad I got the hand,'" Luther said.

Muddy told Luther that he'd play two songs, then he'd call him up to the stage. After the opening number, Muddy called him up. But there was one thing Luther hadn't really thought of till that moment. He had to play Muddy's guitar since he didn't bring his.

When he strapped on Muddy's guitar, Luther realized that the string gauges were very different and the instrument was tuned for more of a slide feel than the burning riffs, which was his style. "So I figured I more or less had to stroke it and not pick it. Then the guys asked me what key I was in? Hell, I don't know what key it's in… I think it was e-flat, but anyway they found it and I started singing and playing two verses of a Jimmy Reed song, 'Red light is a stop light and a green light means go,' and all the while I got my eyes closed. Then I opened 'em and I see everybody dancing and having a good time. From then on, there was no stopping me. I did about three songs, then Muddy came back."

And there was no turning back, Luther had replaced Hollywood Fats at that point, joining Muddy, Calvin "Fuzz" Jones on bass, Willie "Big Eyes" Smith on drums, Bostonian Bob Margolin, who had just joined the band about three months earlier, on rhythm guitar, Pinetop Perkins on piano and Mojo Buford on harp.

Luther said he got a leave of absence from his steel mill job for a year, just in case things didn't work out. But he never went back to a day job. Luther stayed with Muddy's band for nine years and then formed his own band for a while before joining up with the Legendary Blues Band with Perkins, Smith and Jerry Portnoy from Waltham, Mass., on harp.

In 1980, Luther settled in New England and has since carved another career as a very busy touring musician and leader of the Magic Rockers, named for one of his West Side mentors and neighbors of the 1960s, Magic Sam Maghett.

"I played with Sam for two and a half years and back then, you know, I drank a lot just to have fun. I'd drink, get high, then I'd go in the corner and go to sleep. And a lot of nights Sam would fire me 'cuz he'd find me sleeping in a corner somewhere. But he'd tell the others in the band, 'No, no, don't wake him up. As long as he's sleeping he's got a job. But when wakes up he's a fired mutha.'

"When I'd get up he'd say, 'Man, we'd just did 15 songs.'
"And I say, 'So, you don't want me going out there drunk do you?'"
"Then he'd ask me, 'How do you feel now?'"
"I said, 'I feel good.'"
"And he'd say, 'Do you think you can play one?'"
"And I'd know what to tell him, cuz he'd like to hear that song, 'Somebody Have Mercy.' So I'd get up there and be howling and I'd tear the house down, and he'd come by and say, 'Well, you got your job back.'"

Luther said he first got into music as the lead singer in The Spirit of Miller City, a five-member church choir that used to perform at different churches on Sundays in his native Mississippi. Luther was born April 11, 1939, in Itta Bena.

He dabbled with his cousin's guitar and played acoustically in the church choir when he was singing. That combination of singing and playing at the same time, which is Luther's trademark, was how he learned. "I'd always want to sing when I played. And the people'd love that, you know. They'd be throwing things at you from wallets and pocketbooks -- but no paper money'd be in there, that's for sure," he said.

"But when I wanted to play some blues, I couldn't let my mother know -- that was the devil's music. So we'd come back from church and my mother'd go out Sunday afternoon and go for a ride. Then it was guitar and party time for us kids.

Boston's Blues

We'd be playing, singing and dancing all afternoon, till someone would say, 'I think I hear a car coming...'"

In 1955 when he was 16, Luther moved in with his older sister and her two children in a Chicago apartment. So, when he realized that all his blues idols whom he heard on Memphis radio were in Chicago, literally doors away from him, "I'd put on this big hat and a fake moustache, so I could get into the bars. I was a big kid too. And when I got in, I'd go straight to the bar and order 100-proof Grandad. And Howlin' Wolf would be playing... and then the bartender would look at me, you know, and I'd look off... then he'd ask, "You, you old enough to be in here? Let me see some identification."

"Of course I didn't have any, so I'd leave, and go to the next club and do the same thing," he said laughing. "Once I got in Chicago, I knew I wasn't going back to Mississippi."

He and his two other sisters held jobs at a nearby hospital at 707 West Fullerton Ave. for about eight years. And it was about this time that he met Ray Scott, who allowed Luther to be a singer in his band, which also featured Floyd Murphy on guitar, brother of Matt "Guitar" Murphy, when Luther was 18.

During the breaks, Luther would sneak over and start noodling with one of the other band member's guitars and after a while "I got to be where I thought I was pretty good. But I didn't want anyone to know that I was learning guitar."

Luther moved to St. Louis for a year and got into a band with Little Junior Robinson, where at first both men played bass. So he said, "Luther, you take the lead and I'll play the bass, and that's how we worked it. So when I came home to Chicago after a year, I was pretty good, you know, I'm thinking yeah, I'm ready now."

But trying to make it on his own was pretty difficult. "You don't know what I went through. I played for tables and chairs for so long, just tables and chairs. And when I did get people in front of me, I didn't even know how to act. But all through the years, I'd play just as hard for one person or two persons as I do for 1,000," Luther said.

"I try my music out on me first, to see how I'll react, how I feel. I'm doing something that I can feel when I'm playing. Then if I can feel it, then I know that you can feel it. You'd be surprised at how many people have come up to me and said, 'Mr. Johnson, thank you for your music.' And that's the best feeling in the world -- giving a part of yourself to someone else and making 'em happy.

Art Simas

"In Warsaw, Poland, I played for 14,983 people all bobbing their heads like mine. I can sing all day and all night and never play the same song over. And you never know what I'm going to play. My band never knows what I'm going to play. I like it that way. I love playing the blues. It's my music, my roots."

Web: telarc.com/blues

Amyl Justin

Amyl Justin: The minister from the Motor City

Amyl Justin commands the stage with a voice that summons a passionate spirit of his early gospel days. But you'd best stand clear of the stage at his live gigs because this spirit moves in multiple directions simultaneously -- and he swings a mean microphone stand to boot.

Justin was born in Detroit in 1952, and by 15 he was playing the usual high school circuit, armory dances and other social events in the mid- to late-1960s. By 17, he was backing up main acts, such as Iggy and the Stooges, and playing in various dens and lounges in and around the Motor City.

But this whirling-dervish of a vocalist almost didn't get a chance to showcase his then-hidden diaphragmatic talent until he was forced to sing one night at the Muskegon Armory in Michigan. "I was the drummer in the band who was allowed to do back-up vocals now and then, but one night the bass player who was the lead vocalist got sick and they stuck the mike in front of me, and since then I've been singing," Justin said.

Justin's vocal prowess is one of the many highlights on "Pressure Cooker" from Tone-Cool Records. At first, it seems the disc is a hard-driving, seat-of-the-pants romp through familiar territory -- until you hear the nuances in the music from Kid Bangham's often understated guitar. Because the snips and snaps of cogent phrases coalesce so well with the out-front vocals, it forces the listener to pay attention to what's going on. And that appreciation grows with every turn of the disc.

Bangham is very meticulous and knows exactly what he wants to do, Justin said. The duo have been preparing the CD for the better part of two years. They had been doing session work off and on, but their main focus was always on "Pressure Cooker."

Bangham, born in Philadelphia in 1958, said he took some years off to be with his daughter and devote more time to writing "and putting it all together." Musically, he said, he is at his best when he can create something and see it come to life and then try different methods and variations.

Justin said Bangham has been dogged about his approach to the music. Bangham has also gained a convert at the same time. "I love the way he plays. He's one of those guys who can speak just as loud without playing. The guitar is just the icing on the cake," Justin said. "I had wanted things to have a higher energy. I'm sort of a very right in-your-face kind of performer, but he chooses the more subtle route. I kind of like that about him."

During a three-year stint in the U.S. Coast Guard off of Governor's Island in New York, Justin played in many of the smaller clubs in Greenwich Village, "a totally different scene completely" from his Michigan roots, he said. Yet he never lost sight of what he wanted: a chance to make music his life.

After the Coast Guard, Justin returned to Grand Haven, Mich., and went to a community college. He put a couple of different bands together and moved out to Saginaw. But the West Coast and California seemed like a better opportunity.

"I almost starved to death out there," he said of California. So he decided to head East around 1984 and he put together a 10-piece soul R&B revue called the Motor City Rhythm Kings, which still gets together on rare occasions.

When he first arrived in the Boston area, Justin said there was a vibrant scene with a range of places to play which paid bands a reasonable wage. This was about the time that Harpers Ferry was in the midst of a transition from a good ole country watering hole to a happening blues hot spot, with crowds waiting around corners to get a glimpse at the Rhythm Kings.

At various times, the Motor City Rhythm Kings featured Matt Woodburn, Scott Shetler, Steve Brown, Rob Lee, Stu Schiffer, and others. "We played a good amount of original R&B and played to whatever the crowd wanted," Justin said. The main thing on the owner's part was "what's going to get them to drink."

After about two and a half years of no personnel changes in the band, Justin said he felt a need to take a new direction and look for a new guitarist. So the band asked musicians to audition, and "here comes Matt Woodburn in for his audition with this black eye makeup from his Young Guns rock group, and he starts tearing it up. The other guys in the band really didn't want him. They were saying, 'No, no no, we can't have this guy.' But he was exactly what we needed. All he wanted to do was play blues -- Albert Collins, Freddie King and Stevie Ray Vaughan stuff. It was a perfect combination for us and I said, 'You're hired.'"

The band was recorded on a compilation disc called "Botown Does Motown" on Fast Track Records in 1986 or '87, Justin said.

Justin is proud to say that Motor City Rhythm Kings was a spawning ground for so many of the musicians who remain very active in Boston today.

Art Simas

In 1998, guitarist Peter Malick and Justin released "Sons of the Jet Age," a rock-based blues disc that even got the Number 1 spot on Australian radio.

In late 1999, Justin moved to Nashville.

Bruce Katz

Art Simas
Bruce Katz: Digging jazz and playing blues

Musician. Teacher. Composer. Bruce Katz is all of them at the same time in the Boston blues scene and he's been an integral player for a number of bands over the years, including Barrence Whitfield and the Savages, Ronnie Earl and the Broadcasters, and now, with his own band.

Katz was born in 1952 in Brooklyn, N.Y., but grew up in the Long Island suburb of Valley Stream. After the mandatory years of classical training, beginning at age 5, Katz stumbled across a Bessie Smith record tucked deep in his parents' record collection.

"I really flipped," he said. Then it was New Orleans Dixieland jazz and boogie-woogie that fueled his musical curiosity.

"I taught myself blues by listening to a lot of people," he says, "but I didn't talk to my classical teacher about it. I don't think he would have dug it."

A year at Johns Hopkins University was convincing enough that Katz was not made to be a lawyer. "I was into rock and blues bands instead of going to classes." But a second academic career began in 1974, when Katz came to Boston and enrolled at Berklee College of Music.

"That was a time where I was all jazz, jazz, jazz, from 1974 to 1980, I just pursued jazz in a very single-minded way, which is a way to get good at something – focus, focus, focus.

"I graduated Berklee as a composition major. And I composed three-movement piano sonatas, fugues and short works, which was kind of cool. I consider myself a composer because all of my albums are original works," he said.

Berklee provided the solid foundation for his career as a professional musician. Katz said, "If you write a sonata or if you write a Motown song, it's all about writing music -- the same concept is involved. Styles come and go, but the same concepts of what makes a good jazz, blues or rock tune or classical are all grounded in similar types of ideas on melody and how to approach things."

After graduating in 1977, he was ready to conquer the music world and make his mark. But to earn a living and pay the rent, "I was playing in a disco show band. Well, it was better than getting a day job," Katz said.

Boston's Blues

"I played with a lot of different people in the jazz world... Mark Harvey and Aardvark, Search, Jimmy Moser... and then I started falling back into blues again... and playing with Dave Scholl, who was a sax player with Barrence Whitfield and the Savages. And we played with Big Mama Thornton in some of her last gigs, and with Cranky Frankie in a band called the Big City Twisters with Mike Costello (now a fifth-grade teacher) who was one of the founders of the Cambridge Harmonica Orchestra with Pierre Beauregard of Truro, Mass.

In 1985, Katz, Milt Reder of Rear Window Studios and who also went to Johns Hopkins, and Dave Scholl got together with Barrence Whitfield and formed the Savages, which lasted from 1986 to 1990. "That was the most powerful thing I've ever been involved with," Katz said. "That band blew walls down every single night. And we toured constantly, nine months a year. I ended up doing seven tours of Europe and made three albums with the group. But by the end of it, I was pretty much dragging. I didn't know – musically -- what end was up and my chops were down."

Katz went back to the classroom at the New England Conservatory and enrolled in its Masters Program in Jazz Performance, "which was the opposite of being on the road. I could forget about the business end of the music and forget about touring and concentrate on the music, and the teachers there, some of them were jazz legends.

"I was 37, the oldest student in the program. I think I got a lot more out of it because I came from a different angle than most of the students who were there right after college. I was getting a jazz degree, but I was able to put together all of the other stuff. In fact I put together my own band in my second year. I had realized that if I was going to do my own thing, I had to put the effort out and put a band together."

Katz graduated from the Conservatory in May 1992, the same month as his debut record, "Crescent Crawl." Earlier that year, Katz recalls playing background jazz piano with Marty Ballou on bass, for a Best of Boston Magazine party. "When I was playing, all of a sudden I felt like there were laser beams on the back of my head. I turned around, and it was Ronnie Earl. He had just won the Best of Boston award for best guitarist, and I guess he dug what I was doing. So, about 10 months later, he called me to join his band. Even though I had my own album out, I wasn't about to turn it down. So I did that for five years."

In 1994, Katz released "Tranformation," followed by "Mississippi Moan," and in 2000, "Three Feet Off the Ground."

"Mississippi Moan" features "Hanging On A Cross Between Heaven And The Blues," sung by vocalist Mighty Sam McClain. In fact, McClain had written the lyrics six months before, but he didn't know how to present it in a song. So when Katz presented Sam with the music, it was a perfect match.

Katz has also been involved in many side projects for Audioquest Records of California. "I've been on all of Mighty Sam's records for Audioquest, and Joe Beard's (of Rochester, N.Y.) CD featuring Duke Robillard and Jerry Portnoy; (A second Joe Beard record was recorded in 1999 with Per Hanson and Rod Carey who had teamed with Katz in Ronnie Earl and the Broadcasters); Dennis Brennan; a Jimmy Witherspoon record with Duke; and a jazz record for Cercie Miller. (Katz was in the Miller band in the early '90s.)

On "Mississippi Moan," band members included Tom Hall on saxophone, Julien Kasper, on guitar; Ralph Rosen on drums, and Tony Poniatowski on bass with Katz on keys. Mike Costello played harp.

On "Three Feet Off the Ground," the Bruce Katz band includes Katz on Hammond B-3 organ and piano, Kasper on guitar, Rosen on drums, and Blake Newman on acoustic bass.

Today, Katz teaches private piano lessons and is a part-time instructor at Berklee College of Music. Katz covers the history, analysis and composition of the music from various styles and perspectives in Blues Application and Analysis, the first blues course ever offered at the college.

Katz says students listen and analyze the works of bluesmen such as Charley Patton or Big Bill Broonzy, for example. "We'll get very deep into what exactly is going on musically and technically when that person created a song," Katz said.

"Then I have the students write blues in different styles. Right now we're into early jump era and getting near Muddy Waters," he said. "But it's tough to fit everything in one semester."

Web: brucekatzband.com

Boston's Blues
Marian Leighton-Levy: Founder and inspiration for Rounder's Bullseye Blues label

Founded in 1970 on the idea that "if someone could start a record company in West Virginia, then hell we can too," Rounder Records began its musical journey into the heart of America.

Two ex-roommates at Tufts University, Ken Irwin and Bill Knowlin, and Marian Leighton-Levy knew there was a void of American music that was not being played: music of the people in the Appalachian hills, in the bayous of Louisiana and of family get-togethers in alfalfa fields in the Midwest. It was home-spun melodies and the storytelling pathos of folk and blues. In essence, the collective soul of America was being ignored by major record companies and radio stations in the late 1960s.

When they first set out to find these artists and performers, Irwin, Knowlin and Leighton-Levy were simply fans of the music with one unified goal -- let the public enjoy this art for what it is -- nothing more, nothing less. If people liked it, that was cool. Musical appreciation, awareness and fun were tops on their bottom line. Making money was never the ultimate motivation for the trio.

Because the focus was on the music and not the dollar, artists were attracted to this start-up company that had a genuine sense of togetherness and purpose. Over the last three decades, this familial environment enveloped dozens of musicians and propelled Rounder to its status as a premier worldwide record manufacturer, producer and distributor.

In the early days, folk and blues were intertwined, Marian Leighton-Levy says. "We were kind of the same as the other labels that were a little bit before ours, like Arhoolie Records, and grew up doing the folk and blues revival -- the era of the Ann Arbor Blues Festival. So we always considered blues as a part of folk," she said.

As for its blues beginnings, Rounder scoured dozens of tapes from collectors, and from friends like George Mitchell and David Evans, who were doing limited recordings and collecting older country blues material for their own record bins. Rounder set out and acquired these forgotten gems, breathing new life into the roots-based Southern blues.

One of the mainstays in the formative years was Frank Hovington, a Delta-style guitarist who was living in Delaware when Rounder discovered his talent.

103

Art Simas

In the early 1970s, Rounder recruited ace producer Scott Billington, who rekindled the sounds of Robert Johnson through the music of Johnny Shines and Robert Jr. Lockwood. Both had traveled many a muddied road with the elusive Johnson during the 1930s and learned to emulate the master's picking techniques.

Shines' live 1971 acoustic recordings on "Hey Ba-Ba-Re-Bop" plays tribute to Johnson's barebones grit and soul. A follow-up collaboration of Shines and Lockwood on "Hangin' On" furthered the Johnson legacy to a new generation. The album won a W.C. Handy Award for Traditional Blues Album of the Year.

The addition of George Thorogood to the Rounder family solidified the blues as a commercially successful genre. Thorogood was Rounder's first megastar and the company's premier act for several years. The George Thorogood & the Destroyers debut in 1977 jump-started the group's enormous popularity, riding that wave right into the 1990s. The subsequent "Move It On Over" became Rounder's first gold record in 1978.

After the astounding success of Thorogood's releases, Rounder began producing more touring bands, such as Roomful of Blues ("Hot Little Mama," "Dressed Up To Get Messed Up" and "Live at Lupo's") on its sister label, Varrick.

"So at the same time we were working with Roomful, we were doing George's records and the Nighthawks, who were definitely the most happening of the touring blues bands," Leighton-Levy said.

Meanwhile, Rounder started distributing Black Top records and expanding its blues artists' stable to include Anson Funderburgh and the Rockets and Earl King with Roomful. Both appeared on the "blusier" Black Top label, based in New Orleans, rather than Rounder.

"Through that experience, we wound up working with Ron Levy on a number of projects including our 'Modern New Orleans Masters Series.' Some of the grittier records on that series, such as the Mardi Gras Indians and brass bands records, we have Ron to thank for," Leighton-Levy said.

Billington, who spawned the notion of a New Orleans Masters Series, began producing albums for the suave and polished Soul Queen of New Orleans, Irma Thomas, and the prolific and versatile vocalist Johnny Adams. (Note: See the profile on Scott Shetler and his work with Johnny Adams.)

Boston's Blues

About a decade ago, Leighton-Levy and Levy tossed around the notion that since Rounder was making more and more blues recordings, why not create a label exclusively devoted to blues. And that became the inspiration for the founding of Bullseye Blues.

"Both Ron and Scott have been incredible assets," Leighton-Levy said. "They are very different in terms of approach and style. You can hear Scott's approach on all of the 'New Orleans Master Series' whereas in Bullseye, you hear Ron."

Because of his vast musical experiences with B.B. King, Albert King, Roomful of Blues and many, many other artists, Ron Levy strives to harness the essence of live blues in the studio. Like a chemist, Levy works to quickly bottle the musical elixir before it has a chance to mellow or lose its potency.

"He's an absolute master of that," says Leighton-Levy. "That's what we try to capture on Bullseye. I think it will last and people will find the recordings just as exciting in 10 or 20 years as the day that it was released. That's the goal -- not to make something for any particular audience or market -- it's the music for its own sake. It's music-making at its purest and that's Ron's approach.

"For us, the music has always come first. That's why we like what we're doing and why we're in Cambridge instead of New York or L.A. We're also not a bureaucratic company where some portion of it is run by accountants or lawyers. We're made up of people who like the music that we do and as a result, there's a kind of family feeling within the company. I think it's inevitable that having that family feeling with the musicians is a natural part of that whole relationship and process.

"We started out with Ken, Bill and I, with us being a '60s kind of family, then as we get older and have had families of our own, it becomes a further extension and expression of that. And I'd like to think that the same is true of the blues part of our catalog and the Bullseye experience," she said.

"In a sense I feel that Bullseye was our baby at the same time that A.J. (Ron Levy and Marian Leighton-Levy's son) was born. And then it brought it all back home in the sense of bringing Roomful to that label. I feel honored to be working with them again," Leighton-Levy said.

Other notables who have recorded on the Bullseye label include: Charles Brown (the first artist to record on Bullseye), Little Jimmy King, Smokin' Joe Kubek, Otis Clay, Ann Peebles, Jimmy McCracklin, Champion Jack Dupree at the New

Art Simas

Orleans Jazz & Heritage Festivals in 1990 and 1991, Michelle Willson, Luther "Guitar Jr." Johnson, Bluestime with Jay Geils and Magic Dick, and Ronnie Earl.

Because of Knowlin's penchant for forging ahead and using the latest technology (Rounder was the first label to produce roots and blues music on compact disc), the company entered new territory with the first CD-Plus or CD-Pro on Roomful's "Turn It On, Turn It Up." The disc has a video component, so listeners can see a video of the performance on their personal computers if they have a CD-ROM drive.

"It's interesting to think about and speculate where the blues will be going in 21st century," Leighton-Levy says. "What makes the blues what it is -- the great playing, the inspired singing, will certainly be as important and an essential part of it. But I see a lot more opportunities for the music to grow and be spread into many areas.

"One of the things that have happened within the last 15 years is that all musics are kind of interdisciplinary. Categories matter less and less because reaching people through radio stations has become so specialized and rigid that it's almost pointless. You can't count on reaching the public through radio in general," Leighton-Levy said.

"As a result, a lot of the things that are the strengths of blues, such as the 'liveness' of it, will become more and more important."

Web: rounder.com

Ron Levy

Ron Levy: A great influence on modern blues
as a performer, producer and executive

Ron Levy. His name is everywhere. Flip over a blues record and I'll bet you that name will appear somewhere in the credits or liner notes.

Born May 29, 1951 in Cambridge, Mass., little did anyone know that Ron Levy would become a giant in the music industry by excelling as producer, arranger and performer.

Before we get too far, here are some tidbits on Levy. The kid started playing piano in 1964. In 1966 he was backing up people such as Chuck Berry, Freddie King and John Lee Hooker; in 1968, he was playing organ for Albert King; and in 1969, he was playing piano in B.B. King's band.

Levy also has a great eye and ear for new talent, advancing the careers of such artists as Bernard Allison, Smokin' Joe Kubek, Johnnie Bassett, Michelle Willson, Byther Smith, Little Jimmy King, Tommy Castro, Gordon Beadle, Susan Tedeschi, Mike Welch, Pat Boyack, Andrew Jr. Boy Jones, Tutu Jones, Preston Shannon, Henry Qualls and many, many more.

"When I'm looking for new talent, I'm looking for a uniqueness, a vibe, and a message that the person stands for something. Or a certain image, think of the greats. There's a certain visual associated with them. That's what I look for and someone who can deliver a great show. The talent can be developed," Levy said.

And it all started on the clarinet, the instrument of "well it looks easy enough to play" forced choice for many who attended elementary school during the 1950s and early 1960s.

Levy took clarinet lessons in 1959 and also played alto and baritone sax in high school, but admits, "I never could play."

1964 was the watershed year. After seeing Ray Charles deliver a vocal and piano sermon, the first concert Levy attended on his own, the teen started dabbling on the keyboard the next day.

"When I was 14-15, I zeroed in during that summer. It was an awkward growing stage and I kind of withdrew and went straight into my music and practiced every day. I went to a job but when I got home I'd play the piano up to the point where my parents would tell me to knock it off. Doing that every single day, I had improved quite a bit and had a direction.

"And that's when I got bitten by the bug. It was music in general. I was always one of those kids who brought 'James Brown Live at the Apollo,' Aretha Franklin, Otis Redding and Muddy Waters records to teen parties. I just always loved that American music.

"I grew up in Brookline and went to Brookline High, and I was in the same homeroom as Peter Malick; Bob Margolin was a year ahead of us. A lot of talent came out of that school," Levy said.

(Margolin went on to eventually play with Muddy Waters and Malick went on to play with Otis Spann of Muddy Waters' band.)

With everyone around him playing in a band, Levy put together his own group and before they knew it, they were backing up John Lee Hooker, Big Mama Thronton, Albert King, Bo Diddley, Chuck Berry, Freddie King and others at all different places from frat parties to the Boston Garden.

"We opened up for Albert King at Lenny's on the Turnpike and that night Albert fired half of his band. He ended up hiring me and my drummer. I was still in high school, so I played on the weekends with Albert King. After a while we played on a bill with B.B. King. And Sonny Freeman (that was the name that B.B. went by – Sonny Freeman and the Un-usuals) asked me for my number just in case there was an opening. And a few months later, he called me at my home. At first I thought it was a joke being played by Albert King or somebody in his band," Levy said.

"Playing with Albert was one thing and it completely floored me, but B.B. was more intimidating. I was 18 at the time. I was tested but it was good for me... He was strict in a tough-love kind of way, but he'd always give a guy another chance. But if you screwed up he'd let you know about it.

"B.B. is not the king of the blues just because he sings and plays great. He's the king of the blues because he works hard. I can't say any more about his work ethic. B.B. taught you how to conduct yourself and how to be in show business. You learned from the master. And he's such a great bandleader and a great humanitarian. He always treats the fans with the utmost respect. He was great to work for.

"I learned as much from the other players in the band, too, good things and bad things. We had a lot of fun and did a lot of stuff. We had a big hit record – 'The Thrill Is Gone.'

"In playing, the dates were divided into thirds, like Chitlin' Circuit gigs, which don't exist any more, and the hippy houses (Filmores and Boston Tea Party) and everything else from the original Antone's in Austin and the old Tipitina's in New Orleans. And each town had one of those joints, and we did colleges, casinos and lounges. Those were very interesting times because the blues was coming out of that Chitlin' Circuit thing to a more wider audience. And we just played our hearts out every night.

"When I was a kid, there was a mystique about the blues. You had to dig it out, there were only newsletters about the music. Most of the stuff you learned from was first-hand from individuals. Back then it was a rebellious thing to be into that, which is what I liked. But you've got to remember, there were a lot of changes going on in civil rights and all, and by sort of being part of the music, you were part of the freedom movement. And I'm sure that had a lot to do with B.B. picking me. I wasn't the best piano player out there, but a lot of kids could identify with me at colleges, so there was some marketing on B.B.'s part, too.

"B.B. and I usually hook up two to three times a year. When I saw him in the fall of 1998 he said he was proud that I was grown up and a man. He sees me like my parents; I was just starting to shave practically when I first met him at Louie's Lounge. He was about 39 or 40.

"And then I told him in '98, 'I'm older now (48) than you were when I first met you.' That kind of put it in a different perspective.

"So it's kind of funny, he called me son, because he helped raise me. It was kind of like being in the Army, you had to measure up to their expectations.

"When I played with B.B., we'd open up with 'Everyday I Have The Blues' and then go into 'How Blue Can You Get' but the rest of the show was spontaneous. He'd never count off a song, he'd never tell you what key he was in. He'd just start playing. You just had to be psychic to a certain degree," Levy said.

Levy was the pianist and road warrior with B.B. King from 1969 to 1976. "When I left I was the last member of the originals who played with B.B. in 1969," Levy said.

110

Boston's Blues

Levy returned to the Boston area afterward and settled in as the keyboard player in the Rhythm Rockers with Johnny Nicholas, Ronnie Earl, Sarah Brown, Kaz Kazanoff and Big Walter Horton at the Speakeasy in Cambridge. Of course the Speakeasy was one of, if not the top blues club in Greater Boston at the time. So that lasted for five years.

In 1980, Levy joined the newly arrived Luther "Guitar Junior" Johnson and the Magic Rockers as organist and road manager. During the same year, Levy began to do a lot of session work with Rounder Records, working with J.B. Hutto, who had also settled in the Boston area, Sleepy LaBeef, Duke Robillard, Irma Thomas, and others.

In 1983, Roomful of Blues came calling, and that gig lasted from '83 to '87. During that time, Roomful released several classic albums, "Hot Little Mama," "Live At Lupo's Heartbreak Hotel," "Dressed Up to Get Messed Up," and collaborations with Big Joe Turner and Eddie 'Cleanhead' Vinson with Levy and longtime Rounder producer Scott Billington at the helm.

Along the way, Levy kept his fingers moving along the keyboard as the master of the B-3 groove. He released the first of his Wild Kingdom albums in 1985 with members of the Fabulous Thunderbirds and Roomful of Blues as major contributors. He also had an affinity for the New Orleans rhythms and is a player on two solo albums and a session musician, arranger, and/or producer and A&R executive on 18 other albums from 1984 to 1987 with Black Top Records.

He then signed on with Rounder and remained with them for 10 years from '87 to '97.

In 1987, Levy founded his own company, Levtron Productions and Levtron Music and moved deeper into the technical aspects of production and arranging for Rounder Records of Cambridge.

In 1988, A.J. Levy was born to Marian Leighton-Levy and Ron on Nov. 18.

"I was with Roomful of Blues and working for Blacktop Records (associated with Rounder at the time in New Orleans) and I met Marian, fell in love and got married; and started doing session work for Rounder, so I learned my way around the studio.

"Then I got into a situation where I wanted to do other stuff, but it didn't fit in with what Rounder was doing," he said. There was another solution – start a label that was focused on blues and which was easy to identify.

"I was at a party and Paul Rishell and Rosy Rosenblatt was there... and Rosy had this huge dictionary. So I started from A and looking for a name for the label. I went through the A's and then I looked at bulldog, and then I thought of Bullseye. You could do a lot with marketing with that kind of name, and that evolved into Bullseye Blues, a place where I could channel these artists who were playing blues.

In 1997, Levy formed a partnership with Scott Haidle and created Cannonball Records, based out of Minneapolis, Minn. But after about a year and a half, Haidle decided to cut Levy out of the action after Levy had built up a stable of talent including Bernard Allison and Johnny Bassett, and others.

Haidle had a company called Pollstar Distributing, in Minnesota, which was financed by him and various friends.

"We had a good run. We put up a lot of money," Levy said. "But from my personal divorce proceedings (from Marian), he got notice that my shares could not be transferred or sold and that kind of spooked him.

"I think he spent more money than he should have. Looking back on it, I think the return that he expected on releases that were out for a year were unreasonable, and he was in control of the spending, which bugged me because I was getting good prices and I built this thing up... And when the opportunity presented itself to where he could take all the money as a tax write-off and keep everything for himself, that's what he decided to do... I had no recourse when they cashed in all their chips. I trusted him too much. But I guess it's the way of the world. I didn't get any compensation such as royalties or mechanicals from songs that I wrote or published.

"I could have probably fought it in court, but it might have taken five or six years but by that time I may have ended up with nothing. But it was my baby. I created the whole goddamn thing and I found everybody. The whole art look and the marketing gimmicks (the little lead shot inside a CD jewel case) were my ideas.

"He promised more than he could deliver. The staff was completely inexperienced in running a label, and a lot of time and money were wasted through the learning process. We just weren't getting the good product placement. We were competing head to head with labels that were out there for 50 years.

Boston's Blues

"I was planning for the long term. It's too bad because we had a great feeling, and roster," Levy said.

"So I looked at myself and I asked myself, 'What can I do now?' And I knew what I could do, which is write, create music and play. No one can take this away from me.

"But, you know, everything worked out for the best. I'm the happiest I've ever been. I'm back home, close to my son, writing, performing, rehearsing and playing two or three times a week. I feel energized playing again.

"Before, when I was with Roomful and B.B., even with the Ron Levy Blues Band, we did over 250 nights a year, so it was just gig after gig. And then when I was producing, I was doing more, creating music and arrangements. But I was doing it for everybody else.

"Now, I've come full circle -- my band, my arrangements and I'm doing what I want to do -- and people are digging it. It's really satisfying, I'm very fulfilled in that regard," Levy said.

Web: levtron.com

Shirley Lewis

Boston's Blues
Shirley Lewis has got a lot of soul and blues

Shirley Lewis knows the blues. Good blues, bad blues, all kinds of blues. And she continues to live the blues. But the blues will never get her down because she believes in herself and her talents.

Watching Shirley Lewis deliver a gospel show is a spiritual experience. She doesn't profess religion, rather, she lets the spirit move her, and through her, the audience is moved -- to dance, clap their hands, smile. It's a gift she gives graciously and she puts every ounce of herself into her performance -- her blues.

Shirley Lewis was born in 1937 and grew up in southern New Jersey, the third youngest child of 13, six of whom survived. She has five brothers and one sister. Her father was a full-blooded Hopi American Indian and her mother was one-quarter Blackfoot American Indian and black.

She began singing in the church choir when she was 4 and at vaudeville-type festivals and fairs where her father was an entertainer. The family, known as the Lewis Gospel Singers, traveled to these shows on the weekends throughout New Jersey under the tutelage of her father, who taught them various songs, lyrics and harmonies. He died when Lewis was 14 but the family carried on the tradition for a few more years.

Singing came naturally to the youngster. She only needed to hear a song once and she could sing it back note for note. "I guess you'd say I have a photographic memory. I don't know what it is but I've always had it. I know more than 2,000 songs about all the blues. I have no idea how I've done it but I was just born with it. I can hear something once, I know it. If I like it I know it forever. If I don't like it I discard it. Isn't that weird?"

Determined to get away from an abusive husband, Lewis moved to British Columbia, Canada, in the 1970s, with her two daughters. The marriage was marred by violence. "He beat me and he was a drunk most of the time," she said. So Shirley had to raise two babies, Marlene Marie and Minerva Joy, now in their 40s, respectively, by herself, defend herself from a no-good husband, and make enough money to support everyone. It was an awful time in her life. Singing soul, R&B and gospel was her salvation.

"I was young and I put all my effort into singing. I had to because I chose to be a singer," Lewis said. She worked throughout all of the western Canadian provinces -- Alberta, Saskatchewan, Manitoba and British Columbia, and dropping down to the States to perform in Washington and Oregon, too.

She also made occasional trips to the East Coast to visit her mom, who remained in New Jersey. She opened for B.B. King in 1965 in Chileshurst, N.J., one night, which started a lifelong friendship with the King of the Blues. "He's been a tremendous force in my life," she said. "That's when I really started singing blues. Up to that time I sang R&B, Motown and other stuff, but when I found the blues I knew that was for me because that's what I know," she said.

In 1980, B.B. returned the favor and sat in with Shirley on one of her gigs at the Cafe New York in Vancouver, Shirley's home at the time. Today, she has dual citizenship status as a Canadian and an American.

Eight years earlier, she landed the leading role in the "Black Is Beautiful Show," a two-year gig that turned into six, also in Vancouver. She recorded an album, "Black Eyes" in 1975, which followed a popular single, "I Need You," two years previously.

At this time, Lewis was one of the top entertainers in Canada, and regularly played the best houses in that country. "I never wanted to be a big, big star. If it came along, then that was just fine," she said, "but I never went looking for it."

In 1986, she moved to the Boston area to be closer to her mother, who died in 1991. She dove into the local Boston blues scene and attended the many jams with Earring George Mayweather and Silas Hubbard at the 1369 in Cambridge, and Harpers Ferry in Allston. She recorded two albums during the 1990s and has played in just about every club in New England. She's been a featured performer at the City of Presidents Festival in Quincy, Mass., the Portsmouth Blues Festival in Portsmouth, N.H., among others, and is often called to do corporate and private parties. She's traveled to Iowa several times for the Mississippi Valley Blues Festival, one of her favorite spots on the banks of the Mississippi River.

Locally, she teamed up with guitarist City Pete Poirier in the Shirley Lewis Experee-ance, and occasionally does a gospel show with vocalist and drummer, K.D. Bell. She says she'd love to do more gospel shows and record a gospel CD sometime in the next year or two. She plans to release her latest CD in 2001 called "The Blues According to Shirley Lewis."

"I like to do my own thing," Lewis said, "I want to unite people and I talk a lot about togetherness. Everybody should be getting along."

Web: shirleylewis.com

Teo Leyasmeyer

Art Simas
Teo Leyasmeyer proves that dreams do come true

While the road has taken some strange twists and turns for Teo Leyasmeyer, including three brief stints at divinity schools, including Harvard, the musical director for the original House of Blues has been preparing for this opportunity all his life.

And to think of it, Teo may have the most enviable job in the business. He gets to book the performances, occasionally sits in on keyboards, and coordinates dozens of blues projects.

As the steward and caretaker of the most recognizable blues icon in New England, Teo is aware of the historical importance of the House within the community. He also knows he's being watched on a number of fronts: by House of Blues corporate management and its board of directors, other club owners, and potential entrepreneurs who may be looking to emulate the formula.

So is there pressure to come through and deliver the goods?

"It's not a matter of me competing with anybody -- they know where I'm coming from," Teo says. "I'm a blues guy."

What makes Cambridge so special is its rich history of mingling generations, lifestyles and cultures. The community has always nurtured those who are passionate about their music.

From the late '40s through the '50s, Greater Boston was a famous stop for the top-rated jazz musicians who played the best clubs in New York City. There were literally clusters of clubs in the Scollay Square and Park Square sections of Boston, and in the South End off of Massachusetts Avenue near Columbus and Tremont streets. At their height, these rooms, or lounges as they were called, generated as much atmosphere and excitement in Boston as 52nd Street did in New York in its heyday.

In addition to jazz, which was continuously showcased in every decade, the late '50s and early '60s segued into the coffeehouse/folk club circuit. These establishments presented the best in alternative entertainment – poets, comedians, beat jazz, folk and later, blues performers.

One of the favorites was Club 47 in Cambridge. Bob Dylan and Joan Baez were among the regulars to light up the room. And within the same month, it was not

118

unusual to see some of the blues giants play the room during this folk and blues era.

"Blues has unquestionably influenced all kinds of music," Teo said. "We try to explore music that has influenced or been influenced by blues including Country, R&B, soul, funk, New Orleans, African and gospel. For me, blues and gospel totally go hand in hand. To borrow a phrase from my friend Preacher Jack, 'Gospel is just blues with a solution.' Musically, the parallels are many and obvious while thematically, the respective lyrics speak for themselves.

"It would be inappropriate for me to book a lot of alternative music at the House of Blues in Cambridge. I almost have an obligation to maintain another musical tradition -- especially with us being called the House of Blues. To me that's two plus two: the House of Blues presenting blues in an area where blues has always been honored," Teo said.

"What we're presenting is an experience, not a commodity, where one draws energy from the other (artist and audience). It's finally about honoring the transcendence of music, and about being the truest possible caretaker of what you play. In blues, particularly, there's not very much room to hide."

Besides preserving the musical integrity, reaching beyond the walls of Winthrop Street to the community is very important. For example, the Cambridge Chapter of the International House of Blues Foundation sponsors school tours for elementary, junior high and high school students during the school year. Students listen to an historical presentation of the development of the blues and they also examine real American history: slavery, with its oppressive personal, social and economic consequences, and within that framework, the evolution of African-American music and its broad effect on all types of music.

Then someone may talk about the House of Blues art collection; the artists, mostly laborers and everyday people who have no formal training in art; and the rich history and spirit of the work that adorns the walls on all three floors. "That's something the kids aren't going to get in their regular schools," Teo said.

The House of Blues Foundation annually awards a number of arts education scholarships. In addition, guest performers often play for students during their stops in Cambridge, which helps to put everything in a broader perspective.

Being exposed to a variety of blues also happens at the gospel brunch on Sundays. "We want to give the people a true gospel experience. We want to get at the heart of what a gospel service is. You cannot escape the communal sharing aspect or the spirituality of it. That's central to it, central to the message. It's inspiring when individual members of the choir spontaneously speak about their faith because what you're hearing and seeing is how a person's life was changed. It's so powerful," Teo said.

Raised in Philadelphia, the 51-year-old Leyasmeyer knew he wanted to be associated with the blues even as a youngster. "I was drawn to the raw sound on labels such as Crown, Jewel, Riverside, Aladdin, Paramount, Folkways, Arhoolie and Yazoo in my older brother Archie's collection. Artists who really affected me were Leadbelly, Big Bill Broonzy, Lightnin' Hopkins, Wolf, Muddy and John Lee Hooker; Ida Cox, Ma Rainey, Bessie Smith, Sippie Wallace and Big Mama Thornton. Especially of interest to me were all of the rugged, classic barrelhouse, blues and boogie-woogie piano players: Leroy Carr, Jimmy Yancey, Champion Jack Dupree, Roosevelt Sykes, Sunnyland Slim and Little Brother Montgomery, Big Maceo, Otis Spann and Lloyd Glenn, Albert Ammons, Meade Lux Lewis and Pete Johnson.

"While it was different and dangerously exciting, I remember also instinctively feeling that it was somehow familiar, and identifying with it -- knowing that something within you corresponds to that sweet-sad sound you're hearing," he said.

Basic piano lessons followed, along with an urge to participate and make something happen.

In Philly, clubs such as the 2nd Fret and the Main Line were the beginning of that searching-out process. But it wasn't until he moved Boston in the early '70s when he really started to break out as a musician.

"A large part of that was the vast music scene in the Boston area. It was so extensive and I was so often surrounded by great music that I eventually found my place within it. I used to go to Paul's Mall and the Jazz Workshop in Boston -- two legendary adjacent music rooms run for 15 years by Fred Taylor, a prince of a man with a huge spirit and deep love of people, musicians and music."

(Note: Taylor is now the talent buyer for Scullers at the Double Tree Guest Suites Hotel, 400 Soldiers Field Road, Boston.)

"My other haunt was Joe's Place in Inman Square in Cambridge," Teo continued, "a serious hardcore blues room booked by the pioneering and knowledgeable Dick Waterman. At Joe's, I gradually became part of the house band and backed scores of visiting musicians. In those days it was almost like a fever, trying to sit in with as many blues artists as possible. Looking back, I don't know if it was ego-driven as much as a way of experiencing what you were hearing first hand through participation, not just through listening. But there was such a compulsion to it. My old friend (pianist) David Maxwell has a great phrase for it: 'The zen of sitting in.'"

By hanging out, Teo was able to carve a niche as a reliable keyboardist among some of the blues elite. By working in the house band at Joe's, he was able to secure a few national gigs -- touring with Luther Allison through 1974, and East Coast road trips with Big Mama Thornton, John Lee Hooker, and others.

"I'll never forget late one night, Big Mama Thornton and I were sitting drinking in an after-hours club I had taken her to. They had this grand piano there on which I was noodling, and she was entertaining the patrons with her stories. After asking the club owner if it was really Big Mama, one awestruck guy got up the nerve and asked her to sing 'Hound Dog.'

"Without missing a beat, she asked him how much money he had in his pockets. The poor guy took it all out and blurted, 'seventeen dollars.'

"'Well,' she said with a wide-eyed deadpan delivery, 'I'll sing you a verse for seventeen dollars.'

"Don't you know, he handed it over, she counted it, put it away and, pointing her index finger at me on the piano, said, 'Teo, hit it.'"

Perhaps the greatest thrill for Teo occurred when Howlin' Wolf asked him to accompany him to the El Mocambo in Toronto for a week.

"I was living in Somerville at the time, Wolf was in town playing and I had invited him over for dinner one night. Sometime before I had picked him up, he must have gotten into an argument with Detroit Junior, his piano player, because Wolf asked me if I wanted to go up to Canada and play with him. And of course I said 'YES.'"

In Canada for that week, a I-can't-believe-I'm-here Teo roomed with Hubert Sumlin, who was totally gracious, told him stories, and treated Teo like a lifelong friend. "After the gig one night, early in the morning, for hours, both of us were in a locked, dark, function room somewhere in the hotel, with Hubert playing brilliant guitar and me trying to sound like Hosea Lee Kinard on this banquet spinet that I had found. Looking back on it I wouldn't trade those times for anything."

Teo said he looked up to Wolf, much like an uncle and had an affinity for him beyond music. "I had heard stories how he was offish or distant but I never experienced that," Teo said. "He was always really nice to me. I remember him in his hotel room sitting playing acoustic guitar with his suspenders on, singing softly and talking about his farm in Arkansas... Unbelievable. What a way to learn about life and music from someone who was such a singular, charismatic master in his field. A true blues immortal.

"That kind of thing stays with you the rest of your life. I knew then that they were special, exceptional moments -- like Wolf on stage looking over his shoulder smiling, with the gold in his teeth shining, approving of the way his song was being done. My God, that's worth more than a college education."

When the band finally returned to Boston, Wolf and Junior had mended their differences and for Teo, it was back to banging the keys at Joe's Place.

Teo's perseverance eventually evolved into being invited to play as a member of Freddie King's band. In the spring of 1976, he left Boston and moved to Dallas.

"After resettling, my first official gig with Freddie was at the Houston Civic Center where we were on a bill with Bobby 'Blue' Bland and B.B. King. I thought I had died and gone to heaven," Teo recalled.

"One of the coolest things to watch offstage was the way Freddie would regularly win money from other bands, visitors, strangers, whomever, by shooting craps in the dressing room before the gig. He'd take off his pants, neatly fold them and hang them over a chair, and then, on his knees in his underwear, dice in hand, almost always proceed to beat the pants off everyone else.

"On longer road trips, he would advance the band a week's or sometimes two week's pay, and then have poker games for hours and hours on a fold-out table in the middle of his bus. Once again, more often than not, he would emerge the winner. You can imagine the subsequent ferocity in the band's playing once it sunk in that they weren't going to get paid anytime soon. Part of the dues on the road, I guess."

King entertained all. George Benson, Eric Clapton and Leon Russell, who produced King's records under the Shelter label, routinely stopped in at Freddie's gigs, Teo said.

Boston's Blues

"After a rehearsal on Christmas Eve 1976, at the New York Ballroom in Dallas where we would be playing later that night, Freddie invited Deacon Jones, his longtime organist, and myself to his home for what ended up being his last supper. It was a huge, delicious, southern holiday spread. I'll never forget the warmth and generous spirit of his entire family.

"I remember, too, some of his song selections later that evening as being atypical. He played some old mournful stuff like, 'Hey little bluebird, send a letter down South for me,' which he hardly played during that time. Anyway, after the gig in the early morning hours, he was rushed from his home to the hospital, where he died a few days later.

"I never got over those last impressions I had of the man: larger than life... generous, sensitive, tremendously powerful and filled-to-bursting with blues. I felt terribly saddened yet somehow blessed that I had been around him so near the end," Teo said.

After King's death, Teo played or toured with such notable artists as Chuck Berry, Big Joe Turner, Koko Taylor, Linda Hopkins and Buddy Guy and Junior Wells. He eventually moved to New York and became a member of Johnny Copeland's band and later, his bandleader from 1987-90, touring internationally almost a dozen times during this period.

Also at this time, Teo began his bookings and promotions endeavors at the Abilene Cafe in Manhattan, working two-year stints ('85-'87 and '90-'92) at the club's two crosstown locations: 21st and 2nd Ave. and later, 8th Ave. between 13th and 14th. He booked the rooms, led the house band and played with over 50 different headliners while enjoying the best of both worlds.

"Sometimes I just had hunches about things that might work -- and they did more often than not," he said. One shining production from these hunches was the multimedia presentation, "Moanin' at Midnight: A Tribute to Howlin' Wolf," which Teo produced and hosted as part of the Benson and Hedges Blues Festival in October 1991 for George Wein's Festival Productions.

The stage show featured the great Hubert Sumlin, Henry Gray, S.P. Leary, Calvin Jones and horn man Charlie Brown. There was a photo gallery and some rare film footage of Wolf.

Teo recounted the great enthusiasm these ex-bandmembers had for each other as well as the respect they had for Wolf. "It was really a trip... these older cats gathering from Wolf's bands in the '50s, calling each other by their nicknames of

123

40 years ago, and musically sliding into those characteristically greasy grooves that we've all heard a million times, from the Sun and Chess releases of that period. There was real magic in the air."

Before they raised their instruments to replay the notes of their youth, the band formed a tight circle backstage. Someone unwrapped a paper bag that disguised a special blend of North Carolina moonshine. In ritual-like movements, they slowly poured shots into the deep bottle cap, looked at each other with aged bloodshot, watery eyes and individually intoned, "For Wolf," as they passed the bottle and poured the potent concoction down their throats.

The ceremony was repeated again, only this time they didn't drink. Rather, after each had poured his share, with bowed heads, each cast his shot onto the floor, again, individually declaring, "For Wolf."

Teo witnessed from a distance and dared not disturb the moment; he knew this was their time, their personal tribute.

Teo is appreciative of the opportunities he has had with his projects. But he is even more enthusiastic about the future and how, with the help of and through the House of Blues, he can share his artistic synergy. "It seemed that everything I had done up to this point led to this and was being culminated by this job. Now that's a rare thing," he said.

"In my job as talent buyer I personally have found a lot of fulfillment in working in a friendly, supportive environment where professionalism, integrity and cooperation is not only encouraged, it's expected," Teo said. "For the House of Blues to come along when it did for me seemed providential. I'm deeply grateful to Isaac Tigrett (founder of the House of Blues) for giving me the opportunity to promote the legacy of the blues.

"I've settled down a lot, have a family, and stopped drinking that mash. I'm in a totally different place. I feel like I can finally begin to contribute and give back what was so freely given to me in the early years when I was a wild kid experiencing. Part of the giving back process is creating the possibility for others to be inspired, also in appreciating what you have and in being nice to people along the way."

Being committed to the music is Teo's own self-imposed life sentence. Like many musicians who share a kindred inspiration, he said he instictively knew that this was his calling.

Boston's Blues

Teo said guitarist Paul Rishell similarly told him that after Dick Waterman introduced him to Son House in the '60s, it was like an epiphany. After Rishell heard, spoke, played and hung out with House, the man Muddy Waters called "The King," Paul knew that he would do this for the rest of his life.

Although Rishell and harpist Annie Raines play in a deceptively simple acoustic style, to Teo, the emotions that leap from the strings on a board and holes in a can dwell deep within us. "The subtleties that come from doing that style are so engaging. It's not in the complexity, it's in the subtlety -- feeling where to leave notes out, how to change up the rhythm. Tone, attack, color, spacing, dynamics: those are some of the secondary qualities that come with musical maturity."

In evaluating talent, "If as a musician you don't have that emotional conviction, then the real ability never comes out. If you do have that conviction, ability and the passion, you can create and influence your destiny, which eventually leads to finding your own voice. Learning to consistently deliver on the emotional level has always been a tough mountain to climb," Teo said. "For someone like John Lee Hooker, on the other hand, it's as natural as breathing."

For the serious music fan, Teo says, "If you hear something that makes you stop and listen, then it's worth knowing who or what influenced that performer and that song. That starts an historical connection which can then be traced back to see the evolution of a story, a song, a style, a feeling, an artistry, a statement."

"Blues isn't dead," Teo says. "There will be always be people who are reflexively moved by it and changed by it. At its best, there is a fierce, deep, darkly powerful intensity to the blues which lets you know that it is truth. Its simplicity and almost magical hypnotic quality veils the depths of the underlying despair, yet simultaneously, the cathartic release enables the spirit to endure."

Note: In 1997, Teo was awarded a W. C. Handy Award for Blues Promoter of the Year.

Web: hob.com

Bob (Barbeque Bob) Maglinte

Boston's Blues
Barbeque Bob learned harp the hard way

A self-taught player, Bob (Barbeque Bob) Maglinte, born in Brooklyn, N.Y., in 1955, didn't start out as a harp player. He says he was playing "bad" guitar, according to Noah Webster's meaning of the word. So he put his musical aspirations of being another Bob Dylan aside for a few years.

In the 1970s while at Bunker Hill Community College, Bob was listening to Paul Butterfield and, of course, the J. Geils Blues Band that featured Magic Dick on "Whammer Jammer." So he went down to the corner music store and picked up a Hohner G harp, which was the toughest key to learn. "Hell, how was I supposed to know?" he asked, figuring if you've seen one harmonica, you've seen them all. He didn't know that harps come in different keys.

"So I started looking at instruction books in bookshops, not buying any, just reading and trying to soak up as much information on the harmonica as I could. Then I'd practice wherever and whenever I could -- bathrooms, subways, you name it, and I didn't give a damn if I made a fool of myself in the process," he said.

In the fall of '73, he saw Carey Bell, who was with Willie Dixon at the time, and a month later, he saw James Cotton at Joe's Place, which had a terrific jukebox of blues 45s. That set the stage for a more serious introspective and studious endeavor to the music. "I went deeper and deeper trying to find out everything I could," he said.

Bob served his vinyl apprenticeship as an understudy of Little Walter, both Sonny Boy Williamsons (Rice Miller and John Lee Williamson), Junior Wells, Poppa Lightfoot, "who recorded on an obscure label, but he had an incredibly overamplified tone, some of the heaviest stuff I ever heard," and Big Walter Horton.

"I saw a lot of Big Walter in the 1970s, and his pick-up band was John Nicholas and the Rhythm Rockers, with Mark 'Kaz' Kazanoff on sax, Dave Maxwell and sometimes Ron Levy on keys, Sarah Brown on bass... I learned more by watching Big Walter than listening to any of the records. One thing you learn from him is tone control, tonal variety and the element of surprise and dynamics.

"A lot of players are full tilt. They don't treat it enough as an instrument and take the time to learn the musicality of the instrument. It's the easiest and at the same time, one of the hardest instruments to learn," he said.

Bob advises the most important thing is to learn the economy of notes. "There's a right note for the right time.

"Another thing that you have to watch out for is that you don't run out of ideas. You've got to master the tonal control and the dynamics of the instrument first before you attempt to increase speed. I appreciate different players and I can't say that any one particular player is a favorite because they're all very distinctive and they all had their own influences on them... For example, Little Walter, although he never admitted it, was influenced by Big Walter and Sonny Boy and Louis Jordan and the whole jump sax thing. Basically Little Walter played the harp as a sax because he couldn't afford a saxophone.

"And along the same time period, T-Bone Walker took the sax concept and played it on guitar. In those days, guitars and piano players commanded a lot more respect than harmonica players. They weren't accepted. There were a lot of great blues harp players who were known for playing other stuff besides blues. Even Little Walter was known as a great polka player. He never recorded them, but he played a lot of polkas."

Bob first came into his own as a musician with a stint with Elmo Jackson, who used to introduce Bob with every name you could think of, except his own. One day Jackson, who had been listening to the original Bar-B-Q Bob, a 12-string guitar player who often used a bottleneck, introduced him as Bar-B-Q Bob, and the name stuck.

The real break came a little more than 20 years ago with the Hound Dogs, which featured Ronnie Earl on guitar, Keith Dunn on piano, Michael "Mudcat" Ward on bass, and Charles Robinson on drums. For Bob's first gig, they were the back-up band for guitarist Jimmy Rogers at Lupos Heartbreak Hotel in Providence.

"And that first set I was scared to death. I was so scared, I apologized left and right to Rogers, and he said, "Don't worry about it, you're doing OK. So whenever he was around, he was sort of like the big old granddaddy for me," Bob said. (Rogers, one of the original members of the Muddy Waters Band, died in December 1997.)

During this time, Bob got to see and hear a lot of shows -- especially the Fabulous Thunderbirds, who had a big Boston following. They, and many other blues bands, would play a week-long engagement at Paul's Mall on Boylston Street, so many of the local players became friends with the touring musicians.

Boston's Blues

"One night the T-Birds opened for Muddy Waters, and all of Muddy's band got front-row seats. That never happened because they used to hang backstage, but they were taking it in and loving it. One show I'll never forget... Annie Anderson, Robert Johnson's sister came to see Muddy play, and had a scrapbook of Johnson's photos, clippings and letters -- and this is long before Rolling Stone did the big story on him. Muddy of course, had seen Robert Johnson when he was a young man, and when he looked at the scrapbook, his eyes were out of his head and his hands were shaking. So from that reaction, you know it was the real thing.

"Later that night, Muddy did two of Johnson's tunes in respect to him. Oh, what I would give to have a tape recording of that. I can tell you that from what I saw in that scrapbook, not even one-tenth of Robert Johnson's material has been published," Bob said.

In early 1980s, Bob worked a daytime job as an assistant manager in an auto parts store chain. "That experience was good for me in learning to become a bandleader," he said.

But his first attempt at the helm was not storybook material. "I guess when you're young you tend to think that you're a hot shot, and you think you're a whole lot better than what you are. So I've learned a lot of painful lessons. At first you're bitter about it, but once what you thought was bad, is not necessarily all that bad from hindsight, and you eventually learn from it."

The '80s also brought the modern blues jam. Since he wasn't working in a band, Bob became a regular at various jams because he knew he needed to hone his chops. In 1988, he spent three weeks with Luther "Guitar Jr." Johnson on a trip through Canada and down South.

"That kind of whet my appetite for getting out there. When I got to Canada, people would carry your stuff, and they went nuts for us. In the U.S., it's a whole 'nuther ballgame. Here, musicians tend to be looked at as a commodity, a piece of meat," he said.

Bob recalled, "After Luther, I hooked up with the Rhythm Aces. But over the next few months, one by one they left, and I was forced to be the bandleader, learning by the seat of my pants with no one to help guide me."

In 1992, after several personnel changes and three previous tries, "We won the Battle of the Bands at Harpers Ferry, which helped to get the name, BBQ Bob and the Rhythm Aces, out there more.

Art Simas

The last incarnation of the band, BBQ Bob and the Varaflames, had Vas on drums, Tommy Reed on bass, and Craig Ruskey on guitar, with Bob blowing harp and occasionally doing his off-the-wall stunts.

"I never started to do the lying on the back thing until a few years ago," Bob said. It was drummer Rich Lee, who always wanted to be a showman, who egged him on. "We're at a place called Whistler's Tavern, and he gets close to me (Lee would take the snare drum off and hook it on a belt and play behind Bob) and he says, 'Hey, get down, get down on the floor. Go ahead, go ahead, lay down on the floor and keep playing.' So I did it, and people got off on it. They were going crazy. And then later on, he was sitting on my stomach while I was playing. Crowds love showmanship but you've got to be able to back that up, too. Give them a little extra to loosen 'em up and not play at them, and make sure that you're having fun, too."

Note: Bob was diagnosed with diabetes in 2000 and is undergoing dialysis treatments three times a week while he awaits a kidney from a donor. He said he may have to wait for more than four years. But he said he is determined not to let the disease get him down.

Two benefits were held for him, the first in October 2000, at the Yardrock in Quincy and the second in February 2001, at Gilrein's in Worcester.

Peter Malick

Peter Malick: Dealing with the blues

"Hit it!"

Peter Malick has often heard that phrase during his life -- as a musician and Las Vegas card dealer.

Malick was indoctrinated into the blues when he was still in high school, moving to Chicago after graduation and living among some of the giants of the industry -- Otis Spann, Muddy Waters, S.P. Leary, Earl Hooker, Jimmy Reed, Sam Lay. It was Spann who would play the role of musical godfather and spiritual mentor to young Malick and have the greatest and lasting influence on him.

Born in Brookline, Mass., in 1951, Malick started playing guitar when he was 13, just about the time the Paul Butterfield Blues Band emerged onto the Chicago scene, but before the historic Newport performance in 1965 with the electric Bob Dylan.

"After listening to that first Butterfield album and that Chicago blues sound I could identify with it... that was it for me and I wanted to search out more of it, understand it, play it," he said.

Malick says he owes a debt of gratitude to Bob Margolin, also a Brookline native, because "Bob was responsible for me getting kicked out of my first band. I was the rhythm guitarist and I was really bad. That was the best thing that ever happened to me because after that I got serious." Margolin, who is two years older than Malick, was in a band called The Free Born playing rock and had already earned a reputation as cool dude -- so when his word came down, Malick was gone, or something to that effect.

Some former members of The Lost and Buried Remains, two of the better-known Boston rock bands, started their own assembly called Listening (which cut a record with Vanguard), with Malick, 16, on guitar.

"Through Listening, I got to meet a lot of Boston musicians," Malick said. "One of the people I met was Doug Grossman who had a band called The Cloud. Otis Spann used to stay over his house in Cambridge -- The Band House -- whenever he was in town. Some of Muddy's band would stay there, too. So, Doug had set up a gig for Otis at The Ark, which later became the Tea Party. And he hired me to play guitar.

Boston's Blues

"After the first set, Spann asked me to come back to Chicago with him. But I still had 5-6 months of high school left. I told him, 'Sure, I'll come down after graduation.'

"At spring break I went down to New York and played with him. Then June comes around, and I tried to call him, but his phone was disconnected. I didn't know what to do. I really wanted to go and do this. Then after a while I said, 'To hell with it,' I had enough money for a roundtrip ticket and for one night in a hotel, if that was what it was going to take.

"I arrived in Chicago and finally found a cabdriver willing to take me to Spann's address, and I see him outside talking with his neighbors. I get out of the cab, Spann turns and looks at me and says to his neighbors, 'Oh, here's my guitar player now.' Then he says to me, 'Get your stuff son, let me take you to your room.'"

Spann died in April 1970, but Malick got to see the keyboard genius at what he did best, right up until the day he passed on. "He didn't work a whole lot at gigs. I did get to work with Muddy a few times. But every night we'd have some sort of party at Spann's. People would show up with food, booze. Spann and I would start playing and some other musicians would join in. It was just an incredible education," Malick said.

The magical summer of 1969 gave way to a harsh reality in the winter of 1970. Malick returned home to Brookline for the holidays, but it wasn't long before he received word that Spann had entered the hospital. In the meantime, Malick was attempting to set up a gig for Spann at the old Tea Party location at 53 Berkley St.

Malick found out from a doctor at Cook County Hospital that it was terminal cancer. Nevertheless, Spann came to Boston one last time about three or four weeks before he died.

"I wasn't ready for what showed up," Malick said. "He could hardly speak, had no voice. But he played his butt off. He could still play, he didn't have quite the strength but he was such a feel player and that's what he was all about. I don't think nobody has ever come close. As far as blues piano, he is it, and probably will be it forever and ever."

Even during the last few days, Malick said "I'd literally have to help him sit up in the morning and he'd say, 'Well son, do you want to play some?'

'I don't care, you want to?' I'd bring him over his piano and we'd play. That's what he did, all he did."

After his close friendship with Spann, Malick returned to Boston and started backing the Chicago acts such as Big Mama Thornton, John Lee Hooker, Luther "Georgia Boy" Johnson, Freddie King, The Coasters, Chuck Berry, and others.

On a lark, Malick auditioned and got a part in the musical, "Hair," staying with the company for one and a half years. He also met his ex-wife who was also in the production. "It turned out to be a real fun time, nothing more than that," Malick said.

After "Hair," Malick happened to stumble into the James Montgomery Band. "It just so happened he was looking for a guitarist. They held me down and poured all sorts of liquor down my throat until I said yes. I figured I either better say yes or I was going to be dead," he said. "So under extreme duress I joined the James Montgomery Band in 1972 and stayed with them for their first two albums and with him for about three or four years.

"I settled in LA with my wife and daughter, tried to put together some things, but nothing really turned up. So, with my son Peter about to be born and finances weren't the best, we decided to move to Vegas, since my wife was from Las Vegas -- and I became a blackjack dealer. I was thinking, well maybe I'll do this for a little while. I've been in the gaming business up until the time I came back here (in 1996)," Malick said.

Malick said work in Vegas in the 1970s was very different than today. One could work six months, try something different (like attempting to resurrect a band) and if it didn't turn out, go back to dealing again. "It was like, 'Hey, I'm back in town.' 'OK, you're hired.' It was actually kind of cool that way. But for the soul, it sucks."

Malick found a new talent in a poker game called Hold 'Em, and turned pro for a few years while in Vegas.

In the mid-1980s, Malick said he didn't even touched a guitar for three years, until he reflected on where his life was going with the help of LA soul singer Sonny Green, who asked him to join him in LA again. "That sort of forced me to get my chops together. At that point I realized that that's what I do."

While playing as much as possible in LA, Malick said he wanted to eventually make his way back East, which he did in April 1996.

134

Boston's Blues

"For blues to continue and be vital," Malick says, "it has to reflect what's going on today with those people's lives who are making it. I just want the stuff that I'm playing to reflect who I am... For any musician, artist or actor it takes coming from the heart. There's no secret. That what makes the difference."

While in Boston, Malick had fronted his own band of Jason Langley on bass, David Spreng on drums and George Papageorge on the Hammond B-3. He also worked with Amyl Justin for a few years before Justin left for Nashville.

In 2000, Malick released the last concert of Otis Spann, which happened at the Boston Tea Party in early April 1970. Three weeks later, one of the best blues pianists of all time died of cancer. The recordings of that special night were "lost" for nearly 30 years. The CD, with an 18-year-old Malick playing guitar, was nominated and won a W.C. Handy Award in 2001 for best historical blues album.

Malick has since left for the West Coast and is making records under the Conqueroot label.

Web: www.malick.com

Bob Margolin

Boston's Blues

Bob Margolin: Giving the blues to anyone who will listen and learn

In 1999, I e-mailed some questions to Bob Margolin. Below is the electronic chit-chat.

AS: Paint the music scene in Greater Boston in the 1960s... what were you doing, who were you hanging out with... and the type/s of music you were into at different stages and/or bands you were in or led. Other local bands and competition for playing time at the clubs... names of clubs, locations.
Who were some of the national blues people that you really wanted to see?

BM: I was in a number of blues and blues-rock bands from 1966 on. Many of the young Brookline musicians were playing blues -- Ron Levy, Peter Malick, bassman Teddy Parkins, singer-harp player Bill Gleason, drummer Lew Lipson, guitar-keyboard-singer Nick Carstoiu, multi-instrumentalist Spilios Spiros. David Maxwell, a few years older than me, was making friends with the Chicago blues bands that came through town.

The J. Geils Band and the Colwell-Winfield Blues Band were very popular. In the '60s, there were no exclusively blues clubs, but national touring bands would come to the Unicorn Coffee House or Club 47 in Cambridge, The Boston Tea Party or The Psychedelic Supermarket, Paul's Mall and the Jazz Workshop, Sandy's in Beverly, and Lennie's on the Turnpike. Local bands would open. Uncle T and Peter Wolf were on the radio. WBCN was "underground radio."

Around the turn of the decade (1960s into the 1970s) I was working with musicians from the North Shore -- Mitch Weinstein singing, Joe Luise on bass, and Dave Weber on drums in a version of The Freeborne Blues Band. There were a few other versions of that band before and after that.

In the early '70s, a number of local blues bands emerged: James Montgomery, Powerhouse, The Allston Allstars, The Boston Blues Band (I was in that from March '72 'til August '73 when I joined Muddy's band). Speakeasy Pete opened up the Speakeasy in Central Square.

Joe Spadafora opened Zircon in Somerville and then Joe's Place in Central Square. He brought in national touring blues bands -- I saw Howlin' Wolf, Hound Dog Taylor, Willie Dixon's All-Stars, and backed Albert Collins there in '72. Roomful packed 'em in at Brandy's, near the intersection of Commonwealth and Brighton avenues, around the corner from where I grew up in Brookline.

Bunratty's on Harvard Ave. in Allston began to do local and national blues bands. In Worcester, the Boston Blues Band was working at clubs like The Ale And Bun or The Odyssey for a week at a time, filling the clubs every night.

AS: Besides the fact that blues has given you a paycheck for decades, what is it about the blues that grabbed you so hard that you've never let go?

BM: I love the sensual sound and feel and rhythm of the music. It's redeeming to share deep emotions, playing or listening. Blues brings all kinds of people together in love of the music. Blues becomes more meaningful and valuable as the world gets uglier and more unfriendly.

AS: What were the circumstances that led you to join Muddy's band? Describe that first session with him and the other band members.

BM: I had opened shows for Muddy with Luther "Snake" Johnson and with The Boston Blues Band. He could hear that I was trying to play his "Old School" Chicago blues and he was very encouraging to me. In August, '73, I went to Paul's Mall on the first night of Muddy's engagement there and when I came in, Muddy's harp player, Mojo Buford, told me that Muddy had lost a guitar player the night before. Mojo told Muddy I was there, and Muddy told me to come to his hotel the next day and bring a guitar. I had him figured right -- he said, "Play it," and I played some straight, old-style Delta blues. Muddy dug that and gave me the chance that changed the rest of my life.

AS: Lifelong lessons. I know you continue to summarize your experiences in your column for Blues Revue, but could you share some of the lasting impressions of that time with Muddy and the other guys.

BM: I learned a lot from those older, more experienced musicians -- socially as well as musically. The band I was in for most of my time with Muddy was Muddy plus those of us that sometimes tour together now as the Muddy Waters Tribute Band: Jerry Portnoy, Luther "Guitar Jr." Johnson, Calvin "Fuzz" Jones, Willie "Big Eyes" Smith, and Pinetop Perkins. When any of these guys had a problem with another, they'd say whatever they had to and settle it, and the next day, the problem was gone, forgotten. We've got a deep friendship as well as a special sound when we play together.

AS: Your impression on the state of the blues today from your perspective on the road.

Boston's Blues

BM: More bands are competing for less gigs. It's hard to get a good-paying blues gig on a weekday. My band is playing lots of festivals this summer (1999) and much less club gigs. I wonder what will happen in the winter. Everyone's making CDs and most lose money doing it. Blues is more visible today, but few people can make a good full-time living at it. We sure need to get some blues on TV. Perhaps the new Blues Music Association will help.

Musically, you can't replace the legends we lose every year, but there are some fine players carrying it on with originality and depth. I think blues will be around for a while.

Web: bobmargolin.com

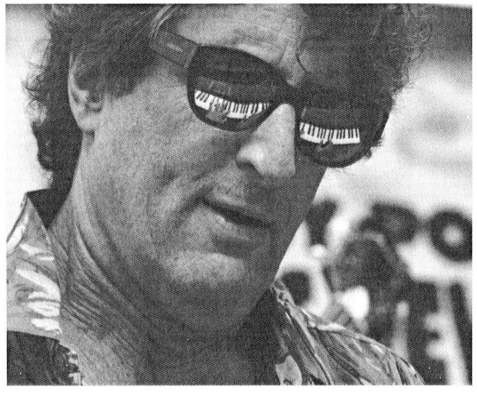

David Maxwell

Boston's Blues
David Maxwell: The consummate keyboardist

David Maxwell is known in the greater Boston area as THE man for side projects when it comes to blues.

Often reverently referred to as the man who inherited the heart of Otis Spann, the deep, soulful blues pianist for Muddy Waters, Maxwell is a precise marksman and creative genius on-the-fly on the piano. Buoyed by years of understanding and nuance, Max's blues dexterity leaps from his fingers to our ears –- and in that instant, listeners know they are listening and learning -- as one generation passes on its spiritual legacy to another.

He was born in Waltham and spent his early years growing up in northwest Washington, D.C., studying classical music with various teachers.

In his teens, Maxwell, who had moved to Greater Boston, met Alan Wilson of Arlington, Mass. Wilson at the time was playing trombone with a drummer in a funk-jazz kind of groove, similar to Cannonball Adderley and Bobby Timmons. The two became good friends and many late-night, early morning jam sessions followed as the music led their way. "I wasn't really into blues then," Max said.

Maxwell entered the University of Rochester in the early 1960s. While he was in school he met up with Wilson, who had changed instruments and was now playing harmonica. Wilson's musical preference had changed too.

"He turned me on to a lot of the pre-War blues, which eventually led to Muddy and Otis Spann," Maxwell said. "And I began in earnest to learn about blues."

Maxwell studied in Paris during his junior year. There, he got to see Spann, Muddy and others who were making the rounds in Europe.

"Seeing Spann made a big impression on me," Maxwell said. "I also saw Thelonius Monk and learned about Indian music. When I got back (to Boston) I started playing with different people."

After Paris, Maxwell decided to head home and he didn't go back to Rochester.

Upon his arrival, Maxwell quickly became a mainstay within the Boston music scene, playing with many of the greatest bands of the era.

Art Simas

In the mid- to late-1960s, the Colwell-Winfield Band (Billy Colwell and Mike Winfield) was the hottest thing in the clubs. They were one of the first groups to call on the emerging blues pianist, and Maxwell played with them for about three years.

Also in the band was a skinny 17-year-old hotshot harp player from Detroit -- James Montgomery.

The band disintegrated after Colwell's attempted suicide. "Billy shot himself in the head, distraught over his girlfriend," Maxwell said. "And he was disabled from that point on."

Maxwell was also in the first incarnation of the J. Geils Band, with Jay, Magic Dick and Danny Klein, for about three to six months. He played on one of the band's early gigs at the Boston Tea Party, a venue which would eventually become Geils' home base, with Don Law, the megastar promoter, as manager of the band.

In the mid-1960s, Paul Butterfield and Charlie Musselwhite were getting a lot of attention as young, upstart blues performers. "But there wasn't anybody in Boston that had that fully formed sound," Maxwell said. "Jay was just getting going and when I was with them they were really slavish in wanting to get the arrangements exactly right. But I was more free-wheeling."

"The sound that Colwell had was more like an Albert King influence with horns," Maxwell said. "It was a pretty good sounding group, and even had a conga player. Emmett Berry (now a sax player with the Weepin' Willie Band) played with them, too."

Maxwell did some session work with guitarist Danny Staroben, in addition to hearing such blues icons as Son House, Bukka White and Skip James ("he was really deep and poignant").

At Club 47, a local blues watering hole, Maxwell was introduced to Muddy Waters, and he heard John Lee Hooker for the first time in The Golden Vanity coffee shop. He also heard Hooker playing with a beat-up guitar in another Boston coffeehouse, and finally got to back him up with Colwell-Winfield at the Catacombs nightclub around 1966 or 1967.

Throughout this early blues period, "It was Alan Wilson (who had formed Canned Heat) who kept me abreast of what was happening on the scene," Maxwell said.

Boston's Blues

Another way of catching up on the latest hot artists was simply browsing in a record store. "At the time, you could go into a record store to the listening booths. It was a nice diversion and a pretty good way to spend an afternoon. I spent many an afternoon in Skippy White's back room listening to early Hooker sides from Crown.

"I used to hang around Harvard Square a lot, too. One time I was hitchhiking from Auditorium Station and a van picked me up and there was a bunch of musicians in it. We were talking and they said they were going to New Hampshire for a gig.

"I told them I was into blues and played piano. And the guy in front said, 'Oh, are you into Otis Spaaaahhhn?' And that was Peter Wolf, who was with the Hallucinations, with Paul Shapiro on harmonica. They used to play at the Playboy Club in Park Square," Maxwell said.

"Peter Wolf had an apartment in Harvard Square. He was a real fan, worshipping guys like Bobby Blue Bland, Bobby Womack, and of course, the blues people. He was really adulating. I wasn't that outgoing. I was a little more reserved.

"I also played a lot at the student lounges at MIT through Dick Stroud. He would requisition the lounge and we'd play all night; we'd get the musicians who were in town to come over… one time Hooker and Spann came over. We used to hang there all night. Those were some great times.

"When Spann would be in Boston, he'd always let me watch him. One time we got him over to Harvard-Radcliffe, where I was working, playing for a jazz dance class. Another time, Muddy and Pinetop Perkins came into a class I was teaching at the Commonwealth School of Law.

"I think it was important to hang out with the bands, and with Otis Spann and all. I'd look over his shoulder and ask him how he did a particular riff and he'd show me how he did it. And with Pinetop, I'd watch him all the time and he'd show me. He'd exaggerate with his right hand what he was doing.

"It was amazing that these guys would go out of their way and do anything for you," Maxwell said.

While backing visiting performers and learning from the greats first-hand, Maxwell used to regularly go to the Jazz Workshop, a nurturing oasis for all musicians, headed by Fred Taylor, now music coordinator at Scullers in the Double Tree Guest Suites on Soldiers Field Road, Boston.

Maxwell wasn't the only pianist who was honing his blues chops and trying to keep a steady paycheck. There was some pretty good competition here.

"There was a thing with piano players in the late 1960s between me, Teo Leyasmeyer (music coordinator for the Cambridge House of Blues), Ron Levy, the former keyboard player with B.B. King's band and producer for dozens of records on a number of labels, and Al Copley, formerly of Roomful of Blues who now lives in Europe.

"We'd go to different bars and the other one would always want to sit in. Of course when you're blasted out of your mind, it just adds fuel to the fire," Maxwell said.

"We all were kind of bad boys. It was a kind of blues band image that was romanticized. Yeah, it was a likeable, friendly rivalry. I think each of us had our strong points but egos were running rampant."

The Unicorn on Boylston Street near the Prudential, The Catacombs, which was four flights down off of Boylston Street, and Club 47 were some of the favorite haunts of the day.

Maxwell landed a job in Luther "Snake" Johnson's band after Johnson left Muddy Waters (who was replaced by Luther "Guitar Junior" Johnson), and continued to back the roving national blues artists.

In August 1969, "we went on the Dick Cavett Show with John Lee Hooker. But I don't think anyone saw us because that was the same weekend Woodstock was going on. We were trying to get out there, but there was no way we were going to get any exposure that weekend," he said.

Maxwell teamed with Bob Margolin and formed the Boston Blues Band, also filling in on the off-nights with other guests such as Big Mama Thornton, Albert Collins, Sonny Terry and Brownie McGhee. And on one of those evenings, Freddie King came through and eventually offered Maxwell the piano seat in his band, which was based in Texas.

"I played with him (King) for a couple of years, and a lot of that stuff is on video (four videos recorded between 1972 and 1973, including one shot in Sweden and another produced by Leon Russell). But you won't hear Maxwell on any of the albums done by King at that time because Russell played piano on those albums produced under Russell's Shelter label.

During 1973-74, Maxwell joined up with Bonnie Raitt and her band. "I first met Bonnie at the Newport Folk Festival when the blues guys were there. It was through Dick Waterman that I joined her band in 1973. She's a wonderful person. She was really serious about music and writing. She understood how special her talents were in reaching an audience. With her voice, she could make that connection, and of course she was doing the folk stuff, too.

"She really had a definite concept of getting a certain feeling behind her, whether it was rock or a more delicate kind of thing. We had a really good relationship."

Maxwell was also with guitarist Johnny Nicholas and the Rhythm Rockers, which had ex-Thunderbirds drummer Fran Cristina, Johnny Ace on bass, and later Sarah Brown and Kaz Kazanoff on harp. A few years later, Ronnie Earl and Ron Levy joined Nicholas and the Rhythm Rockers.

"I first met Ronnie when I was living in Brookline Village. When the T-Birds would come to town, they would sleep on the floor of his apartment and play at the Speakeasy. "We (Ronnie and I) always had an affinity with each other as friends, and we both came out of the same philosophy on how to play blues," Maxwell said.

I eventually joined James Cotton in the late 1970s and then from there it was all kinds of music. Buddy Guy, Jimmy Rogers... Nightstage was really happening and I backed up a lot of people," Maxwell said.

Now, things seem to have come full circle with Maxwell playing once again with James Cotton and Darrell Nulisch, who does the vocals.

In 1997, Maxwell released "Maximum Blues Piano," on the Tone-Cool label and is scheduled to release another CD soon.

Web: tonecool.com

Mighty Sam McClain: Singing for the Lord

The emotional stirrer of the soul. That's Mighty Sam McClain, born April 15, 1943. From his beginnings in the church gospels at the age of 5 to his most recent tours of Europe, McClain is a lightning rod of inspiration to those who hear his message. And that message carries a lot of weight because behind the voice is a man who has lived much more than the cliched "been there, done that."

McClain struggled to get away from an abusive childhood; won fame (but never fortune) in short bursts of success; gambled on other people's trust and lost all in the inhospitable 1970s. He wandered aimlessly on the outside of his career that consumed him on the inside. Now he's back on top of his life and his destiny.

Throughout his career, his voice served two polar purposes: on one hand, it was used by others as a weapon against him. They sought to transform his identity to something he was not. And on the other hand, that voice became his salvation and has literally kept him alive. McClain readily admits he knows no other life, and that if it wasn't for singing, he wouldn't be here to tell his story.

McClain's 1998 CD on Audioquest is aptly named because his is truly a remarkable "Journey" that took him from the edge of despair to the unfathomable triumphs of heart and spirit. "Journey" is a musical autobiography of Mighty Sam McClain.

The performer and the person are one. No hidden agendas, no pretenses cast, no aspirations sought. None offered. "What I am is what I am on and off the stage," he says.

It's easy to figure out Sam McClain; he's happy to tell you. He says his job is to sing from his soul and thank God for his life. Plain and simple. Only now can he say, "It's a good time to be Sam McClain. I'm just getting started. I'm blooming right now. This is the best point in my life."

McClain speaks in short, direct tommy-gun blasts in his native Monroe, Louisiana, tongue. The accent is about the only vestige of his roots from that state -- and he'd like to keep it that way because it's a reminder of the physical and emotional pain he suffered at the hands of his stepfather.

Boston's Blues

"I left home when I was 13 years old and I've had to make all my decisions. I had a little plan to get away from home because I knew I had to stay in school or else they would have put the law on me. So I stayed with my aunt and my first cousins till the truant officer came by and told me I didn't have to go back to school or go back home because there was proof that I had been abused by my stepfather. If I had stayed at home I would have killed my stepfather. I was already contemplating it. And it was so easy to do because he was a hunter and there were guns all over the house.

"At 15 I was ready to go. I knew I wasn't going to be picking cotton with no mule, tractor or plow or none of that shit. I knew there had to be something else. I'd stand at the side of the road and these Trailways and Greyhound buses used to come by and they'd get me high like a drug addict from the smell of the fumes. I just wanted to go. I didn't care where, I just wanted to go. And I never looked back. So actually my stepfather was a blessing in disguise. Because there was nothing for me at home.

"My mother was unstable. She had 13 kids between four men. "But in the last few years, my mother and I became friends. She's sort of put the whole thing (of my childhood abuse) under the rug, out of her mind. She's a tough broad. But she's happy to see that this dream I've been chasing is finally coming true. What makes it come true for her is that I send her some checks. To her, that's reality. She can always use the money. I don't think the music has much to do with it as much as I would like to think that it does.

"I'm just trying to accept things. There's no way I can understand. And that's a hard one for me because I've been making my way, threading my way all through my life," McClain said.

Sam knew he had a vocal gift. "I feel so blessed that God has given me this voice. Even before I was born, God had given me this voice to sing. God knew what would save me. And this the only thing that could possibly save me, so I had to pursue it. I had no choice, it was like a blessing and a curse, it was all or none. But it kept me focused. My ex-wife used to say I was like a horse with blinders on, just looking straight ahead."

McClain got his musical start in the local church gospel group. "I sang, 'On the Battlefield Working for My Lord' as the first song I sang in public, and I got my first pay for singing in elementary school. And I got bitten by the bug since I could get paid for singing. So music's been part of me all my life. I never had no kind of training. I've been singing for as long as I can remember. So I know it's a gift from God. But God had to give me something to sing about because this is

God's voice and I'm his instrument. I know God has allowed me to live longer because I told him, 'If you let me sing, then I'm going to talk about you, I'm going to talk about homelessness and injustice, about what it means to go hungry. I can talk about these things because I've been there.'"

He traveled to Pensacola, Florida, for two days and ended up staying 10 years. He recorded his debut album, "Sweet Dreams" in Muscle Shoals, Alabama, in 1966. Then it was on to Houston, New Orleans and Nashville, where he was tested every day.

McClain had some raindrops of success, but it was always a passing shower. It was in Nashville where he thought he'd take the city by storm.

"But God had to bring me to a place where I had to know that I was no better than anybody else," he said. "I had to do all kinds of things to learn the lesson. Like cleaning out toilets, that's one of the first jobs I had in Nashville. It makes me sick to my stomach to think of some of the things I did. I was broke, I was hungry and I needed a job. That was the only one in sight. I couldn't see me doing this and I couldn't see me eating out of a garbage can either. But there I was.

"You know, everything I've been through I thank God for it now. I can talk about it with pride because I made it through. It didn't kill me to put my hand in shit, to go out to make a living to feed me and my family. It didn't kill me. I could wash it off. I learned something about humility, and I found all the things I couldn't do, I could do. And I did it with pride."

Financial success may have eluded McClain while some his contemporaries enjoyed greater material goods. But McClain was never interested in winning an acquisitions race.

Again, it was the experience and lessons learned from a table-scrap life that are so important to him. "I'm so thankful because just knowing who you are and knowing what you want to do with your life, and having some sense of direction of going about doing it. That's success right there. Life is not nearly as complicated as I thought it was. And as people led me to believe otherwise even in the name of love... Hell, I've been married four times and I know definitely that my music was part of the destruction of some of those other marriages. It wasn't the whole thing, but it played a part. That's why you have to find out who you are because people will lead you to the fucking gallows in the name of love.

Boston's Blues

"I write my songs on the spot, off of emotion, feelings and of reason, so I never know what I'm going to do. So I thank Joe (Harley of Audioquest Music) for giving me the freedom to express myself and be successful. I'm not making any money, but success isn't all about making money. It's about feeling good about yourself, about where you're going.

"I never had no real money, but I understand the power of money. But I don't need that excess that I thought I needed. All the stuff I thought I needed money for, I don't need none of that shit. I'm in debt, but I'm in debt for good things, for my family. Before, I'd go in debt from having a party, that is if I did have any money. So God knew what he was doing when he didn't give me no money back then -- no telling what kind of shit I'd get my crazy ass into.

"This is a spiritual thing. It's bigger than man. I believe that. Once you know that, you'd be surprised to find out who you are, what you can do, and how much power you have because it's given to you. There were a lot of times when it was real hard and I just wanted to quit, and I shut down. Now, I listen to my own lessons.

"So you better know who you are and where you're going, you better know what your name is, because if you don't know where you're going they'll take you to Mississippi somewhere. If you don't know what your name is they'll call you Jack. That's true. If you don't tell them your name, they'll give you one."

Facing the demons head-on was the only way McClain could be true to himself and to his faith. "I'm growing more intense now that I've stopped drinking three years ago, going on four, and it has made such a big great difference in my life. I can think, smell, taste everything. It's so nice to have fun and not think that you have to carry around a bottle of booze. But that's the way I thought it had to be. Every night before I went on stage, I had a little shot of something to give me encouragement because I don't think I had the sense enough to be scared.

"I've been living by faith all my life. I don't know how I'm going to do it, but I'm going to do it. I don't know, but I know I will, cuz God said so. I'm trying hard to keep my word because I know I got to, and nowhere to put the blame. I don't want me to get in my way and I take all of the responsibility," he says. "I fall every day, every day I make an ass out of myself, and I say 'God, I'm so sorry. I know I'm better than that.' But God's a loving God, and he'll say, 'Get up and move on.'"

Because he's in a business where people constantly engage in a tug-o-war for artists' attention, McClain says he's aware of the hollow promises and illusions

149

of grandeur that come with the territory. That's why he's formed his own company, McClain Productions, which include McClain Management and Emily's Son Publishing. His ("fourth and last") wife, Sandra, is at the helm, and Sam couldn't be happier. "You have to trust people, but give them some room to fall, too. If they betray that trust, then you've got to be ready to move on. Don't condemn the person, condemn the act.

"I've had my fill of agents and booking agencies and so-called managers. I decided that I could run my life better than someone else, and since that time, there's been a tremendous change. I've lived a long time waiting for this.

"We've got so many fans in Europe and now we're going to stretch out to China and Australia this year. And all of that is coming through my house, my management company. Ain't no middle folks," he says.

Currently, McClain has two CDs in circulation round the globe. "Joy And Pain, Live in Europe," is available on that continent, and "Journey" is in North America.

McClain says in any endeavor, "You've got to be ready to sacrifice. You could be the best saxophone player or the best writer in the world but if you don't put it to work, it don't mean shit... It's time that everybody take a look inside at themselves and in the mirror because that's where it all starts -- with your own responsibility as a man, as a human being. I'm finally taking on my responsibility. I'm late, I'm way late. I should have done this a long time ago. All we have in the now, the now. That's all we can be.

"I'm very happy that now I have a chance to enjoy and have a better life that God has graciously given me. I'm really starting to appreciate it. I know it's making a difference in my voice, in my life -- in everything. And that's the greatest gift God has given me -- showing me that he is real."

Web: mightysam.com

James Montgomery

Art Simas
Like an uninvited houseguest, James Montgomery just never left. While others grew old, the legend played on

"In The Beginning..."

Well, how else would you describe James Montgomery's tenure on the Boston blues scene? He's been the most enduring blues artist for more than 30 years.

Before blues was once again "discovered," there was James Montgomery, the skinny kid with the long stringy hair out front with his own band at Boston University in 1970, singing the praises of Muddy Waters, Junior Wells, James Cotton, and dozens of other blues greats. Some of the guys who agreed to play behind him said, "You better call it the James Montgomery Blues Band – just in case it sucks."

Within two years, the James Montgomery Blues Band was among the hottest acts in Boston, right alongside J. Geils and Aerosmith, the new upstart rock bad boys.

Montgomery was quickly signed to a multi-album deal with Capricorn Records, and "First Time Out," which hit the stores in 1973, cemented his stature. He was big. He was hip. He was hot.

Montgomery has toured with many major artists, including Aerosmith, Bonnie Raitt, Bruce Springsteen, the Allman Brothers, Steve Miller and many others who were, or continue to be the best in the business. He has jammed on stage with B.B. King, Buddy Guy, John Lee Hooker, Junior Wells, James Cotton, Charlie Daniels, Bonnie Raitt, Gregg Allman, Laverne Baker, Patti LaBelle, and Peter Wolf among others, including an impromptu session with Mick Jagger at New York's "Trax."

Over the years Montgomery's band has been a springboard for many musicians. Members of his band have included Billy Squire, Wayne Kramer (MC-5), Jeff Golub (Rod Stewart), Jim McCarty (Mitch Ryder and the Detroit Wheels), Nunzio Signore (Bo Diddley), Jeff Pevar (Ray Charles Orchestra, Crosby, Stills & Nash), Bobby Chouinard (drummer with Ted Nugent, Squire and Robert Gordon), Jeff Levine (Joe Cocker), Aerosmith's Tom Gambel, and many others.

But somewhere in the 1980s bad deals and bad management tarnished his earlier hard-won national success. It's been a hard, yet very familiar road for Montgomery. He still plays the clubs, still pays his blues dues with the utmost respect to the masters, and he's always been here in New England.

Boston's Blues

While others have grown up, had kids and became grandparents, Montgomery has been singing and playing "Junior's Jump," "Schoolin' Them Dice," "Messin' With the Kid" and occasionally his signature "Train," week in and week out for three decades and counting.

James Montgomery is not built for comfort. He's got to be on the edge. And that's where he is today. He has a new attitude, new band and new commitments to himself, the music and the community. He is involved in many charitable events. If the word fund-raiser is mentioned, Montgomery is often the first to volunteer.

And speaking of community, Montgomery, as president of the New England Blues Society, has spearheaded the effort to bring medical care to musicians without health insurance in the New England area. Clinics north and south of Boston have signed on to treat musicians who have no medical insurance -- no matter their condition or ailment.

In addition to medical services, a rehabilitative clinic has agreed to provide follow-up therapies and even home health care -- all through the efforts of James Montgomery.

"We want to be a model for the rest of the country," Montgomery said when asked about his plan to bring medical care to musicians. "We hope to make this a national trend and have more people and agencies come on board."

Throughout the years, Montgomery has always been the bandleader, the outfront personality who likes the lights, the banter with the band and the audience, and his tornadic solos. Today, The James Montgomery Band is headed back to the roots of blues. He said he plays "what Paul Butterfield would play today, early James Cotton and early Junior Wells. Much of the blues community forgets just how energetic those guys were. They'd turn it up to 10 and took no prisoners. I'm really aiming for that same direction that got me excited in the first place.

"I think there is a tendency for blues musicians to play things a certain way because they hear it that way, and if you try and get them to do something a little more energetic, it's foreign to them because sometimes I think they put blues in a box. If it goes outside of that structure then we're not going to call it blues.

"These people probably never saw all the offshoots of Muddy's band because every person who left Muddy's band and started their own band tried to outdo the next guy, because that's what they learned from Muddy.

"Remember, Muddy's first band was called the Head Cutters. His idea was to go into these clubs and cut heads and try and get the gigs off from the bands that were playing there on the same nights. Muddy was a very competitive guy. And the guys who worked for Muddy – they were his disciples, and when they left and stared their own bands they wanted to make sure that they kicked more butt than the other guy.

"So that's what I'm aiming for," he said.

So where did this living legend of the Boston and New England blues scene come from?

"My brother John and I were always big music fans. Every Christmas we use to go on shoplifting sprees and get all our favorite records until we got busted," James said.

John eventually became a vice president at Warner Bros. Records.

"Anyway, John had started a 'band' in Detroit, years before the Grateful Dead was conceived and the name of the band was The Dead. And he had four guys in the band but none of them really played any instruments, they just posed and had their pictures taken.

"But if you asked anybody on the east side of Detroit who the biggest band was, they'd say, "Ahhhh, The Dead," of course not realizing that they never played a gig or ever played a nightclub and they never played any instruments."

James concedes that John certainly had the all makings of the modern record company executive.

On his own roots, "I guess I was in sixth grade when I won a talent contest," Montgomery said. "These other kids had real talent y'know… they probably took ballet for four years or flute for four years, or piano -- and then I came up at the end of it. I just wanted to get up on stage, and I had a plastic guitar and put my collar up and put on some fake sideburns and 'played' to "Hound Dog" and won the talent contest. That's when I figured you don't have to have talent to make it in this business."

As a young teen, Montgomery was beginning to think about his future. "To show you where my aspirations were, some kids were thinking they were going to be an astronaut, maybe the president of the United States or a CEO for an important company.

"But I'm going, 'Wow! Man! I want to be a harmonica player!'

"I don't know what it was, but I really thought it was cool. So I joined the Milk River Jug Band, which soon changed its name to the Milk River Sheiks, which I thought was pretty cool for a bunch of 15-year-olds. So through this band I started going downtown (Detroit) and seeing a lot of the folk guys. It's nice to look back and know I ended up being friends with Tom Rush, Jim Kweskin and Jeff and Maria Muldaur."

Back then there were six or seven blues clubs in Detroit and they often played Saturday and Sunday matinees, Montgomery said. This was also the time when the folk movement was starting and there were a lot of 17- and 18-year-olds who were really getting into blues.

"I was like 15 and I'd go to the Chess Mate, which was actually a coffeehouse that didn't serve booze which stayed open all night. Murray Weinbaum, the guy who owned it, had a big backstage area, and all the blues musicians knew that when their bar closed at 2 in the morning, they could go to the coffeehouse. Although they couldn't buy a drink, the dressing room used to be stocked with Old Grandad and Jim Bean. None of those guys ever drank beer or wine.

"So I'd usually go down to see (John Lee) Hooker play down there and it wasn't unusual for the last set to have Hooker, Muddy and Cotton and all these guys up at 3 in the morning drinking Old Grandad and jamming. It was great.

"That's when I really started to ingratiate myself to people like James Cotton. I'd go up to Cotton and say something like, 'Gee Mr. Cotton can you show me...' And he'd be over in some corner trying to pick up some girl. And just about the time that he'd be ready to get a room key, he'd hear this little white kid going 'Gee, Mr. Cotton...'

'Get away kid, can't you see what I'm doing here,' he'd say. But eventually it paid off and actually Cotton and Junior Wells became really good friends and I really loved those guys."

After the Chess Mate days, there was the Living End, the Blue Monday, Duke's Playhouse, and the Decanter. "I'd tell my father that I needed the car to go to the high school basketball game. He wouldn't let me go downtown on my own. This was right before the city was burned down in the riots. It was tough.

"Well, I used to go downtown regularly to see Buddy Guy and Junior and all those guys around '66, '67. I mean it was really tough. For me to go down there in my father's car, what was I thinking? My father was an executive at the Chrysler Corporation, and every year they'd give him a brand new car that was fully loaded. I still can't believe nothing every happened to me. It's just unbelievable. But anyways, some of those guys would look out for me a little bit, and it was great.

"I started out in Grosse Point, Michigan, as a folks/blues player in a jug band playing ragtime. I played jug and washtub. I remember Jim Kweskin mentioning something about seeing this group called The Paul Butterfield Band. This would be about 1963. But sure enough, two months go by and they're scheduled to play a gig at the Chess Mate.

"I was still waiting to see this folk band and these guys come up and they're wearing these tattered jeans and I'm like, 'What the fuck is this?' And I'm sitting about five feet away from Butter's amplifiers. Hey, it was a little folky coffeehouse.

"And the announcer says, The Paul Butterfield Band, and before it really registers, Butter starts out with 'Mellow Down Easy' -- and I'm pinned to the back of my chair like those old ads for Maxell tapes. That was it for me.

"At this point I was fronting the jug band and they taught me how to play. Chris Ciao, who's now with the Uptown Horns, he was the guy who was in the jug band who taught me how to play harmonica.

"So the biggest influences on me from where I grew up with my first blues records were Lightnin' Hopkins, Sonny Terry and Brownie McGee and Robert Johnson. And my biggest influence really, when I started putting bands of my own together were James Cotton and Paul Butterfield. I mean, I always loved Muddy and Muddy was obviously far and away the king of Chicago blues. There's no disputing Muddy's dominance of that whole genre. And that's what I really want to get back to right now," he said.

Montgomery has had a band named after him for more than 30 years. And for nine of those years, it was a musical life that centered around Lenny Bradford on bass and Steve Barbuto on drums. Then, Montgomery was mired in his own blues and dealing with divorce.

Boston's Blues

"One of the things really that I had to figure out on a daily basis was to ask myself, 'What are you going to do to make sure that you're on track?' I mean, it was really devastating to me. All I did was listen to like slow Charles Brown songs and slow Delbert McClinton songs and slow blues songs for two months without stopping. It was a very emotional period -- I really couldn't get myself back in line. Eventually, I was able to kind of devote myself to my career again.

"I was working with LB and Steve who to me are like the closest thing to family that I have. They were like my brothers on the gig and I mean it was a very difficult decision (to go off on my own).

"I've been very comfortable for a long time but y'know for a long time, from say 1972 to about 1984 or so, I was really a national act that was playing a lot of national places. I got into this plateau regionally that was very comfortable. So I think a combination of not being able to get the time that I wanted or the kind of enthusiasm that was needed to re-address our careers. Anyway, it was very painful," Montgomery said.

The trio ended around 1996.

Today, Montgomery is very much enjoying himself. He's got a syndicated radio show, "Backstage with the Blues," which features authentic blues music along with stories, told by the musicians themselves, the show provides a bridge between the artists and listeners, reminiscing about the history behind the tunes.

His guests have included John Lee Hooker, James Cotton, Dr. John, Bonnie Raitt, Koko Taylor, Ruth Brown, Otis Clay, Son Seals, Duke Robillard, Rod Piazza, and many more.

"Backstage With the Blues" may be heard on:
Block Island, RI - 99.3 Swing FM, Saturday, 10 p.m.
Newport, RI/Fall River, MA - 1540 AM WADK, Saturday, 4 p.m.
Portland, ME/Portsmouth, NH - 92.1 FNX, Sunday, 1 p.m.
Cushing, OK - 1600 KUSH, Sunday, 5 p.m. (CST)

Montgomery took James Cotton with his band to the Azores in 2000, and a return trip is likely in 2001. The show was so successful that it was on the 6 o'clock news in Portugal and featured in the main newspaper on the mainland.

In 2000, Montgomery cut some sides for Kid Rock in Kid's house in Michigan; he teamed up with guitarist Jimmy Vivino of the Conan O'Brien band at a few gigs in '99 and '00; and played with Les Paul on two gigs at New York's Iridium Ballroom.

In early 2001, he worked with Mark Naftalin, the original keyboard player with the Paul Butterfield Blues Band on several gigs; in May he coordinated an India Earthquake Relief fund-raiser at the House of Blues in Cambridge; and in July 2001, he worked the Woods Hole Film Festival in Bourne, Mass., putting together an an all-star lineup featuring James Cotton, Jim Belushi and other special guests.

Montgomery has recorded several albums. "First Time Out" has been remastered and re-released by MRG/Capricorn. Others include "James Montgomery Band" on Island Records; "Duck Fever," with members of the David Letterman Band, "Live Trax," with the Uptown Horns (the Rolling Stones' horn section); and Tone-Cool's, "The Oven Is On," released in 1991. His latest, "Bring It On Home" was released in 2001 on the Conqueroot label, headed by Peter Malick, who played in Montgomery's band in the 1970s.

Web: jamesmontgomery.com

Sugar Ray Norcia

Art Simas
Sugar Ray Norcia: 'What goes around, comes around'

That's what happening to Sugar Ray Norcia, born June 6, 1954, that sweet and swingin' guy turned gutbucket bluesman with blisters on his lips. Ray is diggin' deep and blowin' the hell out of his harmonica with his original group, the Bluetones. The same guys are back 12 years later -- Neil Gouvin on drums, Michael 'Mudcat' Ward on bass, Kid Bangham on guitar and, when he can make it, Anthony Geraci on keyboards, with Norcia holding it all together while holding nothing back. (In 2001, Mike Welch took over the guitar slot.)

Formed in the fall of 1999, the Bluetones erupted on the New England blues scene and remain one of the prime attractions for blues lovers near and far. "It was always been a dream of ours to get back together," Norcia said of the reunion. He made it clear he likes being back home and close to his roots. "All those years with all the horns, I kinda needed to get back to the basics."

The "horns" refers to his seven-year stint as frontman and leader of Roomful of Blues, a dream-come-true job for Norcia, a kid who followed in his father's footsteps as a multitalented talented singer and musician. Albert Norcia was a music teacher and a vocal coach, was the author of a book called "The Voice" and a harmonica player. "So that's where my roots are," Ray said. "I listened to him."

Growing up in Westerly, R.I., the younger Norcia was busy in school plays and singing wherever and whenever he could. And about the same time, his school buddies were listening to this band that was rockin' the Knickerbocker Cafe in Westerly -- a band called Roomful of Blues -- while forming a band of their own. They asked Ray if he'd be the lead singer.

"At the time I wasn't really into blues, but they laid a few records on me, like Elmore James' 'Shake Your Moneymaker.' That was the first song I attempted. Another guy in the band gave me his Little Walter records. It blew me away and I brought them home and I tried to decipher what Walter was doing. So, from that time on, I'd say I was about 16 or 17, I really dug what I was hearing and I never looked back.

"I graduated in 1972 and I was just singing. One night the harp player called in sick for a gig, so when he didn't show up I became the singer/harmonica player.

"I even played sax for a few gigs. I like to fool around with instruments. I play guitar, too, in fact that's how I write my songs, on guitar and piano. And I started off playing trumpet," Norcia said. "To be able to play an instrument and back yourself up on harmonica is unparalleled. Some of my ideas for the band are formed that way."

With a growing musical resume and vocal chops, it was just a matter of time before Norcia was going to break out.

"A few years later I met Ronnie Earl, Ronnie Horvath at the time, and that was a real catalyst. I met a lot of people -- Mudcat Ward, Little Anthony Geraci and Neil Gouvin. Neil and I've been together for a number of years going back to when we started the first Bluetones in the late 1970s. We played at the old Met Cafe in Providence and at the Speakeasy in Cambridge. We played with J.B. Hutto, James Cotton and many others, and so we'd turn that gig at the Speakeasy into a little road trip and we'd back up these masters. It was like going to school," Norcia said.

The blues scene of the late '70s and early '80s was pretty cool as far as blues go, Norcia said. There were many more places to play and we all tried to make a living at it. "Hell, we're still struggling," he said.

The Shaboo Inn in Willimantic, Conn., was one of several showcase venues where the masters would stop in on their way from New York to Boston and Cambridge. "That was one of the first places I witnessed George Smith, and I went whaoooo, so that's what it's all about!!! And I saw Muddy there, Cotton, and it sort of steamrolled from there," Norcia said.

The original Bluetones were together for about 12 years, he said, and we ended up with Kid Bangham in the band. Ronnie Earl played with the Bluetones for about eight or nine years of the 12. Then he joined Roomful.

Others who had played in the Bluetones included Peter Hi Fi Ward (Michael's brother), J.B. Hutto and even Hubert Sumlin. "So you're talking heavy hitters here," Norcia said.

After Ronnie left, Norcia put an ad in the paper looking for a blues guitarist. "We saw 10 or 12 guitarists and the last guy was Kid Bangham. He just had a guitar, no case and he looked totally unprofessional when he came for the audition. We went through a couple of tunes and halfway into the first tune, my eyes just opened up and I was saying to myself, 'we found him.'"

With the Bluetones' more traditional Southside Chicago blues, Norcia as the leader, was required to provide much of the material. But inspiration doesn't always precede the perspiration, and songs are in various stages of development at any time.

"Usually it's lyrics first or even a title and I work backwards from there," Norcia explained. "Sometimes it takes the course of a year or two. Something will be in the back of my mind, and I'll forget about it for a while. And we'll bring ideas into rehearsals and then the collaboration begins.

"But I do think the blues tells a story and the lyrics are important. It's fun, it's very challenging. I'm writing songs now for a project coming up but I like the pressure. All a sudden the juices start flowing and the ideas start coming. That's how the 'Superharps' session (with Charlie Musselwhite and James Cotton) came about. I got a phone call asking if I wanted to do it and they asked me to bring three songs to the studio and I had about two weeks before the studio date. All of a sudden all of these songs that were laying there, came to life because I was inspired and motivated. That's what gets me going. I do -- literally -- have a briefcase full of blues where I keep all my lyrics in, ever since I was a teenager. I've got thousands and thousands of pages of blues lyrics," Norcia said.

The briefcase came in handy on a late-night session that became "Take It From Me" with Little Anthony in 1994. "He had always said he wanted to do something with just the two of us. So he took the initiative and booked some time. And I came with my briefcase. I pulled out some of my favorite ones, and we played just like we were at his house," Norcia said. "I'm very proud of that CD."

The first incarnation of the Bluetones lasted until about 1989. Kid Bangham joined the Fabulous T-Birds with Duke Robillard around 1990. Since Norcia was freelancing on various projects, Ronnie called him up and asked if he'd play in the Broadcasters.

"I played with Ronnie in 1990 and we had some great dates in Europe, did a live recording with Jimmy Rogers and we had a ball for about a year. Then right after that was the time I got the call from Roomful, in 1991. So I was with them almost seven years and we'd do 200 to 250 dates a year. That's a real test of a vocalist, singing night after night. Once the voice starts slipping, it's hard to rebound. So I really learned how to pace myself in that band. But it's quite an instrument -- the human voice.

"In the meantime, when I was with Roomful, I did two or three other projects: one with Otis Grand, another with Porky Cohen, and Michelle Willson. So I kept busy," Norcia said.

Boston's Blues

"I left Roomful and almost immediately went in and recorded 'Sweet And Swingin' and did a tour with that band, then formed the Bluetones again, first with Troy Gonyea, then Rob Nelson on guitar. But it was always been a dream of ours to get us all back together.

Norcia said the latest Bluetones are playing gigs as a four-piece band -- mainly because Geraci moved to northern Vermont. But he'll be on the record and we plan to go on the blues circuit, going to Europe and doing festivals.

In between the local and extended trips in the United States, Norcia went to England in May 2000, to do a harmonica festival and he was back playing with Otis Grand in August. "It's a never-ending circuit but something I just love to do," he said.

"Back On Top" with Pinetop Perkins and Michael Williams' record "Late Night Walk" provided Norcia some time to stretch out vocally.

He also occasionally fronts a 10-piece band reminiscent of Roomful featuring Big Joe Turner and Smiley Lewis material. "I've always had the desire to sing that kind of stuff, too. So it's a way for me to have that outlet to sing the big band arrangements of Count Basie and Jimmy Rushing tunes, whereas the Bluetones are in a different bag," Norcia said.

Norcia says he feels honored that young musicians look up to his group. "Try to learn the nuances of the music -- whatever music you're playing," he advises. "I've been playing and listening... for so long, it's all a part of me. Something definitely inside of me clicked when I first heard it... I think back to where we all came from and none of it compares with being a successful artist. That's just a wonderful thing."

Web: severnrecords.com

Greg Piccolo

Boston's Blues
Greg Piccolo: Developing the textures for his own sound with Heavy Juice

The hard-honking tenor sax sounds of Greg Piccolo were the staples of Roomful of Blues for a quarter of a century.

Born in Westerly, R.I., May 10, 1951, Piccolo first met Duke Robillard, the founder of Roomful, when Piccolo was 14.

"He became my musical guru," Piccolo said, "and I just followed along with him. We had a rock band together for a while then we broke up and he started Roomful and I stayed with rock. Then I realized what he was doing musically and I wanted to be involved with it.

"He took me back and I joined Roomful when I was 19 and stayed with them for 25 years," Piccolo said.

When Piccolo's group first started out in 1964-65, they rode the English rock wave with The Animals, Rolling Stones -- "We could do all-Animals all night," Piccolo said.

But when Duke and he played together it was a lot of Beatles songs and lots of harmonies. At that time, Piccolo was only a vocalist. "I didn't start playing (saxophone) seriously until I was 19. I had an alto sax, but I never really got into it. I used it on a couple of Traffic tunes, but I never really got into the music -- the real heavy stuff -- until Duke started playing his records. I always had a guitar, but I didn't touch a guitar until after Ronnie (Earl) left Roomful.

"When we were teens, Duke and I used to write songs together. But I thought they were so bad, but we did 'em anyway," Piccolo said.

Because he perceived himself as a poor songwriter, "I told myself never to attempt to write a song again," Piccolo said.

And it was a long time until he attempted to do it again.

But it was Bob Bell, who still manages Roomful, who asked Piccolo to come up with some original material for the group's next project.

"I said, 'Look, I tried before and it didn't work out, but I'm willing to give it a try again.'

165

"And I wrote seven tunes. They're all different but basic R&B, but they're not all the same types of songs. And I realized that I had something that was there that was coming out, and that those songs were really what I wanted them to be," Piccolo said.

"I never had a sense of urgency about it. I'd write an idea down but it's not like I get up every day and feel like I have to write five songs. Some people, they just write continuously. I have different ways of writing songs; sometimes it's a line that will pop into my head other times it might be a title or something will catch me from something that I read on a billboard or in an ad, or a combination of words that I can twist around. Other times I'll say that I want to write a song that has a certain beat or I'll sit down at the piano and I'll put some chords together just to see what will happen. But that (the debut writing on 'Hot Little Mama') happened slowly in one day, but it happened."

Getting the creative and competitive juices flowing is always a challenge for musicians -– especially when they are under deadline pressure and a studio date is coming fast.

"When you go into the studio, you always want to do something different that you've never done before. But you gotta have some driving thing, something that's going to make it all fresh. As a songwriter, I usually have a song in my head and I'll be thinking of it and working it through my head. Then I'll pick up a guitar and let it flow."

Working off another instrument in the writing process is a unique but mandatory exercise for Piccolo. "I don't think people who are great on an instrument should write to that instrument. Just a quirk that I have. I think it clouds the issue... But then there are people such as Duke who are great at all levels."

Piccolo said the approach is the key, which will also separate musical styles. He said he definitely wanted to develop his own sound. "If I do what's in my head and it comes out right, then I like it, but I don't always execute what's in my head properly. I look at myself, when I pick up the guitar, with an approach that's like a horn. My rhythm parts are based more on horn parts rather than on guitar parts. I think that's part of the reason that I might have my own style.

"I joined Roomful in 1970, and in the '70s we had it pretty good. We'd play at Brandi's for six nights in a row or go up to Toronto and play two weeks at one place. The money was flowing back then and the social mentality was different. Social consciousness played a big part in the club scene. But I guess God protects the ignorant and the idiots. We did a lot of crazy things. It's amazing that a lot of people are still here, including myself.

"I didn't care where I was -- as long as we had fun -- Texas, Louisiana, San Fran, New York City. There weren't too many places I didn't like. But I especially liked eastern Texas and the people there. And of course, I was always happy to have gigs in my hometown. I don't think I'd go on the road if we could do well closer to home on a regular basis.

"In 1978, we started traveling more often as the economy got worse and we had to keep moving. That's even the way it is for my small band. You gotta be ready to move... you got to keep going," Piccolo said.

But playing in Roomful certainly had its privileges. Piccolo said he has fond memories of many musicians, such as Eddie "Cleanhead" Vinson, Big Joe Turner, Red Prysock, Jimmy Witherspoon, Bill Austin and Helen Humes who had Ellen Larkin on piano.

"But my favorite collaboration was with Roy Brown. When we played with him, we became transcended. We pulled each other up and it was really a collaboration where we all became part of the greater whole that really no one was backing anybody up. To me that was the best thing we ever did. He knew how to use Roomful, and to get the best out of us. This was in the early 1980s," he said.

"But we never made an album until 1978, Piccolo lamented. "Nobody knew what we should do, and the singer issue came up, plus we were looking for the big rock record deal and doing some demo work with Pat Benatar. We kept looking for the deal and we kept trying different combinations, different songs, demos and kept shopping them.

"Then we realized that the big Aerosmith-type deal wasn't going to happen and we had let a lot of time slip by. And there was a lot of second-guessing at the time and we had passed up a couple of offers which were pretty good, but we kept looking for the big one.

"Finally, we all realized, 'We gotta do something!' since we waited too long, and it didn't make any sense not to put anything out," Piccolo said.

The album with Big Joe Turner and Eddie "Cleanhead" Vinson came out followed by "Hot Little Mama" and then "Dressed Up To Get Messed Up."

Art Simas

Piccolo left Roomful in April 1994 and moved into his own direction with Heavy Juice.

"The original concept for Heavy Juice was to be a seven-piece band, with two keyboard players; a baritone; a percussionist; drummer, and a bass player. And I wanted the baritone player to be able to play accordian too," Piccolo said.

"It's different than Roomful since it's my vision. In Roomful, there was some second-guessing and an uncomfortable feeling of trying to accommodate people in the band. But in this band, I don't have any qualms of mixing it up playing a reggae song, followed by a blues, followed by a New Orleans song. I get to do whatever I want to do, which puts a big responsibility on my shoulders, but I'm giving the audience something that they can't get anywhere else, something that is unique without being strange or weird."

From seven, the band has since been reduced to three with Piccolo; drummer Jonathan Lichdig and keyboard player, Scinichiotsu, who plays bass with his left hand or Piccolo plays bass on his left hand while switching off from sax to guitar.

"If I can pull it off as a trio without losing musicality, it's a brave new world I'm living in," Piccolo said.

In 2001, Piccolo released a CD called "Homage," which pays respect to some of earlier influences.

Web: gregpiccolo.com

J. Place

Art Simas
Getting back to basics with J. Place

There ain't nothing sautéed, simmered or stewed about Josiah, better known as J. Place's music. It's served on the bone -- meaty, raw and dripping in its natural juices.

Place's 1996 debut CD, "High Temperature," was released when he was fronting Nasty J and the Grinders. There's some mighty good blues on that self-produced album: chestnuts such as Willie Dixon's "Mellow Down Easy," "I Wants To Be Loved" and "I Don't Play," to Little Walter's seldom covered, "Temperature" and "Boogie," to John Lee Hooker's "Big Legs, Tight Skirt," Muddy's "Streamline Woman," and Jimmy Reed's "Ain't That Loving You Baby."

But the real sweet stuff is based in the delivery and presentation. On this particular album, the vocals and harp of Place combine with the guitar workmanship of Nick Adams, churn inside-out then back again like playful whitecaps whipped by an Atlantic gale. One is never sure what course a particular song will take or where it will resurface -- only that it will be in a different place from where it all began. Todd Carson on bass and Maylo Keller on drums anchored the controlled tempest on the disc.

Place said that band was trying to stay true to a traditional sound instead of crossing over into rock-based areas. Listening to this type of down-and-dirty roadhouse blues really gets under your skin and into your blood. You can feel it circulate and curdle. When it gets to your brain, your legs and hips start moving and you don't even know it.

In 1997, Adams and Carlson joined the Racky Thomas Band, which won the Battle of the Blues Bands that same year, representing the Boston Blues Society at the International Blues Talent Competition in Memphis. And Place was left searching for a whole new band.

In 1999 he found his players in guitarist Bobby Gus, bass players Jacques Raymond and Brian Rost, and Larry Takki on drums who released "Bettin' On The Blues," a compilation of Place originals, including the title track and more of those B side blues chestnuts with a twist.

"For me it all comes down to conviction," Place said. "The best blues records are the ones that, when you hear them, you think you are right in the same room with a powerful presence of a Muddy or Wolf. It's undeniable."

Boston's Blues

Place accentuates his voice and harp to elongate, drag and literally grind the music to a deeper layer of blues.

For most of the 1980s, Place "toured" Europe, notably Copenhagen, Denmark, with his band, Boogie Chillen. When he returned stateside about 14 years ago, he hooked up with an R&B band called King Bee. But there was more blues desires that needed to be sated. "Plus, I wanted to blow more harp, too," of his decision to slide over and form Nasty J and the Nightcrawlers, which evolved to Nasty J and the Grinders, then the J Place Band.

Place is also a photographer for several blues publications. In 1995, he, Tom Hazeltine, Jim Saley, president of the Boston Blues Society, and Peter Rea exhibited their work at the Blues Visions Gallery in Rockland, Mass., and in 1996, a similar exhibit was held at Harvard University.

Place also plays with the more countrified blues with Bertrand Laurence and The Jellyrollers.

"When you're in a blues band and you're working the circuit, that's an aerobic activity," he said. "Especially being a harp player and a singer. It's a physical thing. I'm just starting to realize that's it's key to your performance and ability and how you can express yourself soulfully."

While Place may front the band, he's quick to point out that he is not the highlight. "The harp thing is cool, but it's not what it's all about. It's the overall authenticity" that is the core of the band's strength.

"Blues for me is a way to express yourself," he said. "It's a very sensual, honest and open kind of music that allows for a lot of improvisation, not only for the notes on the scale but also the notes in between."

Jerry Portnoy

Jerry Portnoy: From Muddy to Clapton and back home

Chicago native Jerry Portnoy, born in 1943, grew up with the real-deal blues on Maxwell Street. His father owned a rug store and, "I used to go down with my dad every Sunday morning and I'd see these people playing on the street, which was really the center of blues activity at that time after the war."

As the commerce commenced, the musical bazaar would blast the latest sounds from new-fangled electronic amplifiers on the street. Harmonica players engaged in volume duels with guitar players for the attention and silver coins from the bargain hunters and the curious passers-by.

"Musicians would rent electrical cords from the shopkeepers for 25 cents for their amplifiers, which were just made after the war, so I heard all this stuff growing up. Little Walter would be playing very close to my father's store, but I really didn't pay too much attention to it. But it put the music in my head at an early age, which may have been responsible for triggering a response later on in my life."

Portnoy said Johnny Young and Little Walter made some of the first post-war blues records on the little label called Oranel, which was run out of the Maxwell Radio and Record store at 831 Maxwell St. "That was right down the street from my father's store. Those were the only two records that company ever put out," he said.

When the '60s rolled around with the "blues revival" and Portnoy heard the incessant music again, "I just went crazy for it," he said. "Sonny Boy Williamson really got to me and I said, I got to learn how to do this. He was encouraging and was such a great person."

Portnoy met Sonny Terry on a trip to California and had a brief flirtation with his style. But it was that native Chicago sound that beckoned him home. So he started hanging around the clubs, picking up tips and seeing Johnny Young, Big Walter Horton, Eddie Taylor, The Aces, Willie Mabon, Howlin' Wolf, to name just a few. "Chicago was still hopping at the time," he said, "and I used to hang out with Big Walter and Paul Oscher. I was totally immersed in it."

Portnoy's first pro gig was with Johnny Young. By now, in his late 20s, Portnoy played with him for a couple of years; then John Littlejohn for a couple of years; for drummer Sam Lay for about six months; then got his own band together.

A few months later, Young died and there was a benefit for his family where Portnoy played harp. "Muddy Waters was also at the benefit and he asked me to play a set with him because his harp player (Mojo Buford) wasn't there. Three days later I got a call from Muddy to join the band."

He played with the Muddy Waters Band for six years from 1974-1980. "There's no way I can adequately tell you what it meant to me. I learned so much with Muddy... how to get in and out; adding texture without overriding his voice; learning time and delays in the old style; learning the meaning of making a note say something. It was invaluable.

"Playing with Muddy not only secured your own reputation, but exposed you to a level of blues that you can't access today, at least not on a personal level because those people are gone now. I was very fortunate to learn from them firsthand. But blues has always been a music that has been passed down and people passing their gifts from person to person based on people's relationships. And I've tried to do the same, certainly through my own instrument in teaching others."

The Legendary Blues Band was formed out of a core group of ex-Muddy Waters members. People such as Pinetop Perkins, Luther "Guitar Junior" Johnson, Willie "Big Eyes" Smith and Calvin "Fuzz" Jones, carry on the legacy. Portnoy played with that band for six years; took a year off; did a tour on his own; then joined Ronnie Earl and one of the first incarnations of the Broadcasters for a year and a half. He broke away from Earl and formed his own band for about four years. Then he traveled the world with Eric Clapton for four years and contributed to Clapton's blues tribute to the masters, on "Back From The Cradle."

In 1997, Portnoy developed refined instructional lessons on how to play blues harp. The material is contained in three CDs and book called Jerry Portnoy's Master Class. "It's like sitting in my living room and having me explain the ins and outs of playing that instrument at a detailed level. I wanted to capture the definitive method of teaching blues harmonica, and I think I accomplished that. I'm very proud of it and it'll be a legacy for me that will be around long after I'm gone."

If one aspires to be a harp player, Portnoy says, "You've got to bring certain natural gifts and musical talent and you've got to do your homework and do a lot of listening to establish a context and a frame of reference."

When he was a youngster, Portnoy said, "I fooled around with everything, guitar, piano, accordian, and it all felt foreign to me. But when I picked up the harp, I

Boston's Blues

knew right away. I had a good ear for listening and a physical affinity for the harmonica as an oral instrument. It suited me and felt natural. I had a sense of the instrument. I believe certain instruments are for certain people. So then I had to work it out and learn how to properly operate it."

Portnoy arrived in the Boston area in 1977. "This area has always had a lot of great players. So I knew I could have a chance to play. I was in Muddy's band at the time and we did a lot of East Coast work. And there were a lot of good players around here at the time, John Nicholas, Dave Maxwell, and there was a pretty thriving little scene with the Speakeasy, and Boston was a regular stop along the way for musicians with Paul's Mall, and places like that. So that made it an easy fit."

Paul Rishell and Annie Raines

Boston's Blues
Paul Rishell and Annie Raines: Keepers of traditional blues artistry

"Blues is music to a person waking up to themselves" -- Paul Rishell

Country blues requires a very different approach to the music than any other type of blues. There's a commitment on the part of the artists to keep the tradition of the early masters of the genre intact yet move on to higher ground in the development of personal style.

Paul Rishell and Annie Raines are undoubtedly the tops in New England in this demanding and sometimes underappreciated blues mode. They've been playing together for about six years now and enjoying their mutual love for the music.

Rishell, born in 1950 in Brooklyn, N.Y., initially started playing drums in garage bands in the early 1960s in the bars in New York and Connecticut. "I was listening to a lot of jazz drummers and musicians. At the same time I was learning to play other kinds of music. So I was listening to a lot of black music but not really playing out at this time."

Growing up in New York, Rishell said, "I was pretty much left alone and wasn't expected to learn to play anything... not coming from a musical family."

But his life was altered forever when he first listened to the Library of Congress recordings by Alan Lomax when he was 13 in 1963. That was the first time he heard Son House and other Delta artists who spoke of life's trials and tribulations in the Deep South.

After hearing House and the true country blues, Rishell searched for the source of that inspiration and wanted to find out more about the man and the music.

"I finally got to meet him in Somerville in 1973 and played with him. Dick Waterman, his manager asked me if I would sort of take care of him and be his 'trainer' while he was in Boston, which meant that my job was to gently wake him up and make sure he made his gigs on time."

Through Waterman's encouragement, Rishell played with many of the first-generation blues players who came through Boston such as Johnny Shines, Howlin' Wolf, Sonny Terry and Brownie McGhee.

Art Simas

Annie Raines, born in 1969, grew up in Newton and took piano lesson in elementary school before taking up the harp at age 17. By that time, "I learned more music than I thought I knew." She learned from one of the best in the business -- Jerry Portnoy.

Like Rishell, "something went click" when she first heard Muddy Waters, she said. "Actually, a kid who was playing harmonica in the hallways in high school asked me, 'Do you like Muddy Waters?' and I said, 'Sure, I've heard of THEM.'

"So he gave me three Muddy Waters tapes and I immediately got right into it. And I'd say within a month of first listening to that I went to the 1369 jazz club in Cambridge. I knew I wanted to play but I also knew I wasn't ready. But it was the sound that captivated me," Raines said.

Soon after, Raines joined the Cambridge Harmonica Orchestra under the direction of Pierre Beauregard, which allowed her to fine-tune her chops. "So within a year I started to play I was very much involved. I had the privilege of playing with people like James Cotton, Pinetop Perkins and Jerry Portnoy. It seems sometimes as if you're destined to be in a certain place, and events conspire to show you that you're doing the right thing," she said.

In 1992, Frank Capella from the Atlantic Bar and Grille gave Annie a call and said he needed a band for that Saturday night. At the time, Raines had been working on her own and freelancing but wasn't associated with a band. "But of course I said, 'Sure, we can be there," she said. "So I figured I'd better give Paul a call. We had played together before in a band situation and I had always admired his playing. It turned out to be a very fortuitous night. We had an instant rapport and chemistry. I was really psyched. We had the same approach to the music and we've been working together ever since."

Their first collaborative recording appeared in November 1993 on Rishell's "Swear to Tell the Truth," just about a year after that first gig at the Atlantic.

Because of the nature of country blues, Rishell says that individual creativity -- the basic ingredients that comprise a song -- are the essence of its creator. "Subtlety in music is the personality of the player. The subtlety is there to be used whether it's recognized or not. And the same is true for the listener." In other words the listener reaches his or her own interpretations based on the artist's interpretation of things that are there and some things that are imagined.

Boston's Blues

For example, Rishell said Ronnie Earl uses dynamics to get his subtle points across to his audience, which is something others may never use. But he uses that subtlety to his advantage to make people understand.

On songwriting, Raines says every song is different and is a process in itself. On her originals from "I Want You To Know," (Tone-Cool, 1996) she says some lyrics were written years ago ("Got To Fly" and "Little Dove") and the framework was built around them. And on others, such as "Old Heartbreak," Paul would begin with a chording line and the song would evolve from that point.

Often a song will begin from instant inspiration at any moment. There is no specific time when either of them will deliberately say they will write a song at this or that particular hour.

"My late wife Leslie, got the idea of putting us (Annie and I) together. She talked me into it. And she knew me very, very well. She knew that Annie and I would work well together and we started to get creative as soon as we started working together. It's a lot fun," Rishell said. "And it's certainly much easier putting an album together. Annie has a lot of ideas and she brings a lot of perspective."

On the current blues resurgence, the two musicians agree to disagree. Paul says there was a larger blues scene in the Boston area in the early 1970s. He says he doesn't get a sense that there is a strong foundation of blues from club owners or the public. "I think today it's mostly held together by the musicians and a few others who are sympathetic to blues. But I don't see Boston as being particularly celebratory of blues culture."

On the other hand, Raines says, "I think Boston has had a lot more interest in the blues than other cities. It has a lot of resources and it's supported a lot of people in the business. There's such a high caliber of musicianship overall. It's been very good to me. I received a lot of support when I first started out and I could see this thing (resurgence) forming in the mid-'80s. And son-of-a-gun, I was right."

Blues musicians rarely become commodities overnight. Normally they have to work for several years and be ready to tour when the opportunities come along -- if they come along. "The blues is a grassroots thing," Rishell said. "You go out and play a gig and you walk out with 20 or 30 people who will be willing to see you again, then you're doing OK.

Art Simas

"The cost of touring for Annie and I -- we can only do to a limited degree because I have to take care of my daughter (Vanessa). But a lot of times, Vanessa takes her schoolwork and comes with us on tour. Thank God she has the ability to do that. If you have records out, it behooves you to go out there to promote them.

"But to tell you the truth, I'm not sure if I'd buy my own albums. The kind of music I listen to is the blues of people who've been dead for 60-70 years. I'm not really sure what people are thinking of when they come to blues shows. Annie and I try to give them music that is made well, music that has a lasting quality.

"I'm not really sure that people know what blues is. People are sort of being programmed by some of the radio shows and record companies where they can market something and they can all make money from it. That's the bottom line," Rishell said. "So I'm not sure how much the integrity of the music suffers. Does it suffer any more from neglect or from overexposure or a whittling away of the more interesting facets of it so that it will fit into a certain mold of merchandising?

"I don't worry about that because the music has already been made. But I do worry about the progression of it in terms of what people regard as blues. It's a funny thing to define. But I kind of wonder sometimes when people talk about blues and you listen to what they're playing. Man, they're not really playing blues. It may be the form. But you're not telling any kind of story. And blues is a story. I just don't hear a lot of storytellers out there. I hear a lot of flashy guitars.

"Blues is music to a person waking up to themselves. It's a person coming to a certain realization, and you are with them for that moment. It's a spontaneous thing, and if a performer is doing that art of it, of finding new things or relating that to the audience, that's exciting to see. It's not exciting to watch someone memorize stuff and do it over and over. So I get confused about what's blues and what people think is blues. I'm not really sure that I know. I know what it is to me but I'm not sure what it is for other people."

Rishell said, "The greatest thing about playing is when you don't think at all. The greatest part about being here is not being here. It's freedom…"

NOTE: The duo of Rishell and Raines won a W.C. Handy Award for Best Traditional Blues Album in 2000 for "Moving to the Country."

Web: paulandannie.com

Duke Robillard and Gerry Beaudoin

Art Simas
Duke Robillard: 'After 30-plus years
I feel like I'm going somewhere'

Guitar icon Duke Robillard, born in Westerly, R.I., in 1948, has achieved legendary status among guitar players in his career. The founder of Roomful of Blues, Robillard in the 1980s replaced guitarist Jimmy Vaughan in the Fabulous Thunderbirds.

He has appeared on over 125 recordings in his burgeoning career.

Two recordings were nominated for Grammy awards in 1998: Bob Dylan's "Time Out of Mind" and Ruth Brown's "R+B= Ruth Brown."

He was nominated in 1998 and 1999 for a W.C. Handy award as Best Blues Guitarist, and picked up that award in 2000 and 2001.

During his years as bandleader, Robillard mixed blues and jazz idioms. His jazz recordings, "Swing," with the Scott Hamilton Quintet and "After Hours Swing," with members of the original Roomful of Blues, are classics. Both recordings were re-released as a package on the Rounder label.

Robillard also has a very successful "Hot Licks" video on jazz and blues styles, and released two new videos on the guitar styles of blues legends Freddy King and T-Bone Walker.

Robillard has produced and played on two recordings with Kansas City jazz legend Jay McShann, and continues to produce dozens of records for the best in the business.

Robillard said, "As far as the music of the 1940s and 1950s, it's the music that I love the most. I express myself well through that form. I hear things melodically and that style of music -- blues with a jazz interpretation -- the most expressive form. I really crusaded for that in early Roomful. As far as the blues, this is an area that is most beautiful. And it needs to be kept alive."

Rhode Island:
"A lot of jazz and blues people have come from Rhode Island, from the '30s on in jazz -- Bobby Hackett, Scott Hamilton, Roomful, and many relocate to different areas. I'm proud to be from Rhode Island and I'm proud to represent the music that comes from the smallest state in the country."

Boston's Blues

Approach:

"I envisioned myself doing this forever. I never really thought of the future. I was caught up in what I was doing at the time. I used to have a desire to know what I would sound like when I was 50 years old -- and I got my wish. I hoped I would have improved with age... I'm still on the same course.

"I've been through quite a few changes as to what I let influence me and what I was trying to do. I spent a period of playing roots rock 'n' roll. So I let the rock 'n' roll creep into my music and the roots rock sound and a few years of doing stuff where I played a lot of different types of music. It's been good in a sense for songwriting. When you're a songwriter, it's nice to have an open format. That way you can express a lot of different things and different types of sounds in music. I've been concentrating on writing an album of songs that are my own but have the sound and influence of classic R&B.

"I'm working about 240 days a year... gotta pay the bills. I enjoy my work and I love playing. I don't know what to do with myself when I'm not playing -- something I've just been conditioned to do.

"Photography is a hobby. I've done covers for Jimmie Witherspoon and Jay McShann and I did the photography for my albums "Temptation" and "Duke's Blues." I don't have the time to really devote to it because it is an art form and takes a lot of dedication and practice. But I spend whatever time is available to me."

Songwriting:

"I've got two ways: Either I get an idea out of nowhere when I'm not looking for one and I'll write it down and complete it later. Or, when it's time to do an album, I'll just cram. I love doing it because I get caught up in the whole idea of what it is I'm trying to say. It gets the creative juices flowing because you know you've got to go into the studio. It's a little dangerous, too. I wonder, what if I don't think of anything? But I've never run into that. I've been recording that way for many years. "Temptation" turned out that way and "Dangerous Place" turned out that way. I had a few ideas for songs that I finished but most of them came up really quick."

Band Cohesiveness:

"The more we play together, the more open I can be free to go in any direction I want. It takes a long time to develop that. And I need that freedom. Some nights I'll play some rock and roll, some nights I'll play a lot of jazz, others nights will be a more Chicago blues sound. It's whatever I feel at the time. I'm really subject to that. When I work for somebody else, I'm really good at being a sideman. But when I work for myself, I have to go with what I feel at the moment."

Leaving Roomful:
"There were a lot of reasons why: Just a dozen years with one group and also there was a little discrepancy in direction between Greg and I. I was the musical leader and Greg Piccolo was the kind of manager and we had some disagreements. I was writing a lot of material and it wasn't getting recorded and I just knew it was time for me to start recording my own material and I think Greg was threatened by that. Whatever it was, it was just obviously time to go.

"And I was really going to start another band with the same instrumentation. But a lot of people said, 'Try something different. Try something different.' And a lot of musicians were afraid to be compared to Roomful of Blues, which is really funny. When we'd rehearse, we sounded just like Roomful, only because if I get the right players, then it's going to sound like that. But I decided to put my guitar more in the forefront and take a little more contemporary direction and explore, which was a very good learning experience. I think I got a lot better as a guitar player."

Practice:
"Well, I practice to write and I practice to warm up. But I learn on stage. I'm the type of player things just come to me. I don't practice scales. I know how to get what I'm trying to say. And when I teach people, that's a real learning experience. I learn more about music when I teach (such as at the annual National Summer Guitar Workshop in Milford, Conn.). I usually do a couple of days with master classes and clinics, and demonstrate the styles.

"It's all fun in doing the Jazz-Blues Guitar Summit with J. Geils and Gerry Beaudoin, Robillard said. The trio started out doing two or three shows a year at The Rendevous in Waltham, the Sit 'n Bull in Maynard and Scullers in Boston in the late 1990s but took the act to a national audience and received rave reviews and acclaim.

"I really don't consider myself a jazz player, but I do play some swing-style jazz. I'm really a swing and blues guitar player. I'm not a really

Boston's Blues

accomplished jazz player, but there is a lot of swing in my playing. I did a session with Herb Ellis, a legendary jazz guitarist, which is another project of mine where I want to play with a lot of jazz guitarists that I admire. Herb Ellis is one of the first, the other is Les Paul and hopefully within the next year we can get him to do a session. I did enough with Herb to do a whole album. But it probably won't be my next album, it'll be a side project for some label. It's a guitar album -- a conversation between two guitarists playing back and forth.

"I don't see what the big deal is about categorizing one style or another. Blues-based music is blues-based music. Whatever kind of feel it has behind it is just the character of the song. There are a lot of things (blues, soul, R&B, Chicago, roots-rock, jazz, swing), lots of things that have or can have a blues base to them and that's what we concentrate on, that feel."

On the Future:
"You can see that the audience has grown for this type of music. It's been to my benefit that I've been out there working, it's a grassroots thing. Word spreads."

His advice: "Be persevering through it all even though there's nobody there. You work and you just try to do the best you can and make an impression on people. In this business, unless you're lucky enough to hook into a mainstream connection, and that only happens to a few people, you have to really love what you do and be willing to work hard at it for years.

"For me, things are just getting to a point to where I feel everywhere I go, I do pretty well. And that's after 30-plus years. I feel like I'm going somewhere, feel like I'm creating a strong base for my music around the world.

"Music is not a race. It's not a contest. Everyone has their own thing to say and some things touch some people more than others."

Web: rosebudus.com/robillard

Art Simas
Roomful swings into middle age with a band that defies time

Roomful of Blues, now more than 30 years old, is very much alive and doing well in every corner of the world. While the band has been a mainstay in New England, growing up in the smallest state in the union, Rhode Island, it has blossomed into one of the most influential bands in the country. Dozens of musicians, from founder Duke Robillard, Al Copley, Porky Cohen, Matt McCabe, Ronnie Earl, Preston Hubbard, Sugar Ray Norcia, Greg Piccolo, John Rossi, Carl Querfurth, and many others, have benefited from their associations with the band.

Why does Roomful continue to thrive after so many other bands have veered off track? Why do a dozen or more people cram into a bus and travel thousands of miles year after year?

According to three current members of the band, Chris Vachon, Rich Lataille and Mac Odom, they do it for, and because of, the music. It's the beat and sound of a timeless generation. The music never gets old, far-sighted or bald. And because of the musical commitment of Roomful's talented cast of characters, the music is given new life every time the band takes the stage. The players may change, but the concept of Roomful remains.

"In today's musical climate there's something to be said about that," said lead vocalist Mac Odom, who joined the band four years ago, replacing Sugar Ray Norcia. "Yes, a lot of people have come and gone, but through all of that Roomful is still there."

For many years, Roomful was one of a handful of bands that consistently employed a horn section with its own style and sound. "We've always offered a wide variety of blues and it's always been kind of a nice show, I think," said guitarist Chris Vachon, an 11-year veteran of the band.

"I always liked blues a lot and ever since I heard Roomful I wanted to be in it. It's always been a good outlet for me and I'm able to play and make a living from it," he said. "And I've learned how to play with a lot of the guys. Instead of being in a three-piece or four-piece, you learn how to listen. You're not stuck playing solos all night. There are other people (in the band) who are doing things that are more interesting, and I was interested on and off for 17 years. I was just looking to get into something that I thought was great… and I finally got there."

Boston's Blues

Saxophonist Rich Lataille, a veteran of more than 26-plus years with the band agreed that the music drives the musicians of Roomful, and not the other way around. "We're all committed to the music and when people have left, we've been able to attract good players who are of a similar mind, basically, and it's a tribute to the music itself. We play a wide variety of styles and we can delve into different styles and that keeps it interesting for all of us and for the audience, too."

Asked why he keeps coming back year after year, Lataille admitted, "I didn't realize it was going to be this long. I joined the band when I was 19. I remember Roomful without the horns, so when they added the horns, they asked me to join and I said 'yes,' which was what I wanted to do. And here I am and I haven't gotten sick of it. The music has always been strong. We've gone through a lot of changes over the years, but we've kept the same attitude."

Another reason for Roomful's longevity is its professionalism. Odom said, "The group always seeks out good players. You've got a certain level of musicianship and you want to keep that level. We've been fortunate enough to get the players."

Lataille and Vachon said the group always seems to make its gigs, no matter the circumstances. Vachon recounted one episode where the "shuttle bus" that was used as the mode of transportation before the band bought a more accommodating bus, had a little trouble getting across the country. "We broke down seven times between New London, Conn., and Santa Fe, N.M.," he said. "We ended up driving all the way to Santa Fe, N.M., straight through a snowstorm. Even the opening band, which was from Albuquerque, didn't even show up because of the weather, but we made it all the way from Connecticut.

"I just couldn't believe it," Vachon said. "I thought I had joined a garage band because we basically spent all of our time in garages. That... shuttle bus was definitely not built to do what it was doing."

Lataille recalled another cross-country excursion during the summertime on the same shuttle. "We were in Arizona in July coming from Phoenix and going to San Diego, and our shuttle bus broke down just outside of Yuma. It was about 110 degrees early in morning, and we were all standing alongside the bus trying to stay out of the sun. Well, the sun kept getting higher in the sky and the shade was getting smaller and smaller. We've got some interesting pictures of that encounter," Lataille said. "That was the end of that vehicle."

"Another time, we were in Europe and we were coming off our last gig in Belgium and had to make it to London, England, to catch a flight back home. We had to take a bus about 6 a.m., then take a ferry across the English Channel, then take a train to Heathrow Airport," Lataille said. "Because of the bad weather, the boat was delayed and when we got on, everyone on the boat got sick. When we got to England, we decided to take the underground (subway) train to the airport, with all of our equipment and luggage. We got to the airport five minutes before the plane took off, literally running with our stuff, but they actually held the plane for us. Then we had a seven-hour flight. By the time I got on I was drenched in sweat and the people were probably pissed off at us for holding up the plane."

Such mishaps are commonplace in the life of a musician on the road. As long as the commitment is paramount, musicians can withstand the misfortunes with a smile.

"Anyone who can do what you love to do and make a pretty good living is very fortunate," Odom said. "And you count your blessings. That's the whole beauty of it. Roomful is a team and that's what it's all about."

And that's why, even though the players may change, there will always be Roomful of Blues.

Web: www.roomful.com

Richard "Rosy" Rosenblatt

Richard "Rosy" Rosenblatt keeps the tone very cool

"There is some great music happening in this town and people are starting to notice."
-- Richard Rosy Rosenblatt

Richard "Rosy" Rosenblatt has always been a blues guy. From playing in the Speakeasy house band 30 years ago, to promoting the next generation of blues artists, Rosy's heart is in the music, and everyone knows it.

Born Nov. 7, 1951, near Hartford, Conn., Rosenblatt grew up with an interest in playing harmonica. Bob Dylan was one of the first people he tried to emulate when he was around 11 or 12.

But it was blues of Koerner, Ray and Glover ("Spider" John Koerner, Dave "Snaker" Ray and Tony "Little Sun" Glover) that would eventually steer his music career and his life.

Like so many other teens who gravitated to the blues when he saw Paul Butterfield in 1967, the experience opened up his eyes and ears to a kick-ass harmonica style. Before Butterfield, he thought Bob Dylan was the way harmonica was played. "Someone, somewhere clued me in to playing cross harp... that you play second position harmonica, not first position and play in different keys. And that opened up a whole thing for me and I started playing in all different styles," Rosy said.

"I came to Boston University in 1969 and was in the same dorm as Seth Justman (keyboardist for the J Geils Band) and James Montgomery was attending school at the same time... and people had Buddy Guy and Junior Wells, Muddy Waters, Little Walter, and Charlie Musselwhite records," Rosy said.

Of course, he got swept up into it too. Maybe a little too swept away.

"I kind of knew my college days were numbered when I stayed up all night studying, went into the exam, was handed the little blue book, and all I could hear was the entire 'Hoodoo Man Blues' album note for note coming out of this hissing radiator that was next to me," he said. "I went back to college years later through the Harvard Extension program and received a French degree."

Boston's Blues

Ah yes. College in the late '60s. Boston. Blues. The pursuit of academics and the pursuit of blues could not be done simultaneously. Although there is that rare exception -- James Montgomery graduated from BU with a degree in English literature.

Settling in an apartment on Commonwealth Ave., Rosy immersed himself into the scene. The Candlelight Lounge on Western Avenue in Central Square, Cambridge, was a second home where "there were some wild times when Montgomery played there," Rosy said. "The Candlelight was a funky little place that was basically a hallway. After it closed (as a music venue) it was a funeral home then a pizza joint."

In 1970-71, "I put together a little blues band with Peter Goff and David Bain, got some gigs at the Candlelight and some gigs at BU," he said.

That first taste of being in a band led Rosy to join The Allston All Stars, which had several incarnations as a group with Terry Bingham, Joe Foy and Dick Eckman. "It was started by Dick Eckman, who was later murdered by a hitch-hiker," Rosy said. "We had a little rehearsal joint behind the Brookline Liquor Mart.

"Someone from the group went into Cambridge and got us a gig at this place on Norfolk Street called the Speakeasy. I think we were one of the first bands that were hired there. Pete Kastanos (Speakeasy Pete) hired us for six nights for incredibly low pay."

Before the group played their first night at the Speakeasy they decided they'd better legally protect themselves in case things went astray. "So we came in on the first night and beforehand, we had drawn up this little contract to be sure that we were going to get paid. And I remember this laughter from Pete when he saw the paper. 'Which one of you kids made up this contract? I'm not signing no contract. If I don't like you, you're out of here.'"

So much for the F. Lee Bailey approach.

"But we wound up playing there for a while and it turned out to be one of the best blues clubs in the area," Rosy said.

The second incarnation of the Allston All Stars had Bingham and Foy and Rosenblatt with Peter Goff and Steve Berkowitz, also known as T Blade. "And we had Bonnie Raitt's first piano player, a blind guy from Connecticut, and

191

played up and down the East Coast. That band lasted for a while and we did a lot of crazy frat parties," Rosy recalled.

Rosenblatt played harp with Billy Colwell (who had an album out with the Colwell-Winfield Band) and Billy Mather, who was also in the James Montgomery Band.

"I also did a few gigs with Luther 'Snake' Johnson, Dawna Rae and Sunnyland Slim. We put out a record on Airways, 'Tired But I Can't Get Started' featuring Ronnie (Earl) Horvath, Bob Margolin, Dawna Rae and Sarah Brown. That was my first record and it was also Ronnie's first record," Rosy said.

After Colwell, there was Joyride, a mix of blues, R&B, disco and Marvin Gaye tunes, which fell apart in mid-1970s. "So we went back to the Speakeasy and did some pickup gigs, backing Otis Rush and Hubert Sumlin and others. Then we started doing Sunday jam sessions, and later Pete gave me some Sunday nights, and I put a band together called the 11th Hour Band, because we were available at the last minute. Joe Livolsi was on drums, Paul Carter on bass, Paul Lenart on guitar, then Billy Mather and Chuck Purro (from James Montgomery's original band). We started in the late '70s and we were pretty busy every Sunday into the early '80s.

"At the time, I had a small recording studio in my basement and we had enough material to put out an album," he said. "So we pressed the LP 'Hot Time In The City Tonight,' and I named it Tone-Cool Records. That was in 1985 and Tone-Cool's first release."

The 11th Hour Band still exists in theory, Rosy said, although the gigs are few and far between. But every now and then, and usually on Nov. 11, they'll play at the House of Blues in Cambridge.

"During this time I was also doing gigs with T Blade, essentially the 11th Hour Band plus him, and one or two horn players, usually Kaz Kazanoff and/or Derek Dyer (who played with Joe Cocker and Tina Turner) and Larry Luddecke on keys," Rosy said.

T Blade was also very busy managing The Cars, "and we put out T Blade and the Esquires 'I'm A Business Man,' on Tone-Cool," Rosy said.

T Blade eventually moved to New York and became a Sony executive. "He was also managing a band called Push Push with Dennis Brennan, a great soulful singer, but it was more of a pop album," Rosy said. This was released by Tone-Cool in 1989.

Recording Push Push was a mistake, Rosy said. "We weren't prepared to deal with a pop record. I didn't have a clue how to market it or put it out to radio. Then the guitar player quit and the band broke up after the record came out. And that was sort of the end of that."

It also looked like the end of Tone-Cool.

Because of Rosy's friendship with Duncan Brown of Rounder Records, and others at the Cambridge record label, Rounder agreed to distribute Push Push, and that was the beginning of the Rounder/Tone-Cool relationship. The same distribution deal was made for T Blade record.

Tone-Cool recorded Paul Rishell's "Blues On A Holiday" in 1990, followed by Earring George Mayweather's "Whup It! Whup It!" the "Boston Blues Blast Volume I," and James Montgomery's "The Oven Is On," in 1991.

In the meantime, Rosenblatt was helping Rounder start its Bullseye Blues label.

He and Ron Levy, who was married to Marian Leighton, one of the three founders of Rounder, recorded Luther "Guitar Junior" Johnson, and that became Bullseye Blues' first record.

"Levy is a great finisher of projects. I'm a great starter, but he's a great finisher," Rosy said.

Over the formative years of Bullseye, Levy was the master of producing dozens of records for the label.

The formation of the Rounder-Tone-Cool alliance was a critical and historic moment for Boston blues. Without that connection, many local artists such as Toni Lynn Washington, Paul Rishell and Annie Raines, Johnny Hoy, David Maxwell, The Love Dogs, Mike Welch, Susan Tedeschi, and others would likely not have had their records produced here.

Rosy said, "In 1993, we signed a national distribution agreement with Rounder to work with them where they would do all of our manufacturing and marketing. Essentially all of our records would be manufactured and marketed alongside their records, which was a great deal for us because I could really step up production and I didn't have to wait to have one record to be made and sold and wait to get some money back before starting another."

Prior to 1991, Tone-Cool had produced, on average, one record every two years, Rosy said.

"After we had built a profile for the label, we got some interest from artists who were more established, such as Mark Hummel, Rod Piazza and the Mighty Flyers, and Terrence Simien," Rosy said.

All of this was possible because of the strength of the Boston blues scene. "There's a great wealth of people here and beyond," he said. "The Boston blues scene has been a major part of everything that Tone-Cool has accomplished.

"It's still a great local scene, and I get to play a little bit (Rosy appears on a couple of Luther 'Guitar Jr.' Johnson's records). I'm an active harmonica player, but not as active as I might be."

Others who have helped Rosenblatt in establishing Tone-Cool over the years are Alizon Lissance, keyboard player and vocalist for the Love Dogs, and David Bartlett, who started as an intern, working out of Rosenblatt's home, and is now the label's president.

Tone-Cool keeps adding to its musical family. The label signed Rick Holmstrom, the lead guitarist for Rod Piazza and the Mighty Flyers, in early 1999 and released CDs by Toni Lynn Washington Mark Hummel and Gordon Beadle in 2000.

It has since added Bernard Allison, the North Mississippi All Stars and Double Trouble to its stable.

Web: tonecool.com

Scott Shetler

Art Simas
Scott Shetler: Arranging his life according to the blues

Scott Shetler didn't take any shortcuts in his rising career as one of the best musical arrangers and writers in the business. On the contrary, it's been anything but a smooth ride for the lean saxophone player who is a staple of Michelle Willson's Evil Gal Festival Orchestra, the Hot Tamale Brass Band and his own C'mon Man organ trio.

Shetler grew up with classical music. His father, a professor of music at the Eastman School in Rochester, N.Y., indoctrinated the youngster at the age of 5 by insisting he learn trumpet, piano and how to tune a violin.

Maybe it was too much too soon. Because when he was old enough to bolt, Shetler did. Like many musicians, Shetler had to live his blues before he came to play his blues.

He ran away from home (several times), and at 16, he hitchhiked his way from upstate New York to the French Quarter in New Orleans in 1969. This was before he seriously took up the sax. He worked the streets for meal money and lived a threadbare life.

But the music he heard -- seeping out of dark, winding do-not-enter alleys, through iron-latticed doors that led to patio porticos, or wafting on the breezes from a pungently perfumed manicured garden -- stayed with him forever.

"Man, I had never heard shit like that R&B, soul and blues sounds before," he said. It was music that electrified the muggy mists of the Crescent City.

In New Orleans, "I subsequently got arrested and was put in the kiddie jail, which incidentally had some of the best food I had eaten all my life. When they were driving me to the parish jail, the two guards turned to me and said, 'You're gonna love the food in this place,' and I said, 'Yeah, right.' But sure enough, when they put me in the cafeteria, here are these two cops sitting there with knife and fork waiting to chow down... and they brought out the chicken, the mashed potatoes and gravy and everything.

"The reason why I got arrested was because I was standing on the street outside of the French Market and I had a great big Bowie knife that I was cutting a piece of French bread with. An unmarked police car pulled up and the cops asked me whose knife it was... Actually it was my friend's knife and he was an older cat who had a police record. So I said, 'It's my knife,' and they took me -- first to the local jail then to the parish jail, since they saw I was a juvenile."

In 1992, Shetler returned to New Orleans under very different circumstances. He was a member of the Johnny Adams band, which was booked at the Jazz and Heritage Festival. "That was a kick. I hadn't been there since I was literally swept off the street by the police when I was 16, and here I was playing at this great festival with a fabulous artist. It really made me feel good. And the music was starting to happen. It was funny how it all worked out," he said.

He stayed with Adams for several years.

At the same time, he was also playing in Gene Pitney's band, occasionally doing a European tour and all the musical tent venues on the East Coast. He even played Carnegie Hall, actually opening the show with a greasy solo of "Town Without Pity," Pitney's theme song from the 1960s. His father attended the performance and loved it. The elder Shetler told Scott that he thought his work was very important.

"So that was a real come-around for me," Scott said. "Now, I send him all my stuff and he just adores Michelle Willson's stuff."

Before he got to Carnegie Hall and before the steady work with Adams and Pitney, Shetler paid his dues learning his instrument in the Prime Rib Band in Vermont. "I didn't even play blues until about 1985 when I moved to Boston. I figured I wanted to get a little more expansive in music, and Boston was the place.

"I didn't have any work, didn't know anybody. Nothing. And everything was so expensive here compared to Vermont. So I started playing in the subways, playing clarinet every day, like a job. I got these permits from the Cambridge Arts Council and I used to go down to Government Center from 7 to 10 a.m. then I'd go back from 4 to 7 p.m. I used to like Park Street and Arlington Under, too. And I'd make about $40 to $50 in change.

"Then I met Amyl Justin. He was in a band called Tremendous Richard, a real early R&B horn band (with Latin grooves). I auditioned at City Side and I hopped up on the bar and Amyl hired me on the spot. That was about 1986," Shetler recalled.

The call to play with Adams, who died in 1997 from prostate cancer, came from Mike Duke of Mike Duke and the Soul Twisters, who, at the time, was Adams' musical director.

Duke called Shetler and said, "There's this guy Johnny Adams who needs a sax player now, to go to Sicily."

"So I took the gig," Shetler said. "And that's where I met Ed Scheer (lead vocalist for the Love Dogs), who was the drummer in that band, a fabulous drummer by the way, and Kenny Harris was the keyboard player with Adams.

"At this time I first started getting into the arranging. On the gig there was a great trumpet player called Walter Platt, who plays with Mighty Sam McClain. And Walter used to get paid for arranging. So I used to kind of ghostwrite these little arrangements for some of the tunes that didn't have horn arrangements. I really didn't know how to do it but I was really infatuated. So I'd sort of slid them onto the music stand. And if it made it through, meaning if Johnny didn't stomp his foot or glare at me, which meant the arrangement is outta here, we kept the arrangement."

In December 1992, "I went on the first Rhythm and Blues Cruise -- and everybody was on that boat -- Albert Collins with his own band; Buddy Guy with his band; The Persuasions; Bernard Purdie; Houston Person; Etta James; the Johnny Otis Orchestra, it was unbelievable. And it became clear to me the depth of the music and the depth of the musicians," Shetler said.

That year was also critical because Shetler got to play with Harry van Wall, who had played on all of Ruth Brown's early stuff. And then Michelle Willson called Shetler after she had heard of some of Wall's music and said she wanted to do a Women in the Blues Show at the Tam in that same style. And that was sort of the beginning of the Evil Gal Orchestra, with Gordon Beadle, who had also played in the Hot Tamale Brass Band, and David Limina on keyboards.

"So we started writing and the thing took off like a shot," Shetler said. "The following year, we went down to Memphis, and it had been years since they saw anything like us. We came out with the jackets and the ties and the horn section… It was wild. And we took every freaking award they had that year."

On Willson's "Tryin to Make a Little Love" on Rounder, Shetler gets his due on the horn arrangements in the liner notes. "We had skeletal arrangements of the material that we were going to do. But it wasn't like we were rehearsing them or playing them out. And we weren't real sure what was going to happen with those

Boston's Blues

guys (other musicians from New Orleans who did the record with Shetler and Limina on keyboards) once they had they're own interpretation of it," Shetler said.

For Shetler, it was a real learning experience because there was some stuff he had to completely rewrite on the spot. Shetler said producer Scott Billington would say, "I like what you wrote but it's not fitting what we've done with it now."

"So I'd have to sit down between takes in the back room and I'd be rewriting. It was crazy, man. At night, Billington and I would go back to the Rounder apartments and sit at the kitchen table and write... and get up the first thing in the morning and write. Literally, I was either constantly writing or recording during the four days that the record was made -- six days with the vocals.

"That was a real experience for me. They kept everything and they loved it... Actually, I was pretty flattered that Rounder sent me down there to play with those musicians and let me do the horn arrangements," he said.

In congratulating Shetler, Billington said tongue-in-cheek, "I guess we've gotten really good in making good records on a low budget."

And in return, Shetler said of Billington, "I think he really knows how to work with and back a vocalist, to make sure that she or he is front and forward. And (Michelle) really dug into that record. She's scary these days. I get the same feelings I get with Michelle that I used to get with Johnny. No bullshit, no histrionics, just singing."

Somehow or another, the conversation always comes back to Johnny Adams. Shetler said he was his blues mentor who told him, "Close it all off and look inside of yourself for the notes."

Shetler said Adams would often say that playing an instrument was like singing. "He would look at you and give you that expression that said, 'Well, if you can hear these notes and you know what they are, then find them on your horn and play them.'

"Johnny was a hard-ass to work for on stage. And a real sweet guy off stage. But the reason why he was so hard was that he was trying to get you to play just from your heart, and he'd want to hear the parts played correctly," Shetler said. "But he was also asking for more -- a commitment to the music. And it took me a long time, a few years, before I figured out what it was he was going for."

Shetler is still searching for that distinct sound that will separate him from other musicians and arrangers. It's coming along. Three years ago Shetler penned arrangements for three CDs -- "Grand Union," a collaboration of Otis Grand, Debbie Davies, Anson Funderburgh and others; Vykki Vox's "Woman's Touch" and "Can You Feel It," and the 2000 W.C. Handy award-winning CD for best traditional blues album, "Moving to the Country," by Paul Rishell and Annie Raines.

"That was one of those ('Moving to the Country') where I wrote 'em all up the night before," Shetler admitted. "From the New Orleans experience, I got so much quicker at the writing. Someone can bring me something today and I can have it studio-ready by tomorrow. Before, I'd want a week with it."

There is also K.D. Bell's debut CD, "Something's Wrong" on Thrillionaire Records; horn arrangements for Amyl Justin and Kid Bangham's "Pressure Cooker;" the Radio Kings "Money Road;" "Keep on Movin'" by Mighty Sam McClain; and Shetler played baritone sax on Greg Piccolo's "Heavy Juice."

"I really felt great when he called me. Greg just kept saying, "Kick the butt on it, kick the butt on it."

Shetler also likes to play with Mickey Bones and the Hot Tamale Brass Band because he's fascinated by the historical roots of how horns were first used in bands. "I really get a kick out of it," he said.

Reflecting on the current state of the blues and live music, Shetler said, "I spent several years of the opinion that blues, R&B and jazz were not being listened to and the musicians weren't really playing it. But my attitude is not that now. I really feel that it's in good hands. If you talk to someone like Mike Welch, man, he knows this shit. He really knows it. It's really heartening is what it is, and it makes you feel that everything is going to be just fine, that the music is staying alive and it's going to move on."

Susan Tedeschi

Susan Tedeschi: Going places

Take a gifted vocalist/guitarist/pianist, mix in a lot of street-smart business grit and a competitive nature that just won't quit, and you have the multitalented Susan Tedeschi. But even that combination of resources is not enough in the musical cutting-heads classrooms of the blues road and studio. Someone is always ready to take something away from you -- and someone will always ask to give a little more.

Living between the difference is where musicians make their living.

Born Nov. 9, 1970, in Norwell, Mass., Tedeschi first began her career as a singer/actress. Her dream at age 7 was to dance down the aisle at the Academy Awards ceremony and hug her Oscar. "I thought I was going to go to college to be an actress. But during the summer between high school and college, I figured I'd try Berklee College of Music in Boston, so I actually started college even before I graduated from high school.

"I was very fortunate I did a lot of things that I really wanted to do," she said. Like many competitive music schools, "you had to audition to get into the courses that you wanted to take, such as recording ensemble. As a singer, you had to go into the studio twice a week with a band and record the song. And there were other students in the studio who were going to be engineers and producers, so it was a great experience, which really helps you in how to make records."

She said singing in the gospel choir and learning about the legal aspects of music, including entertainment law, was especially good for her. "I also arranged for big bands, which was a lot of homework and a lot of transcription of all the parts. So even though I liked doing it, I didn't have any time because I spread myself real thin wanting to do everything. But I just can't do everything. People keep telling me I can't do everything, but I guess I don't learn."

With a go-go fall and spring academic schedule and two summers of studies, she graduated from Berklee in 1991.

Boston's Blues

Tedeschi said she was prepared for what was to come because of her Berklee experience. "You know a little bit of what people expect you to do. I'm thankful for the stuff that I've learned up to this point because it's helping me keep my head straight. I take my music seriously as a career. It's really overwhelming the amount of stuff that's going on. And I feel that I'm prepared for it. I don't care if I make millions and millions of dollars. Sure, it would be great but I'm not planning on it. I'm not going in with that attitude.

"There's a lot of things that go into it -- taking care of yourself; having a strong business mind so everyone else doesn't take your money; and having people who will look out for your interests," Tedeschi said. "I feel lucky that I have Rosy (Richard Rosenblatt) and Dave Bartlett with Tone-Cool, which put out her 1997 CD, "Just Won't Burn.""

"When I first moved to Boston from Norwell, Lou Ulrich and Mike Piel from Berklee and some other friends told me to go down to Johnny D's to sing (blues). But I didn't do it in '90, '91, or '92. I like to sing that type of music, but wasn't doing it professionally. I was doing other types of singing, originals in more of a folky Neil Young kind of tune but in a different vocal style -- kind of like Linda Ronstadt and Bonnie Raitt used to do where they'd take covers and put their own voice to it.

"But that's why I love to sing so many different styles of music. I love blues and gospel and certain types of country and folk that's not real hick or twangy. I appreciate a real pretty song that has a nice melody line that tells a story. Anything that tells a story or that preaches, that'll make me happy," she said.

In 1993, she moved to Somerville and started attending the Sunday night blues jams at Johnny D's in Davis Square so she could brush up on guitar. Tim Gearan, guitarist for the Toni Lynn Washington Band and leader of the jams, taught Susan how to use her ears as much as her musical instruments and her voice. "And if I had a question, Adrienne Hayes (lead guitarist on Tedeschi's debut self-produced "Better Days" CD) would show me, or Ronnie Earl or Paul Rishell," she said.

"So I started to write my own songs. And I put the band together in '93 with Adrienne, Little Annie Raines and Jim Lalond, and we used different drummers (Mike Aiello from The Radio Kings, Chuck Purro, and Lorne Entress of Four Piece Suit -- with Dean Cassell, Milt Reder and Dave Scholl). And Tim was a major link for me.

In 1994, Tedeschi came in second in the International Blues Talent Competition in Memphis, mainly because she went over her time limit by a few seconds in the finals. The audience and the judges were impressed by her talent. They, and she, knew it was just a matter of time.

"I just started getting into the scene with so many people who knew each other. It's a really small tight-knit community… and it was a cool scene. At the time, the blues people were tight with a lot of the original-type of writers -- Dennis Brennan, Laurie Sargent, Paula Cole -- people who were trying to do their own thing which wasn't necessarily blues. But yet they were all tied into the blues scene because that was how you could make money -- working steady. In fact, Rick Russell and James Montgomery were the first guys who allowed me to get up on a stage when I was like 17 and sing blues with them. They were very supportive and they've always been sweet to me ever since," she said.

Sweet or not, seeing and listening to Susan Tedeschi can be an intensely moving experience, even for her, because of the personal depths that she draws from.

"I have a lot of different security blankets… and I get very emotional at times when I play, and I use it as my outlet. In order for me to be able to play, which is what I love to do, sometimes it strikes a little closer to home than I would like."

On the other hand, there's the side of Susan Tedeschi that says, "I also need to be very strong as a business person so I can get to each level. I'm not in this to become the next Jewel or whatever. I used to look at it like that when I was younger. The music to me is so sacred. I wouldn't really go with the times and be switching from pop to rap or to whatever is hip. I couldn't do it. I've got to be true to more soul and roots music, and blues and gospel at all times. That's the only thing that makes me sane, I think.

"There's nothing wrong with being part of the times. But why not be a part of what you are for that time period? Maybe you can make an influence on the time period. Maybe not. But at least you're being true to yourself.

"For me, having players who are the real thing, who are real soulful blues players in a real true form, not because of the culture that they were raised in, but because of the way they were moved by the music and how they learned the music and history of the music and they respect it and are truly faithful to it. That is really cool, I think. People want honest artists. They don't care if you're not perfect," she said.

Tedeschi said she is very pleased with the diversity and the way her platinum-selling CD, "Just Won't Burn," hangs together. And she was quick to thank everyone for a great job: producer, drummer, vocalist and co-writer, Tom Hambridge, who is on drums except on "Found Someone New," which has Mike Levesque on the kit; Norm Demoura - vocals; Jim Lamond - bass; Sean Costello - guitar on most of record; Adrienne Hayes - guitar; Tim Gearan - slide guitar on "Angel From Montgomery"; Tom West - B3 organ; Buck and Bird Taylor - backup vocals on "Little by Little"; Ian Kennedy from the group, Groovasaurus - violin on "Angel from Montgomery" and "Looking for Answers"; and Annie Raines - harmonica on "Little by Little" and "Friar's Point." Tedeschi plays rhythm guitar and vocals throughout, and piano on "Found Someone New."

"We started this one in April or May 1997, and finished it in October because I was on the road a lot. That's how I make my money just for rent, food, car insurance and health insurance. It's expensive as hell because you don't get any benefits. It's funny how all other businesses, except the entertainment industry, is considered work. I think if you tour for a record company, it should be mandatory that they pick up your health insurance or at least a portion of it. It would be a lot easier for the artist."

Besides the expenses, the road can be a dangerous place. During a trip to Memphis in 1997, the band's van was stolen outside of the hotel where they were going to play that night.

"Luckily, all of the equipment was in the club except for Sean Costello's reverb-a-rocket amp and his master tapes to his first record, 'Call The Cops,' as well as about 300 CDs..."

205

Just a few days earlier in Pittsburgh and in Washington, when she opened for Jonny Lang, she was selling her own CDs to a long line of waiting fans, chatting and having a grand time. But the venue management put a stop to it after a while. "There was a big line waiting to buy (my CD) when Jonny Lang was playing. They wouldn't even let me stand near the table because I was detracting a lot of sales from Jonny. They wouldn't let me sell my own CDs! Then they took 25 percent of the cost. You gotta be shittin' me. I'm here making no money, they're paying us crap, and the payoff is supposed to be on the sale of your CDs, and they're trying to gyp me on that. That's what's paying for my hotels.

"They don't give anything to you. You have to work your ass off at everything. That's one thing Berklee taught me -- they're not going to hand you anything either -- and they (Berklee) never did," she said.

Update: This article appeared in the Boston Blues Society newsletter in May 1997, the year which catapulted Tedeschi into the limelight. Boston fans had an inkling of what was to come when she was named Outstanding Blues Act in Boston in 1995 and 1996. But that was just the beginning.

She has since played alongside B.B. King, Buddy Guy, Delbert McClinton and the Allman Brothers, among others, at numerous festivals in the U.S. and abroad; played the Lilith Fair in 1999, singing duets with Sheryl Crow; and played in the "Concert of the Century" with musicians such as Eric Clapton and Aretha Franklin for VH1's Save the Music Foundation benefit.

Also in 1999, Tedeschi walked away with two W.C. Handy awards -- Contemporary Blues Female Artist of the Year and Best New Artist of the Year. It was her first nominations in both categories. She has been on several late-night TV talk shows and on the cover of many regional and national blues publications.

In January 2000, Tedeschi was nominated for a Grammy Award for Best New Artist of the Year. Right before she made the trip to Los Angeles for the awards, she said, "I want to enjoy it, and then when it's all over, I just want to get back to work."

Boston's Blues

Britney Spears won.

Later in 2000, she picked up her second W.C. Handy award for Contemporary Blues Female Artist of the Year, and kept a grueling tour schedule. She also worked with Double Trouble (Chris Layton and Tommy Shannon), Little Milton, Willie Nelson and several other artists who welcomed her with open arms.

Brian Templeton

Boston's Blues

After two songs, Brian Templeton
was a professional vocalist

The multitalented Brian Templeton, who plays harmonica, accordian and is a vocalist and songwriter, was born in Boston on Sept. 17, 1963. It's not surprising that music eventually found him as the leader of the Radio Kings because he was brought up hearing everything from Big Band jazz arrangements to three-part harmonies to doo wop ditties.

"My parents (David and Sylvia) were musical fanatics. They'd take us (me and my sister Becky) to see live music all the time, places like Debbie's; Pooh's Pub; Jazz Workshop; Paul's Mall; and Sandy's out in Beverly. My mother, sister and I always sang and we taught ourselves harmonies in the car. I saw a lot of heavy people such as Santana with the Mahavishnu Orchestra. And Art Blakey gave me drums sticks. I was only a kid, but still, it put things in the back of my mind," Templeton said.

"We first lived on Kempton Street, near the former Ed Burke's of Huntington Ave., then went to Brookline, then moved to Woburn," he said.

First it was Top 40s from WRKO's Dale Dorman for Templeton's taste. Then it was rock. "I saw Queen with Freddy Mercury, who really knew how to perform, in Boston Garden with Thin Lizzy; J. Geils, I saw them all the time. But I missed a lot of the great ones, and I wasn't into the blues yet," Templeton said.

"Eventually, it was the white guys who steered me into the blues.
Then Stevie (Ray Vaughan) came around just about the time we could go to clubs.

Joey Pappas (of the Paramounts) took me to see Roomful at Jonathan Swifts, when they had Ronnie (Earl) and Al Copley on piano. Ronnie just totally tore my head off. He was standing on tables; he was on his knees; and playing the most unbelievable blues I've ever heard. That was my first blues awakening -- when the music fully hits you.

"I became a Ronnie and Roomful groupie and then I got hip to Sugar Ray and the Bluetones and Duke Robillard, and it spread out after that. Then I met Jerry Portnoy and Kim Wilson. I was just into the scene and I loved it. If Kim was in town they'd go back and play at someone's house. Unbelievable. That was better than the clubs," Templeton said.

He started to play harp and went to a blues jam and heard the group Rockin' Jake and the Roller Coasters, which was looking for a lead singer.

"The singer was Rod Carey who went on to become Ronnie Earl's bass player. He went to play bass with Dave Howard and the High Rollers in Providence. So I went up and sang a couple of T-Bird numbers and the guitar player was Craig Ruskey, who played with BBQ Bob, and Jake hired me after two songs.

"And that was the first time I got up in front of people I really didn't know. So I joined Jake's band in December 1989. I was working in the post office at the time," he recalled.

"About four months later it sort of took me over. I was liking the attention, and I felt it was something I could do well. Before then, well, I dropped out of high school. I was smart enough to pass, but I was just being a dummy, a young kid. I didn't know what to do and was bouncing in and out of jobs after high school. And I finally got a job in the post office, which was nice, but it was tedious and boring. I was late to work all the time, I just wasn't into it. After I started to sing, I felt that that was something in my life that I could do," Templeton said.

Jake eventually went to New Orleans and the band broke up. (Jake usually travels to make the annual Portsmouth, N.H., Blues Festival every August where he hangs out with his old buddy, T.J. Wheeler.)

"I had heard of a band called Billy Blue and the Blazers, so I went and checked them out, and the guitar player was Mike Dinallo. He was with Billy (Blue) Strauss and Jordan Lash on drums and Andy Stoller on bass, who is now with Tracy Chapman.

"One of the connections was that Joey Pappas was rooming with Jerry Portnoy in Waltham, and I was singing with Joey. In the meantime, Jerry was putting together The Streamliners, who had broken off from Ronnie Earl, who was also putting his own band together. So it just happened that me and Mike Dinallo auditioned for the Streamliners. The first time we ever met was at that audition for Jerry Portnoy. Neither of us got it, though," Templeton said.

"After Jake's band broke up, I did a short stint with Little Frankie and the Premiers. And that was a lot of fun, a three-part harmony thing with cool funky stuff.

"Then Billy Blue's band broke up and we joined forces. With Frankie, we were doing all styles but I wanted to get a really strong blues band together. So they

Boston's Blues

asked me to join. That was March 1991, and we changed the name to the Radio Kings, because Jordan Lash played Radio King drums. So that was the birth of the Radio Kings.

"That July we came out of nowhere and won the Battle of the Bands at Harpers Ferry, which was a very exciting time, because we were playing Harpers and Ed Burke's -- it was like playing the Ritz to me. Just having gigs in those clubs was really exciting, and we got great support from family and friends.

"We were going up against George (Rockin' Shoes) Leh, Little Annie, and Blues by Butch, so it was a tough competition. But we won it all, and it just floored me," Templeton said.

"Then I started missing a lot of work because I had to work Friday and Saturdays. I have to say I definitely had a bad attendance record at the post office.

"When we won the battle and I got my name in the paper, my boss saw it and he told me that I should seriously consider what I wanted to do. So that was when I made my boldest decision to be a full-time musician and devote my life to music.

"George Lewis got us involved in the Blue Monday shows at the House of Blues. I sent out 100 promo kits and only got back one reply, a denial from Bruce Iglauer of Alligator. But nobody else ever said anything.

"In 1992, we did the whole year with Jerry Portnoy. Then he went off with Clapton. We played the Stanhope House in New Jersey and then went down to Nashville at the Boardwalk Cafe where we played for the door -- made absolutely no money -- then we were going down to Blind Willie's in Atlanta and our bass player quit.

"He was so pissed at us… It was a really tough road trip in the middle of summer in a car with no air conditioning. But me and Mike, we just wanted to go out on the road because we wanted to do it. We just wanted to play," Templeton said. "Darrell Nulisch had suggested getting in touch with Jay Sheffield at Icehouse Records in Memphis and we had sent a demo to him."

During the southern tour where everything seemed to be going in the wrong direction, the Radio Kings drove to Memphis and played at the Blues City Cafe owned by George Paul, a good friend of Jay Sheffield. In fact, they are both from Helena, Arkansas.

"George remembered the demo we had sent to Jay and he reminded Jay that we were a good live band. And that's why we were signed to Icehouse -- on George's word to Jay. Icehouse signed us up without them ever hearing us play, except the tape," Templeton said.

"I learned how to love the road... even though my Blazer broke down but I learned so much of how to keep your cool and keep going. I knew then that I was going to be a road musician. I really enjoyed doing it. This was summer of 1993.

"In August of 1994, we recorded "It Ain't Easy" and from then on, we became a national act. We had Jay booking us out of Memphis, and on most of our tours we'd start and end there. We played in Arkansas, Mississippi, Louisiana, and all around the Delta. We also got to play at King Biscuit Blues Festival in Helena, too.

"When you drive these roads in the South you really feel that you're on sacred ground. You're inundated with the whole feel and vibe of the whole thing. It's amazing. That's why we named our last album "Money Road."

"We happened to have a day off and we went off looking for Robert Johnson's grave. And there were a couple of spots where Johnson may have been buried... Little Zion Church... so when were driving north out of Greenwood, we went down this road that goes to Money, Miss., the Old Money Road, and we saw the church and took some pictures and there was this guy there who had to be 90, raking in the middle of summer. And we saw this old radio station boarded up and I couldn't believe it... Here I was driving these guys around on these country roads in Mississippi with no air conditioning, and all they wanted to do was get back to the hotel with some AC and a pool.

"But because I had gone to that church, we found the old radio station that we had wanted to find for years. So I was flipped out.

"So the fact that Robert Johnson supposedly sold his soul for fame and fortune and money, and eventually died because of it, and was buried in an unmarked grave, halfway to Money. That's what the (title) song is about," Templeton said. "When they recorded it, it was recorded through an old outdoor movie speaker and recorded from the DAT through that speaker."

Note: The Radio Kings broke up in April 1999. Mike Dinallo now plays in the roots-based Hillbilly Voodoo Band, featuring vocalist Barrence Whitfield. Templeton is aligned with Stone Cold Records out of York Beach, Maine. He

Boston's Blues

released a CD in 2000 called "Home," which features originals by Templeton and covers by Hank Williams, Marvin Gaye and Little Milton. "Home" was produced by Mike Welch.

Web: stonecoldrecords.com

Racky Thomas

Boston's Blues
Racky Thomas: An inventive traditionalist

New Hampshire, Boston, Denmark, back to Boston and on to Memphis.

It's an unusual route for a fledgling bluesman. But that's been the road for singer/guitarist/harpist/bandleader Racky Thomas over the last 12 years.

The Memphis part actually happened in November 1997, as Thomas and his self-named quartet were the representatives for the city of Boston and The Boston Blues Society at The International Battle of the Blues competition, having won the Harper's Ferry Boston Battle of the Blues Bands in July.

For Thomas, who returned to Boston earlier that year after honing his blues craft while living in Denmark for about 15 months, the opportunity to showcase in Memphis seemed a natural progression for his musical career.

"While I was in Denmark," said Thomas, "I played a lot of cafe gigs, and a lot of solo-acoustic gigs. And I really learned how to represent myself by working that circuit and the kind of close contact with audiences you get from playing a scene like that. By the beginning of this year (1997) I really wanted to get back to Boston, and once back, I managed to put together just the kind of band and sound that I wanted. This time around, the timing was right, and now, I think, everything is falling into place."

The twist to this story is that before he left for Denmark in December 1995, Thomas recorded and released an independent CD under his own band name. The disc, self-titled and recorded at Boston's Second Story Studio, featured The Racky Thomas Band in its then trio form of Thomas, bassist Todd Carson and drummer Ted Larkin.

Making guest appearances on the album were guitarist Nick Adams and keyboardist Ron Poster, who, along with Carson and Larkin, are full-fledged members of Thomas' current Harper's Ferry Battle-winning band. Also doing guest spots were harpist J. Place (who also did the cover photography) and organist Elizabeth Steen.

The current Thomas band is a reunion of sorts for Thomas, Carson and Larkin. Along with performing as a unit on the CD, the trio had been among each other's first collaborators when Thomas first ventured into the local blues scene during winter 1994-95. Thomas (vocal, guitar, harp), Carson (guitar, bass) and Larkin (drums) performed in this period as a threesome for the Sunday evening blues jams at The Abbey in South Boston.

"This, if anyplace, is where we really cut our teeth on the local scene. We'd just boldly get up onstage and hammer tunes together," Thomas said. "A lot of the time it was really spontaneous and improvised. It wasn't really the best of conditions for playing. But it was where we bonded and got to know each other, and found we had similar concepts musically."

Before this, Thomas, a native of Wolfeboro, N.H., had first come to Boston as a student at Berklee College of Music, where he graduated in 1991. This is where the singer/instrumentalist found what he calls his "discovery and awakening to the blues."

As Thomas recalled, "Through various guitar teachers and other students, I got to know for the first time people like Muddy Waters, Elmore James and Stevie Ray Vaughan. Up to that point, for me it had been mostly modern rock 'n' roll -- Springsteen, Tom Petty, Bob Seger, etcetera. I really had no knowledge of any of the old or newer blues guys and it was just amazing to hear some of them for the first time."

From The Abbey, the Thomas trio moved to The Midway in Jamaica Plain, where they landed another regular Sunday night blues jam gig. There, the band met Adams, who would more often be found sitting in on live sets with Thomas and his mates. This lasted from June to November 1995.

Shortly thereafter, Thomas packed up for Denmark with his Danish-born wife, and Adams and Carson spent the next year-and-a-half backing "Nasty" J. Place with the Grinders on the tough-rocking CD "High Temperature."

On stage, the Racky Thomas Band displays a rare combination of subtle blues nuance and raw electric power. This is the winning form that brought the band a hands-down triumph at the Harper's Ferry competition, with sets ranging from well-chosen covers such as Freddie King's "Love Her With a Feeling" and Joe Turner's "Roll 'em Pete" to jump-bluesy originals like "Fine As Wine" and "Fightin' Woman."

Thomas' voice has a deep, resonant tone worthy of an older, more weathered blues veteran while Adams' hollow-body '53 Silvertone riffs and Poster's barrelhouse piano stylings add swing to the atmosphere.

Boston's Blues

"We've all grown musically in this band, and altogether I think we have more maturity now as a band," said Thomas, whose first name is a shortened form of Radcliffe, given to him by his family after a grandfather's name. "Our aim is to do whatever it takes to go out, hit the road and entertain. We'd like this band to be a permanent thing. I think we're close and strong as a unit and there's a common musical thread that runs through the band."

Web: rackythomasband.com

Ed Vadas

Boston's Blues
Ed Vadas: Playing and living his blues on his own terms

The burly 6'5" multitalented artist from Northampton, Mass, who plays guitar and harp in his group, The Fabulous Heavyweights, gives you his blues from his own perspective, personal and up close, both physically and emotionally -- if you listen.

The Heavyweights material ranges from a playful take on "The Thrill Is Gone" as "The Ganja's Gone" to "Start All Over Again," a laconic commentary that gnaws at the bone of biting social issues such as rape and child abuse.

But don't get the idea that the band is preaching from a pulpit. Although it delves into some serious material, Vadas says, "we basically have a good time. We try to give the audience some meat to go with the potatoes."

The main thing is having fun in a band that seldom, if ever, holds a structured or traditional formal practice, according to former bassist Steve "Junior" Toutant, who was with Vadas for about five years.

Vadas, who admits he is not the second coming of SRV on guitar, nor wants to be, is very comfortable and at command with folk stylings or uptempo rock-based blues, and everything in between.

For someone who seldom had thoughts about earning a living as a musician, Vadas now finds he can't get away from it. "I don't have any choice now. I'm 51 (in 1996). What the hell else am I going to do? I think I'll be playing and drop dead on stage. I just hope it's somewhere where people like me."

The deadpan humor fits him just fine. A portion of his Vadas' life resume includes stints as a stand-up comic and bit parts in three movies -- "The Money Pit," "Svengali" and "Nothing Lasts Forever." The movie "career" allowed him to buy a 1985 van, which he still has.

But for the past 35 years or so, blues has dominated his life. "I've always been doing my own either original music or roots music. I glean no pleasure from copying something. I'd rather hear somebody fall down the stairs hitting all wrong notes trying to do something original rather than somebody who plays all the notes just like Albert King. It has no redeeming value to me unless it's Albert King."

What drives Vadas is the chance to hit that spot that resonates with true emotion and suspend that feeling through the night. Vadas calls it being in The Zone, a seemingly out of body cosmic experience that lifts Vadas above the stage to where he observes on a metaphysical level, his body coordinated based on the feeling that communicates through his instrument.

"When you hit the zone, it's truly magical. A couple of weeks ago we were in the zone for about one and a half hours, and everyone knew it. At the end, I just wanted to take that and sign my name to it and hang it on the wall -- a Picasso.

"I play for purely selfish reasons. I want to find that spot where the dirt opens up and the little seedling comes out. I don't care if the seedling is poison oak. I'm not necessarily growing great flowers here. They could be weeds. But I want to be at that spot where that seedling pokes through and I want to feel that," Vadas says. "Sometimes I'll be in the zone by myself and I'll be looking at the band and they're not with me. It's like a soap bubble, it's so fragile, first you see it and you look back and want to say, 'Hey guys look, look over here.' Then it's gone. It's such a meditative thing."

On the "South Side of 50" CD, The Fabulous Heavyweights play some chestnuts from Willie Dixon ("300 Pounds o' Joy"), Muddy ("Goin' to Louisiana" and Wolf ("Killin' Floor"). Yet it's on their eight originals that Vadas' personal Blues is told on songs as "Empty Pocket Blues" and "Please Mr. Bill (Clinton)."

Never one to follow the crowd, Vadas was always the rebel as far as music was concerned. Weaned on his brother's 78s record collection, the 2-year-old Vadas would sit in the middle of his Worcester living room with a record player, and the little DJ spun everything from Sonny Terry, boogie woogie piano, jump blues, acoustic Delta blues, and upbeat swing shifts. "Of course I didn't know that these blues records. When I was 20 and saw my brother again, I found out what they were.

"So, when I was 13 in 1957 and rock 'n' roll was really happening, I was primed for it. I was crazed. Everything was blues-oriented. Now I think it was a subliminal thing that drew me to boogie woogie and blues because of what I had listened to as a child.

"But I hated the British Invasion. I was the kid on a beach fighting in every trench to keep them out," he said.

The early '60s also spawned the folk and blues revival, and Vadas was right there in the mix, coaxing others to share his enthusiasm. "I used to go down to the

Boston's Blues

library and listen to the Alan Lomax Library of Congress recordings, and again this was the same stuff I had listened to when I was two. I'd bring friends down and I'd say, 'Hey you gotta listen to this,' and they said, 'What are you crazy?'

"In 1965 or '66 I saw Howlin' Wolf at Newport and it changed my life. Up until then, I thought blues music had to be acoustic music -- Bukka White, Robert Johnson, Joe Spence, Rev. Gary Davis, Blind Blake and Gus Cannon, then I'd try to link it all," he said.

Vadas did a tour of duty in Vietnam in 1966-67 and won a number of Army-sponsored talent contests. As part of a contingent of entertainers for their peers, Vadas performed about 85 shows. "We did carriers, camps near the DMZ, had a few hairy moments... but it was rewarding. We put on about an hour to an hour and a half show. I played bass, did about a 15-minute comedy monologue and a little guitar and a little harp," he said.

After his Vietnam service, Vadas attended the University of Massachusetts from 1969-70 and played numerous gigs here and there honing his skills as songwriter and musician. He said he never gave it a thought to become pro until 1970, a watershed decision which, for him at that point, there was no turning back.

"I'm going to give myself seven years of playing music. And I'm not going to question my decision for those seven years," he promised himself. "Then I'll evaluate it on a yearly basis. I checked every year until about 1981- 82 then I said, 'Oh, forget it. I doomed to make $50 and a sandwich for the rest of my life.'

"I don't have any dreams of making a million dollars. But I would like to get up to that next bracket. My biggest frustration is finding somebody who will say, 'Here's a guy who's traveling and doing 200 gigs a year. Let's take a chance.' All I need is a record label and the slightest bit of support.

"When I'm on stage, I want to find the spot, that special groove, that little place where everything becomes an expression of accidents. All these little cosmic accidents happening," he said.

Vadas says that all performers must strive to hit that high all the time. "When I see someone perform I want to genuinely feel that they're trying to get down and try to make me feel something... even cry. They may not, but I want to feel that they are trying to get to that spot. I want them to get down to the buck naked to where I can feel their raw energy."

The music of the blues today is under pressure -- pressure to continue its new-found success in the commercial market. Where once honesty and expression formed the cornerstone of blues, today it has been transformed and packaged for its entertainment value. "Now the trick and the art is to have a show that incorporates something real in there," Vadas says. "But I think a lot of people miss the point. To me, the public doesn't give a damn -- they just want to see a show."

Then again, most people are not as passionate about the music as Vadas is. And that has been a problem of sorts. Interpretation takes many forms and some people want to hear something that is familiar and safe. But Vadas has never stayed close to shore. He'd rather build his own boat from his own plans, steer his own craft and travel beyond the horizon -- if he doesn't sink on the way. And if he does, so be it.

"A truly good musician takes the musical skills he has on an instrument, couples it with his life's experiences and tries to express the person that he is through that instrument," Vadas says. "You've got to have a good sense of yourself and where you are in the world -- in the universe, on the planet, in the town, on the stage, in the song, and how that radiates out. It's intrinsic... it's not something you do consciously. But the better your sense of self and your torments, the better you will be in touch with that angst. Blues deals directly with that -- no money, no love, no alcohol, too much alcohol, and life's ironies."

In 1998, Vadas released "Bluez.com/Ed Vadas and the Fabulous Heavyweights" on Bluez Records of Melbourne Beach, Fla. He has also been performing as a solo acoustic act.

Neal Vitullo (Young Neal)

Art Simas
Young Neal rips and rocks the blues on every gig

The hard-driving Neal Vitullo, Young Neal to most, may have started out as the typical teenager with a guitar. But there is nothing typical of Vitullo's desire to strum a few chords now and then. He shreds the damn thing every time he straps it on. That's what works best for this powerized trio with Hub O'Neil on bass and Billy 'Bamm Bamm' Donahue on drums.

A self-taught master, Vitullo grew up in Warren, R.I. "I kept banging away at it with Chris "Stovall" Brown and Madeleine Hall in the late-1970s when I was still in high school," he said.

The first incarnation of Young Neal and the Vipers came about in 1982-83. In 1984, fellow Rhody native, Dave Howard joined the band on bass and harmonica. That group stayed together for about eight and a half years, Vitullo said.

"We'd got burnt with Atlantic Records around 1987," he said. "We kept getting bounced from one A&R guy to the next. They just didn't get it. And anyway, it wasn't my style."

Vitullo was forced to try his hand at vocals around 1992 when Howard left to form his own band, The High Rollers. "I had sung a few songs before, but it wasn't for a whole night. But I was at the point where I couldn't have someone else fronting my band any more. Physically (singing) it's a lot... it'll eat you up. One year, I did 300 shows. I still do over 200 a year... that's still a lot."

Vitullo is a definite blues/rocker type. "I can't deny it. What moves me is guitar and all the different aspects and styles. Most times I write songs as an excuse to solo. That's what makes it fun for me. If it's not fun for me, then it's not fun for anyone else. And that works because the music is directly related to the audience. But it's got to be cool-sounding guitar."

Because of the intensity and pressure of being "on" every night and of the nightly grind of playing over 200 gigs, Neal says, "burnout is always looming. That's why you've got to try to find other things. You got to try to find some kind of life."

For Neal, fishing is that peaceful drug that works wonders. "Yeah, I mean just getting outside, on the water where it's nice and quiet, where you can clear your head and get a different perspective at it and hopefully grow, and get new inspiration."

Boston's Blues

His boat is appropriately named, "Played For It." He started a chartering business during the summer of 1997. You'll find him on Narragansett Bay and other ports of call from mid-April through October.

Besides being the captain, Vitullo doubles as his own secretary doing bookings, mailings, phone work, and all of the administrative work that goes into running a band.

"I've always been fishing. With the grind of the nightclub scene, you gotta get a balance. Laying on the couch and flicking channels or some kind of sedentary lifestyle just isn't me. I just got to get up and get out. It's escapism.

"So many guys run into escapism through alcohol and all the other pitfalls, of which, I plead guilty. And that almost killed me. I'm lucky to be around. That was an accepted way of life (in the '80s). Basically we didn't know any better.

"Then you feel like crap and you can't do anything. You start losing interest in the things you love to do because physically you feel so bad.

"You gotta give it up. It wasn't that tough a choice for me and there's not a day that I regret it," he said. "You just got to have some other outlet if you're going to be creative."

Vitullo says he hopes blues continues to grow on its own without outside interference. "You wouldn't have guys who are our influences (Freddie King, Albert King, SRV if they listened to the critics) because they didn't know what the hell they were doing in the first place. They were just going with the feel too. Blues never would have got beyond the acoustic guitar. I'm glad to see things going in a positive way with the creativity and continuing to find new ways to express human emotions in a soulful manner.

"It's something you can't buy or teach. If I could bottle it and sell it, I would. I'd like to share it with you, but it's just a God-given gift. Any way I look at it, it's what I was meant to do," he said.

Young Neal and the Vipers debuted with "Hooloovoo," in 1990 on Big Noise of Providence and "Finally Alone," in 1992, also on Big Noise. The band then signed on with KingSnake Records out of Memphis and produced "13" 1996, and "One's Enough" in 1998.

Web: kingsnakecd.com

Vykki Vox

Boston's Blues
Vykki Vox: Big voice, big talent

You'd never know it, but Vykki Vox, a dynamic vocalist and songwriter, was once shy and reserved about singing. When she was growing up in Montgomery, N.Y., and later in Billerica, Mass., she said she was reticent about singing – even in front of encouraging family members and friends.

Singing in the dark to her blouses and bellbottoms with the door shut Vykki admits, "I was very afraid to sing at parties. I was a closet singer for many years."

Vykki's father, a multi-talented musician, was her first main musical influence. He taught her piano and the one, four, five classic blues chords, and let her experiment and learn on her own. The whole family was heavily into music. Her grandfather played drums and violin in Depression-era bands and was the only person who had a steady job during that lend-me-a-dime time; her mother, Alice MacKenzie, was a vocalist, and her older brother, Philip MacKenzie, played guitar. Philip is now an illustrator and artist and did the artwork for Vykki's debut CD, "Soul Searching," which was released in 1996.

When she was 18, she decided to forge ahead and see if she could make it in the music world as a singer. "It was now or never, and I knew that those years that I had been developing my voice that I had something there -- or at least I hoped I did -- but I wouldn't know unless I gave it a shot."

In the early 1980s, she answered an ad in the Boston Phoenix for a rock-based cover band that was in search of a vocalist. In the band Dagger, she developed her vocal range and diversity in singing a variety of styles and moods. Vykki was naturally drawn to the sounds of Led Zeppelin and Janis Joplin, and the more she sang, the more she gravitated to the blues-based artists. She also listened to Bessie Smith, Big Mama Thornton, and many other blues masters.

"That's what definitely pulled me in. Whenever we'd just jam with friends we'd jam in something that was 1, 4, 5 and pick a key and I'd just make stuff up as I went along. That just kind of confirmed how much I enjoyed that freedom of expression and being able to just let it all out."

She especially likes Etta James, who uses her voice as a powerful instrument. "From my experience, I think a lot of people don't consider the voice an instrument, which I think is so funny because you have to keep very well tuned and you have to know where you're going with the music, just like fingers working an instrument, your body and your muscles work to make the sound that comes out of your voice."

Vykki spent two years with Dagger as a requisite musical apprenticeship. Toward the end of that stint, her brother Philip joined the band. "That was nice to be singing with him after so many years of being in that scene and of watching him in his band," she said.

Brother and sister eventually formed their own group, an originals band, while they played in and out of other bands, but they always came back to writing together.

The writing tandem continued periodically for 10 years, Vykki said, "and we were probably together in three or four bands during that time. He got frustrated with the industry because of all the breakups with the bands. He put so much time and effort and he was so close to making some headway, he just got tired of the whole thing and decided to do his own thing and not rely on anyone else."

Vykki said she also was frustrated with the process of being in so many different situations that had potential, but didn't work out for one reason or another.

"I tried to help and be part of running the business, but being a woman in the industry, especially a few years back, although it's getting better now, I was looked on as the girl in the band and not really given the credit for having a brain or having business sense, which I got from my mom and I got the music sense from my father. So the bands would just break up and I didn't have any control over it."

She took a year off from the rock scene. But she admits she was dying to play again in the late '80s and early '90s. Her brother nudged her a bit in the direction of a three-piece horn band, The Mill Town Rockers, which featured an R&B sound. After a successful tryout and a few gigs, "I really delved into the blues and started learning more, not just feeling it, and learning the background of the players, such as Freddie King, who was so talented with his voice and guitar. That really drew me in," she said.

After two years, Vykki found the same cyclical situation was happening again. She was trying to promote the band and get them more gigs in Boston. But like every one before, the band broke up and she was back where she started.

Before the demise though, the band wanted to name the band after Vykki, but she said she was very uncomfortable with it.

Boston's Blues

"Then later on, I realized that no one knew who I was after being in the music scene for 10 years. Maybe they were right... maybe I should use my name for a change. I wanted to get more into Boston. But the group didn't want to make the effort to get known in the Boston area."

After a few other projects, Vykki said she wanted to focus on originals and/or blues because blues would allow her to express everything she wanted to get across in her music. "I could say my own words within the context of the song or change the melodies. Blues gave me the freedom to do whatever I wanted to do because it is the most expressive music."

Finally, with an enough-was-enough determination, she decided to front her own band, with her own name and not have it dissolve without her input.

She hit the jam circuit in Boston around 1992 and kept both eyes open for potential complementary players. When she first arrived she saw Gordon Beadle, Toni Lynn Washington and Scott Shetler and thought to herself, "Yes, these people are great, these are the types of people I want to be playing with. You could see the energy and what they were putting into the music."

"It was hard at first because they saw this small girl and thought this wimpy voice was going to come out," Vykki said. "But I fought my way through and I got to know the people who ran the jams like Jose Ramos who was very helpful, Chris 'Stovall' Brown and Rick Russell, who asked me to sing at his first House of Blues jam, along with many other people in the area, and I was finally getting the recognition after more than a decade."

She eventually hooked up with Chris Fitz and the two were booked for a regular Thursday gig at Waldo's on Boylston Street in Boston. From that exposure, Vykki said she started working hard to break into more places in and around Boston.

If there is one thing that Vykki knows, it's that the music business is a constant public relations relationship with everyone -- casual listener, club owner or fellow musician, and a nonstop promotional effort.

With a discriminating eye and ear focused on improving her band now, Vykki said she wants to advance and keep the music moving. "I'm trying to work in the originals more than ever, melding all of the influences with the blues being the base for all of it... Hopefully I can continue to grow and bring that sound into the 21st century."

Art Simas

The first incarnation of the band Vykki Vox with Fitz lasted a little more than a year. Fitz said that Vykki wanted to move into a different musical direction and, at that time, Fitz was interested in fronting his own band.

The name Vykki Vox was actually coined by her brother as a nickname when they were youngsters. "At first I was against it, but I knew Vykki MacKenzie just didn't make it... Some people think it's like a dime-store novel or cartoon character. Over time I came to realize that it's a good thing," she said.

"Sometimes people will joke with me and say I smile to much to sing the blues, but I try to focus on the positive things. But the blues has helped me express the pain I've experienced, and I've had had a lot of painful experiences, but I just choose not to focus on those. And where I let that out is through the expression of the music. That's why the blues is so, so close to my heart."

Update: Vykki and keyboardist Dave Osoff form the main songwriting team of Vykki Vox the band. The two have teamed up since the first CD in 1996 and have been a formidable duo.

The band released "Woman's Touch" in 1997 and "Can You Feel It" in 1999 on Webrock Records.

Vykki and the band have branched out beyond their New England roots and were featured at the South by Southwest festival in Austin, Texas, in 2000.

Finally, the word is getting out to others around the country that this is a very talented group of musicians with a very original sound that defies categorization – just call it great music.

Web: vykkivox.com

Toni Lynn Washington

Toni Lynn Washington: A blues diva virtuoso

By Art Tipaldi

Toni Lynn Washington performs magic with every breath she exhales. No sleight of hand prestidigitations, instead Washington enchants audiences by turning carbon dioxide into eloquent music. Within the broad spectrum of wind instruments, Washington works the purest, a voice.

Her keyboard player and friend since 1989, Bruce Bears, recognized her expertise immediately and was stunned that she was still out there. "The minute I heard her, she just blew me away. People that talented don't sit in with bands like this. I thought I gotta work with her," said Bears.

"I said to the band, 'You can fight with me if you want, but we're hiring this woman!' It meant a real change in direction from rockin' blues to more Ruth Brown and swing stuff. I had to put together a whole new band with guys into playing that style."

Up until then, Washington had been a vocalist for hire doing Top 40 and jazz in and around Boston. When she heard of Bears' need for a vocalist, she pursued the spot. "They kinda liked me and I liked the way they played. I never thought I would have my own band. I assumed that people like Ruth Brown or Dinah Washington had their own bands, not me. I always saw myself as a featured vocalist with a band, but having the Toni Lynn Washington Band is really great," said Washington.

Bears explained Washington's vocal enchantment. "She has a midrange alto soul sound that I had never heard anybody else with. Mavis Staples is the closest thing I've heard to it. Toni Lynn has more jazz in her voice than Mavis. It was obvious someone should have picked her up a long time ago. It doesn't make sense to me that she slipped through the cracks like that. I hear people from that period, Ruth Brown, Nancy Wilson, Dinah Washington, and they're really no better than she is. No one ever really picked up on what she was capable of."

Washington is a blues diva virtuoso with no mechanical instrument between her inspirations and the audience. She commands what other instruments seek to imitate. "The voice is the most direct instrument. You can squeeze a guitar note for all it's worth, and yet, she can sing this one low note that's got all this body and soul to it. It'll just smoke the other sound. Her sound has got so much experience in it, it's not really fair to compare," continued Bears.

Boston's Blues

Live is where Toni Lynn enters the unique zone performers search for. At times, she will try to reach a note a different way or experiment with different inflections or phrasing. "My inspiration comes from my heart. The place I sing from is a very free, unstressful place. It is a world all its own and it's my world. I like to watch the expressions on the faces when I sing a certain line. Sometimes I'll direct a line or two at a particular person. This band gives me a chance to release things I have never been able to release before. To do things that I never felt I could do before."

Part of the reason why this gifted voice slipped through the musical cracks may be Washington's life on the move. Born in Southern Pines, North Carolina, in the '40s, she was weaned on the radio tunes of Ella Fitzgerald, Nat King Cole and Louis Jordan. Her formal training came in gospel choirs and while doing chores.

"We were taught you could enjoy the so-called devil music, the blues, six days a week, but on Sunday you better be singing 'Precious Lord.' I always had visions and fantasies of being a singer. When I was a little girl I listened to all the jazz tunes on the radio and I'd learn them. Then I'd put on my own show while I was doing the dishes. My grandmother wondered why it always took me so long to do a chore," she said.

Like all children eager to please parents, Washington led her siblings and cousins in shows for the family. "We'd put on shows for our grandparents. We'd harmonize. I've got a very good ear and I'd give out the parts for everyone to sing. I'd drill those parts into them. I'm the only one who turned out as a singer. After I drilled them, I guess they wanted no part of the business."

In the '50s, she became aware of Ruth Brown and Dinah Washington and moved to Boston where the need to vocalize took hold. Singing in Beantown nightspots like the legendary Hi Hat, Washington discovered the spell her voice cast. A move to New Orleans in the '60s hooked her with the great pianist Edward Frank where she wrote and recorded "Dear Diary." "It was a dumb tune I wrote when I was in my 20s. A little doo-wop tune that everybody liked. It even made the billboard charts. That's how I got the opportunity to open for people like Jackie Wilson, and Sam and Dave in the '60s."

When she landed in Los Angeles in the '70s, Washington was part of USO shows that toured military bases in Japan and Vietnam. Later she teamed with two of Ray Charles' Raelettes in a group called Sister Love. Though not on the big time circuit, Washington remained optimistic about the dream she pursued. "I knew I had given it my best shot. I just guess it wasn't my turn. There are some really

233

talented people I've seen who nobody knows about. Now I'm really going all out for it."

Two years after the release of her Tone-Cool CD, "Blues at Midnight," Washington is acknowledged in the same breath as Koko Taylor and Etta James as one of five nominated by the industry as Contemporary Blues Female Artist of the Year.

The charm and grace of her mentors flows easily from her sleek vocals. Washington's smoky cover of T-Bone Walker's "Evening" combines her smoldering vocals with Paul Ahlstrand's gut-wrenching tenor sax. Her knockout punch is always her riveting cover of Roosevelt Sykes' "Driving Wheel."

When Washington testifies, "Every time I see my baby, I feel like a leaf shakin' on a tree," nerve endings tingle. Whether she belts the blues or coos sensuously, Washington transforms simple statements like, "I'm tired of being Miss Goody Two Shoes" into scorching demands.

"I like to sing songs that have really good lyrics. Then I like to deliver it in my way. I can get really involved in that interpreting. I feel if I can reach people with a phrase or word, they can testify with me. I love singing about a no good man, and watching women point their finger at the man they're sitting with and yelling "Yeah!" laughed Washington.

Bears' respect for Washington runs deeper than keyboard player and guest vocalist. "I can play the technical stuff, but I wish I could play one note with as much soul as she can sing it. It's that ability to get the most out of so little that keeps me in awe of her. That's what I'm learning from her."

Web: tonecool.com

Mike Welch

Mike Welch: Through it all, he's still Mike

In a sense, Mike Welch is a paradox. He is a sage in a 20-year-old body, a guitar wizard who struts the stage with nervous energy while playing it with piercing precision.

He's also a friendly spirit who loves living life in the present tense -- always.

While he's been playing guitar for about 11 years, and working professionally for seven, Welch is an accomplished and very adept blues man.

The beginnings of his pole-vaulted career started in the late-1980s at Johnny D's in Somerville, Mass., where an open blues jam format on Sundays allowed the youngster to flex his fingers on stage alongside future musical partners, collaborators and provocateurs.

Weekend gigs became more frequent for Welch, who was supported 150% by his entire -- and I mean entire -- family who ventured weekend night after weekend night to see him perform.

His elementary education in the blues was structured by listening to his dad's collection of blues records -- Magic Sam, Earl Hooker, Elmore James, T. Bone Walker and many, many others. Those artists spoke to Welch in their own language that was full of riffs of angst, passion, tenderness and heartache.

Welch names B.B. King, Ray Charles, John Lennon and just about every 1950s guitar player who toiled in the blues and R&B business as his musical foundation.

Practice. Practice. And more practice. Even when he didn't have a guitar in his hands, he'd be in a trance walking through his house fingering an imaginary instrument, not unlike others who can't get enough of the music that constantly churns in their heads.

With more exposure in the clubs around Boston, Welch was called upon time and again to share the stage with veteran players, such as Ronnie Earl and Luther "Guitar Jr." Johnson, who were willing to adopt him as one of their own.

His mother, Jan, says she is forever grateful for the blues community -- Amyl Justin, Matt Woodburn and Cheryl Arena, David Maxwell, and many, many other musicians -- who nurtured Mike during his formative years. "Above all, they were good people. And I will always be thankful for what they did."

Boston's Blues

At the grand opening of the Cambridge, Mass., House of Blues, Nov. 23, 1992, "Little Mikey," as he was then known, tore down the house and was dubbed Monster Mike by Dan Ackroyd that night. Mike dropped the Monster monikor in early 1998 in favor of simply Mike Welch.

Playing just about every weekend and touring the U.S. during the summers of '93 and '94 as the Monster Mike Welch Band, Welch, with writing partner and rhythm and Leslie guitarist, George 'Leroy' Lewis, drummer Warren Grant and bassist Jon Ross (and later, David Hull) prepared the band for the debut CD. "These Blues Are Mine" was released under the Tone-Cool label in January 1996.

It was an immediate national and international hit. European tours, interviews with Rolling Stone, People Magazine, USA Today, and others solidified Welch's stature as a rising star.

The second CD, "Axe To Grind," was released in early 1997. It drew similar accolades from reviewers and accelerated Welch's popularity. Again, the national media came calling quite frequently, from Lifetime/ABC-TV, Guitar Magazine, Billboard and others.

During the spring of 1997, Welch returned from his fourth tour of Europe even before he reached his 18th birthday. He appeared on French television, was featured in Rock and Folk Magazine, the French equivalent of Rolling Stone, and got to play with his idols, B.B. King and Ray Charles, in Norway.

He attended the University of California at Berkeley during the fall of 1997. But came home after less than one semester, realizing that New England was closer to his heart than late-night study marathons at Berkeley. "It was so much the wrong move for me," he said. "I think the first college experience was more of a reaction of not getting trapped" in doing the same things all the time.

Welch said the West Coast scene was strictly delineated into rock/blues and swing/jump blues -- and there seemed to be no middle ground for performers. You were either one or the other.

In comparison, he says the New England scene encompasses more diversity and wealth of talent than the San Fran-Oakland area. "I couldn't even get a decent keyboard player when I was out there. Here, you've got some of the best players in the world right here in Dave Maxwell, one of my all-time favorite musicians.

He is one of the few people who can legitimately put the word genius on a job application; and Bruce Katz. I mean, it just doesn't get any better than that."

Welch and the band released their third album for the Tone-Cool label under the vigilant eye of producer Richard "Rosy" Rosenblatt in June 1998. "Catch Me" caught the eye and the fancy of many in and out of the blues community and it was back on the road for Welch for another year.

After "Catch Me," Welch formed another band that had Brad Haleen on bass and Jack Hamilton on organ. "We had some great shows and during that time I worked with James Montgomery and Brian Templeton to keep my chops up but I wasn't saturating the blues scene as I had been. The beautiful thing that came out of that was Brian Templeton's record, "Home," which was produced in 1999 and released under the Stone Cold Records label in early 2000. Welch was the main producer of that project.

"Brian and I were going through pretty much the same thing," Welch said, since the Radio Kings dissolved in 1999. "Neither of us knew exactly what we wanted to do. We had all these ideas. I put together a band for him, which more or less was the Monster Mike Welch band, but that was a great experience.

"The other thing I did was go into the studio with Tom Hambridge whenever I could. Tom was recording all these songs he was writing but I didn't know what they were. Some of them were songwriting demos. So I didn't know what it was going to be -- and it turned into 'Balderdash.' And it was great to be part of a record on a major label (Artemis Records) that wasn't going to be released as a blues record."

Welch admitted that "Catch Me" strayed from the mainstream blues. "My mistake was in trying to play those songs to a hardcore blues club audience. That's not the place to experiment.

"There is definitely a part of me that says at some point I'll put together an originals rock band," he said, "but certainly not right now."

In September 2000, Welch started school as a freshman at the Berklee School of Music in Boston. "I returned to school for the right reasons this time," he said.

He said he's learning jazz guitar, a much more technically challenging genre than blues. But that isn't a knock on blues because blues is so much more emotional than jazz, and not everyone can do both, he said.

Boston's Blues

In March 2001, Welch, Brad Haleen and Warren Grant and invited guests began a residency on Monday nights at Jake and Earl's in Waltham.

Looking back on his phenomenal personal and musical growth, Welch said he is very proud of his accomplishments in the Monster Mike Welch Band and that music from 1996 through 1999. He especially thanked his songwriting partner and mentor, George Lewis, for teaching him how to run a band and be a leader.

"It was remarkable that we (the return of the Monster Mike Welch Band) could get it all together again at the House of Blues (in February, 2001) after three years of not playing that music. So in looking back and giving my body of work a reassessment, I'm proud of what we accomplished, and I think it's pretty good.

"... I've managed to stay true to the blues tradition while at the same time trying to forge original things. It's a tradition that I love being a part of," he said.

In looking at where or how the music will lead him, Welch says there is no definitive answer. "I'm much more prone to let things happen if they are going to happen. If I start making conscious decisions, such as, 'I want to make something that is going to cross over,' then probably it won't cross over and I'll probably be disappointed.

"And if I choose to play straight, traditional blues, well there are other people playing that stuff really well and I'd become one of several thousand," Welch said. "What I'd rather do go is let the music go where it's going to go. As long as the music is honest, that's all I can hope for. The music will change in ways that I can't predict right now."

Web: mikewelch.com

William Lorenzo Robinson, Weepin' Willie

Boston's Blues
Weepin' Willie: Boston's entertainer extraordinaire

A man moves with an unsteady gait toward the stage. Supporting his stature is a black linear cane, a reminder of a neck/spinal cord operation nearly a decade ago that now causes his left leg to be a half-step behind its partner's lead. He looks frail, almost vulnerable.

He is impeccably dressed, resplendent in a black tuxedo. A matching, perfectly knotted bowtie perches above a starched white-ribbed shirt. The shirt starkly contrasts with the neatly pressed, cuffed black trousers and eye-aching shine cast from patent-leather shoes. He personifies aged sophistication, elegance and style -- nouveau chic at 75.

On stage he moves quickly to his spot, a place he knows well after more than 50 years behind a microphone and in front of an audience. A glance back to his bandmates and he is ready. The music starts. With a flick of his wrist as if shooing away an insect, he discards the cane and manhandles the microphone by its invisible throat. Everyone stops his or her private conversations in mid-sentence and their collective heads turn toward the stage as one. It's time to see and hear Weepin' Willie sing his blues.

William Lorenzo Robinson, better known as Weepin' Willie, was born in Atlanta, Georgia, July 6, 1926. His early years were mostly spent outdoors in the fields of Winter Garden and Belglade, Florida, under a humid and unyielding sun picking tomatoes, potatoes, beans and assorted crops.

After his mother died when he was 10, Willie and his father migrated with the harvest seasons in a canvas-covered truck, driving from Florida through the Carolinas to Virginia. Throughout this time while he traveled on the muddied back roads and labored in the fields, Willie knew there had to be another way to make a living. "I didn't like this. It was too hard," he said.

On one trip to Cheapside, Va., Willie's father had arranged to have him and a family friend head further north to Trenton, N.J. "My father said he'd join up with me in a few weeks. But I haven't seen him since," he said. "I was just a kid, 15."

He went to work on a Trenton farm milking cows, driving tractor and truck, doing the usual chores of the day.

"I got sick of picking potatoes and the rest, so they let me drive the truck. It was better than picking," he said.

After a year or so, he moved into the city and became a dishwasher. When he was 17 he enlisted in the Army.

"I told them I was 18, but I was really 17... In the Army they told me to listen up and pay attention, because if you don't pay attention you'll have to take basic training all over again and not get a chance to go overseas. So, I didn't pay attention and I didn't go overseas. I wasn't mad at nobody."

After three years in the service, Willie met a friend who booked bands in Trenton, and he started working as a master of ceremonies in a nightclub. The club booked such luminaries as B.B. King, Bobby "Blue" Bland, Jackie Wilson, and Little Richard. While King, Bland, Wilson, and Richard carried their own MC, Willie was the house MC who'd tell jokes, dance, sing, and generally warm up the people before the main performers came out. "I got to know a lot of people personally this way, B.B., Bobby Bland, Big Joe Turner, they all came through."

When Willie first started emceeing in Trenton, the owner said he needed to change his name. They first tried Willie the Weeper, but that didn't really fit. So Willie shortened it to Weepin' Willie, and has been ever since.

B.B. King was most responsible for the development of Willie as an entertainer. King told him that if he wanted to sing, "Then just sing. The rest will take care of itself."

"But I don't know any songs except your songs," Willie told King one night.

"Then sing 'em," King said.

"So I got up there with his 21-piece band behind me... Now I've never been around anything more than four pieces in my life, and I didn't know nothing from a hole in the ground. But I was lucky. B.B. said, 'That's all right. Keep on singing. Learn one song. Then learn two, and so on. Learn enough songs to where five people will like you. Maybe after a while 30 people will like you. Just keep on going. That's how I started out.'"

King also advised him to always sing so that women will like you. "Because if you sing to the women, the men will always follow," he said. "Do what you can do, the best you can do. After that you ain't got no control over it."

Boston's Blues

"Well, I must have done all right because no one ever asked for their money back whenever I sang. I never had any formal lessons or anything like that. I just sing what I feel," Willie said.

"I never say that I worked for B.B. King or Jackie Wilson or anyone else. I tell people that I worked on stage with them. And I worked with a lot of people -- Jimmy Reed, Chuck Jackson, Otis Redding, Joe Tex, and Solomon Burke," he said.

In 1959, a young woman from Louie's Lounge in Roxbury came to Trenton and asked Willie, "I like your band, do you want to go to Boston?"

"Yeah, we'll go to Boston," he told her. "And we've been here ever since."

Willie worked at Louie's Lounge as the house emcee for several years and fronted the house band. "That's where it was happening -- Roxbury -- in those days. It was hot. All the players came through there."

He then worked at Basin Street South as assistant manager for a few years, and then moved over to the Peppermint Lounge. Around the corner from the Peppermint were the Golden Nugget and the Palace, nightspots that jumped every night of the week. This was about 1962-3.

In 1964, Tommy Hunt, author of the then mega-hit song "Human," hired Willie as his emcee and entertainer at the Ebb Tide. "When I come on, I want the stage hot," Hunt told Willie. "If it's not hot, then you're fired."

So it was up to Willie and a man called Herky, who was known as the Monkey Man because of his ape schtick, to whip up the crowd for Hunt. "We stayed on the stage and had to keep moving all the time. If he looked over and saw we weren't moving, he'd fine us $10. Sometimes he'd play for two hours straight and we'd have to be up there moving with him the whole time. I used to say, 'Oh, my God this guy is going to kill me.' But he paid good money. The money I make now is what I was making then."

When Hunt was on, he was a good entertainer. But he had a reputation as a fickle performer, one who often feigned himself sick if he didn't want to work on a particular night. Willie said he did have a slight heart attack one time, but after he recovered it became a favorite excuse to duck gigs he didn't like.

"I figured I'm not going anywhere with this guy," Willie said. "But he paid good, I'll say that about him." Hunt eventually moved his entire band to England, where he still resides, and raised a family and did pretty well for himself, Willie said.

Still a migrant in the musical world, Willie then worked at Club New Orleans in Boston's Combat Zone on LaGrange Street. Then he moved to play at Jacob Wirth on Stuart. That's when guitarist Buddy Johnson joined Willie's band, forming an association as The Buddy Johnson/Weepin' Willie or the Weepin' Willie/Buddy Johnson All Star band. (Johnson died in 1997.)

By this time, his experience as a showman was evident to every nightclub owner, and it seemed everyone in Boston knew Weepin' Willie as a class act.

Other jobs included the International Lounge, Ben's Lounge, and performances at just about every watering hole in and around the city.

Willie's charismatic personality takes over when he's on stage, a commanding presence that brings immediacy to his audience. "They like that one-on-one contact. They can feel it, and that's what he brings to every show," said Peter Lembo, Willie's former manager. "I call him the Dean Martin of the blues. Martin wasn't the greatest singer in the world but he had that personality that could bring a song across."

"I never called myself a singer," Willie said. "To me, I'm just entertaining. Whatever I do, people seem to like it. I can't sing like nobody else, I just sing like me."

Willie says that in addition to singing, he was quite the dancer in his day. "I don't look like it, but I can dance too. Back then I could run through the house singing and dancing. But now, forget it."

In looking back over his career as an entertainer, Willie said he'd like to be remembered as someone who "did what I liked to do. And somewhere along the line I hope someone liked what I'd done. If you like what you're doing, just hang in there. I never worried about no big money. I never did it for the money, I just did it 'cuz I liked it."

Update: In late 1998, Willie recorded his first album, "At Last – On Time" with the help of Mighty Sam McClain, who now lives in New Hampshire. It was a dream come true for Willie, who had told Sam a year before, "Before I die, I'd

Boston's Blues

like to make a record." Susan Tedeschi, another Boston-based blues performer, is also featured on the CD, which was recorded at Blue Heaven Studio in Salinas, Kansas.

Web: acousticsounds.com

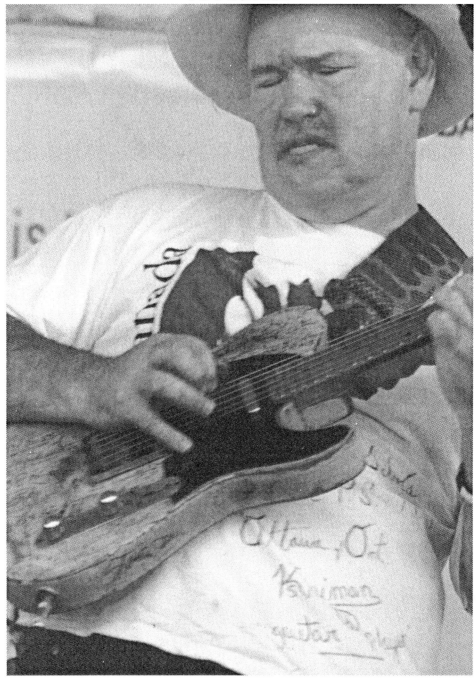

T.J. Wheeler

Boston's Blues
T.J. Wheeler: The ambassador for blues education -- everywhere

Like a medieval troubadour, Thomas James (T.J.) Wheeler carries a song and a message as he criss-crosses U.S., Latin America and Europe -- open up, learn from the music of the blues and apply the lessons to your daily life.

Sometimes it's easier said than done. Wheeler, 49, has had to struggle to get various bureaucratic funding agencies to listen to him. Finally, after 20 years of trying to crack the system, he is reaching thousands through his Blues in the Schools and Blues in the Prison programs. As expected, his audience ranges from toothless-grinning wide-eyed first-graders to suspicious, steely-eyed criminals. He talks of racial diversity, being aware of other cultures and breaking down barriers between peoples and generations.

"When I first started in Seattle, I didn't have the know-how to go about it. So I basically did things independently. But most people just didn't get it. At that time I only got to do about six or so programs per year in the schools," Wheeler said.

Wheeler and his wife, Nadine Perry, live in Hampton Falls, N.H.

But in 1989-90, three things made Wheeler's avocation of spreading the blues possible. He was selected to participate in the Ben and Jerry's Foundation Hope, Heroes & the Blues in the Schools tour, which covered 3,000 miles in three weeks; he was accepted as a member of the N.H. State Council on the Arts and its Artists in Residency program (mainly funded through the federal National Endowment for the Arts); and his founding work in the nonprofit BluesBank Collective organization allowed him to do inner city programs, attend workshops, symposiums and conferences in his work as the unofficial ambassador of blues in New England.

Wheeler estimates he has taught over 125,000 students. And he always delivers the same message to all students -- use the blues as a cornerstone to learn from the past. Because he usually encounters predominantly black or predominantly white students while in inner city or suburban schools, Wheeler bends his delivery according to his audience.

"In the predominantly white schools, I talk about how racism is still very much alive today. I try to challenge the students to broaden their perspectives and get in touch with their humanity," he said.

Wheeler contends that traditional education methods "with its tunnel-vision has subconsciously reinforced a notion of white superiority" by teaching that all of the important contributions made in society have come from the white, Anglo-Saxon European heritage.

In addressing students at inner city schools, Wheeler says, "I tell them they should revel in their culture and take pride in how revolutionary and ingenious this music has been for the world, as well as its healing power and hope. I try to negate the negative stereotypes that have for so long been attached to blues and jazz. But I don't try to turn them into saints. I want them to learn from the mistakes of the past and that means getting their own business together, whatever that may be."

Having the students relate to the history of the blues while finding a link to today's problems is another challenge. "Education can show the way, but the answers depend on each individual to seek them out," he said.

When he is on the road, and the road can include stops in Memphis, New Orleans and Finland, day sessions usually last from one to two hours per class. That includes the animated lecture and a mini-concert featuring the many guitar styles of Wheeler, who fronts his own band, T.J. Wheeler and the Smokers.

"During the last few years I participated in The Magic Bus, sponsored by the University of New Orleans, Eisenhower Center," Wheeler said. "Winners of New Orleans schools essay contests went on a two-week trip that included highlights of the civil rights movement through the Deep South. And I was asked to be on it as a resident blues musician and educator. Not only did we visit highlights of the civil rights movement, we went to places that had a lot of blues history, like Leadbelly's grave outside of Shreveport, La. And when we arrived at the grave, relatives of Leadbelly greeted us at the site. And we went to Rufus Thomas' 75th birthday party, stopped in Little Rock, Ark., with Melba Beals, one of the original Little Rock 9 -- the kids that integrated the Little Rock school district. And it marked the first time that anyone of the Little Rock 9 addressed an audience about what happened 40 years ago when they were escorted by National Guardsmen. So whenever we could we'd connect with a greater audience in each area we went to.

"We did another trip with a wider range of students from other parts of Louisiana -- so that was a fantastic experience that I've been involved in," he said.

Locally, he's a regular visitor at the Portsmouth (N.H.) High School and Middle School and elementary schools in his hometown of Hampton Falls. New England residencies last from one to six weeks and at the end of the course at "graduation ceremonies," the students entertain their parents and the public with a mix of musical performances which could include a jug band, kazoo band, choral group or a blues/jazz ensemble.

"My biggest reward is in hoping I've actually helped students broaden their minds and open their hearts and ears, not only to the music but to the message beyond the music," he said.

In 1993, Wheeler received a W.C. Handy award for his ongoing work in blues education.

Inspired by B.B. King's work on "Live At The Cook County Jail," Wheeler said he wanted to bring the blues to the people behind bars. Again, after years of diplomacy and insistent persuasion within the various bureaucratic channels, Wheeler a few years ago was selected by the N.H. State Council on the Arts to teach a three-week course at the Manchester Youth Development Center for adolescents.

Because the course was optional, "On the first day one person showed up. I'm thinking, 'Man, what am I in for here? This is not happening.' So I told the kid, 'Pass the word, tomorrow we're going to do some cooking -- Creole cooking.' I used that as a metaphor for teaching diversity because Creole cooking takes in all kinds of cultures.

"The next day, I think 30 kids showed up. So, while I was cooking and making the barbecue sauce, I'd have zydeco and Cajun music in the background, trying to show the similarities between the music and the food. That way I got some rapport with them and I didn't have to pull any punches with them as far as racism, drugs, government and surviving. I tried to focus in on making new beginnings and leaving people you knew behind, because sometimes you've got to make a clean break in order to survive," he said.

For this particular group, Wheeler said he wanted the students to absorb the blues, listen to its frustration, know where it came from, and then take their anger and animosity and turn it inside out -- recycling the music into something that relieves them of their self-destructive energy.

For the culmination of the two-month workshop, the inmates staged a play based on Alan Lomax's interviews with several Mississippi blues musicians who spoke candidly about Jim Crow laws and life in the South before civil rights in the famous musicologist's seminal book, "The Land Where The Blues Began."

Wheeler noted that the only reason the real musicians spoke so openly to Lomax was because they thought that their conversations would never get published. Back then, the wrong words said at the wrong time could be fatal, and the musicians wanted to protect their families. "That really seemed to hit home to them."

Wheeler says he's been doing more education and blues in the schools programs than ever before.

"It's kind of a paradoxical time for blues in the schools. On one hand more people are hearing about it and I've received a fair amount of attention and awards for the programs and I've been traveling, such as doing the first blues in the schools program in England about two years ago. And I've done blues in the schools in conjunction with several blues societies -- Nashville, Jackson, Miss., a cool thing for the Delta Blues Library where they invited me down to do a how-to session of blues in the schools for musicians. So that was a real honor to be asked to do something like that because it really felt that I've come full circle being that's where I went, to the South, as a young man to study at the feet of these cats -- and then 30 years later to be asked to help the performers.

"But on the other hand, there have been so many cutbacks for arts and education in general and also the climate for arts and education and the message that I use the blues as a way of teaching black history and dealing with the subjects of racism and using blues as a window to look at those untold stories of black history -- the climate for that is not as receptive as it was a few years ago.

Because of politics today, Wheeler said teachers and administrators are reluctant about bringing in any type of controversy.

"People are getting more tentative about what they're doing, which is a real shame. Saying that kids can't handle the truth just perpetuates the problems," he said.

Whatever the future political outcome, Wheeler remains devoted to making people stop and think about their actions and hopes the message from his own song, "Let Me Be Me" off of his "Storybook" CD, is taken to heart:

"It's all right if you're friend is white.
Don't turn your back if your friend is black.
True friends are rarely found.
And if color is all you see, just stay away from me and let me be… let me be… let me be me."

Boston's Blues

Update: In 2001, Wheeler was off to Cuba, bringing his message of hope through the blues to the people. He continues to preach and sing with his group and as a duo with Pat "Hatrack" Gallagher at various clubs around New England, and in the classrooms.

Web: tjwheelerandthesmokers.com

Parker Wheeler

Dennis "Fly" Amero

Art Simas

Parker Wheeler and Dennis "Fly" Amero: Gracious hosts at The Grog

For the last 10 years, Sundays at the Grog in Newburyport, Mass. -- a town that still has a real soda fountain pharmacy that makes milkshakes and ice cream sodas in tall, thick glasses accompanied by long, skinny, silvery spoons -- has been a special place thanks to harp man and vocalist, Parker Wheeler, and guitarist and vocalist, Dennis "Fly" Amero.

Wheeler began the weekly open jam format in 1990. "When I first started," Wheeler said, "I felt there was no place where anyone was playing any kind of adult music. Blues became the common denominator because it's a style of music that can bring a lot of people together on stage. If we put something together that is listenable, people would come.

"So I talked with Doug Johnson, who does the booking for the club, and called as many people to come down that first time -- and they've been coming back ever since," Wheeler said.

"For the first six, seven or eight months, we were getting the guys who work with the 'name' players, such as Chuck Chaplin who played keyboards with Matt 'Guitar' Murphy. And from that it evolved to, Why not approach Matt Murphy or James Montgomery or whomever?"

While the open jam afforded budding musicians a taste of the spotlight, more often than not, Wheeler was forced to play the moderator role, and not his harp. "I'd get to play the first set, then not play for three and a half hours. And that's not why I started it."

So, with Fly Amero arriving on the scene along with drummer Tom Hambridge in 1992, the gig evolved to a more structured format, with invited special guests. This allowed more time for everyone to stretch out musically and not hurry or worry about who's on deck.

"What we wanted to do was to get the cream of the crop of the players that were around here and make it a fresh show every Sunday," Amero said. "The players became the show."

Wheeler also noted that the audience has really supported the Sunday night shows over the years. "We have a strong group of regulars, and we get a diverse crowd of anywhere from 21-year-olds to people in their 60s."

Boston's Blues

Amero, learned guitar "backward" by playing a right-handed guitar upside down since he is left-handed, at age 11, in Essex, Mass. He spent two years with the pop group Orleans in the early 1980s; met and played with other famous artists, such as Billy Joel, Hall and Oates; wrote the musical score to the John Sayles' movie, "City of Hope," wrote and sang dozens of jingles for radio and television (Somerville Lumber, The Ground Round and the WCVB-TV Channel 5's "I Like Mike" promo spots in the 1990s featuring sportscaster Mike Lynch), and he continues to write comedy music.

In 1995, "Twisted Christmas," a collection of holiday comedy written by Amero, Brian Silva and former disc jockey Bob Rivers, went "gold," paving the way for a 1996 version, "Cracked Country Christmas," another collection of country novelties such as, "Santa Smells Like Daddy's Glass of Beer," "WANTED: Kris Kringle, Deadbeat Dad" and "Don't Serve Beans on Christmas Night."

"I first got into the blues when (Paul) Butterfield came on the scene with the 'East-West' album with Mike Bloomfield," Amero said. "It just seemed to tie everything together for me and through them I discovered Muddy Waters and Doc Watson and all kinds of acoustic blues.

"I played backstage with Buddy Guy and Junior Wells at the Newport Jazz Festival in 1966 when I was 14 or so. Actually, I picked up a guitar that was leaning against a railing and started jamming when they were in the back. That was something I'll never forget," he said.

Wheeler was born in Exeter, N.H., and grew up in upstate New York. He started playing seriously at around age 16 or 17 and began earning a paycheck at 19 in 1966.

"I kind of backed into the blues thing. I joined a band as a singer in 1965. And they said, 'If you're going to be a singer, then you've got to play the harmonica.' So I bought an E harmonica, because back then everything was in the key of E, all the simple rock songs, not having a clue about a cross harp. That didn't work too well. But then Paul Geremia straightened me out about playing cross harp. And I took to it like a duck to water."

After seeing Muddy Waters with George "Harmonica" Smith perform at Club 47 one night in Boston, with Paul Butterfield and Elvin Bishop in the audience, "I crashed the dressing room. And that kind of got me started," he said.

Wheeler started playing New York gigs, then hit the road on his own magical mystery tour in 1969 that brought him cross country, eventually landing in

Art Simas

California. He returned home the following year and joined the band Swallow, which was under contract with Atlantic at the time. The band switched affiliations and signed with the Warner Brothers label and did many major shows and projects with people such as B.B. King, Traffic, John Mayall, Earth Wind and Fire, to name a few.

In 1973, Wheeler moved back to New England and met Amero at a roadhouse called the Sunnyside in Ipswich.

Their paths would intersect every now and then from that point throughout the next two decades. Now, they form a formidable musical duo -- with the best in the business backing them up (or the other way around) every Sunday for people who are hungry for great blues at the Grog.

Michael Williams

Michael Williams balances jazz, blues

Guitarist Michael Williams likes to live on the edge -- where blues and jazz socially intermingle in an afternoon cocktail party.

His music is unique and definitely not the same old 12-bar blues. On the contrary, the music literally cannot be defined. Is it blues? Is it jazz?

The musical astigmatism suits Williams just fine. That's where he wants to live -- on the fringe of both worlds while integrating the deepest mainstream influences from each genre. "My thing is halfway between blues and jazz. I like to mix the ingredients together," Williams, said. "I'm trying to create a little niche for myself. I want to be known for that."

A native northern Californian, Williams settled in the Greater Boston area in 1984 "after spending about 10 years of my life trying to be a be-bopper," he said. While he was in the Arcata, Calif., area, he played in a variety of bands that backed national artists such as Little Charlie and the Nightcats and Robert Cray, on the northern California circuit.

"By time I moved out here, I was familiar with the players and wanted to work my way into the scene. But it's kind of been a long process, meeting different players and hanging out and playing with different people," he said.

Williams plays lead guitar on his own "Late Night Walk" album and is the main string man for David Maxwell's Maximum Blues Band, in addition to other side projects. But his main job is holding down a teaching seat at Boston's Berklee College of Music. 2001 marks his 15th season at Berklee.

"I'm teaching guitar at Berklee three days a week," Williams said. "It's taken the stress off of playing only to pay your bills. I feel fortunate. I've got a guitar in my hands all day long and I love it. The way the school is now, they expect you to bring in and teach your own music, called Teaching Your Own Studio.

"The school expects you to be developing as an artist and not to shut yourself in and only be a teacher. I have no desire to just teach. I think you need a balance in your life, teaching and playing. So it offers me a sense of balance," he said.

In teaching, Williams also tries to impart the emotional side of the music, especially in blues.

Boston's Blues

"Sometimes students will come and have a lot of chops physically and they think all they have to learn is three chords and then they can go out and play blues. But they are not ready because they don't have the respect for all the nuances in there and for everyone's style of playing. That takes a lifetime to do that," Williams said. "So I get a lot of pleasure teaching that and passing that on and trying not to let people underestimate what's involved in the music because it's far from being a simple thing. The technical aspect doesn't really have that much to do with it. It's much more personal. So I feel that it's my responsibility to teach that."

In creating his CD, "Late Night Walk" (www.bluetempo.com), which features harp man Sugar Ray Norcia, sax man David "Fathead" Newman and B-3 keyboardist Bruce Katz, Williams said the rigors of recording fueled his imagination, sometimes at odd hours of the day. "I'll tell you, there was a serious lack of sleep on that album. I got up in the middle of the night often, so it's an appropriate title for the record."

Williams said the spontaneous inconveniences were actually great motivational moments. "For me, I've got to create the challenges that make you get up in the middle of the night. But I also need deadlines to push me. In any event, one can't be a 9 to 5 jazz or blues player."

In September 2000, Williams conducted a very successful fund-raiser for the cleanup of Hardy Pond in Waltham by calling on some of his friends, who also happen to be some the best musicians in New England. Darrell Nulisch, David Maxwell, Brian Templeton, "Sax" Gordon Beadle, Per Hanson, Paul Rishell and Annie Raines, and Marty Ballou and others contributed to the cause at Prospect Hill Park, in Waltham with a torrent of great music.

Michelle Willson

Boston's Blues
Michelle Willson: The Evil Gal who loves to sing

Michelle Willson is one of the brightest stars in the Boston area. A talented vocalist, she sings with sass, class and pizzazz in her Evil Gal Festival Orchestra. She is signed with Rounder Records and has made four records for them since she won the International Blues Talent Competition in 1993. Her latest, "Wake Up Call," was released in the summer of 2001.

Yet behind the success there were years of distress.

This interview was done in the spring of 1998.

Michelle Willson was born in 1958 and grew up in Arlington, Mass.

"My childhood was pretty troubled and there was a lot of bad stuff going on in my house, and I was always looking for places to escape to. My refuge was The Friends of the Drama in Arlington, a community theater group where I did acting and backstage activities. I spent my entire childhood there.

"I was also active in the children's choir at Unitarian Universalist Church in Arlington. Again it was something to get me out of the house. It wasn't that I was particularly religious or enjoyed the music. It was acting that I was interested in the most, you know, you can pretend for a few hours that you're somebody else.

"So when I was about 10, I auditioned for the 'Sound of Music' and got the part of one of the children. So that was it. I pursued that pretty vigorously and didn't take private singing lessons until I got to junior high. I was pretty serious about it, and joined the glee club and all that.

"When I was 12 or 13, I studied voice with Rene Rancourt, the singer who sings the national anthem at all the Boston Bruins hockey home games. He was very supportive of me and told me I had a great gift.

"But things around the house were still very, very strange and got worse. It was pretty much a constant nightmare growing up. I'm sure both my parents will be delighted to read this but that's the truth.

"In retrospect, my singing was sort of pathetic because it was the only place where I could get any attention paid to me -- and I got a lot of attention that way. So it seemed like the thing to do because it was the only way to get anyone to notice me. So that's how it started," Willson said.

She tried out for all the musicals and was determined to learn as much as she could about singing.

"I went to the New England Conservatory when I was in high school to get extra voice lessons. When I got to be about 17, I loved singing and I loved knowing how to sing properly. That was important for me at the time.

"So I went to an audition so I could go to UMass-Amherst on a scholarship, but I screwed up the audition so royally because I was so nervous I couldn't even sing. I couldn't count, couldn't sing, couldn't do anything.

"At the end of the audition, a person on the committee told me, 'I don't know what you're doing here, but you have no musical talent whatsoever and you should stop doing this right now.'

"At the time I was just starting to be interested in jazz and they had a couple of really great people over there on the faculty at UMass.

"So something had happened. I'd go to my high school classes, but whatever I had that was special about me was gone. I think I was so traumatized by the audition process that I hid out for the next few years.

"Previously in high school I had joined a band and we did about two gigs. We were all the younger siblings of another group that had a band, and we'd end up hanging out at their rehearsal gigs. We thought they led the most glamorous lives because they could stay up late, smoke pot, watch The Three Stooges, and eat pasta," she said.

Around 1978, Willson and two sisters, Jackie and Nanette Child, formed a three-part harmony group called Mimi Jones. "We even opened up for Sandra Bernhardt at the Inn Square Men's Bar in Cambridge. And we had a following and developed a reputation.

"But then Nanette got involved in Scientology and that was the end of that band," she said.

"At this time, I was pretty much into group singing. I'd stand on stage with my eyes closed and my hands in my pockets and just open my mouth and sing… and people dug it. But they always hoped that I would be a little more extroverted. But I couldn't. I was so incredibly inhibited, but I had to do this singing thing.

Boston's Blues

"Then I met Ken Harris, who was with the Martels, a popular blues band in the 1970s. This was in the late 1970s, and Boston was a really happening blues scene, much like it is now. And he liked me and my singing. And DiDi Stewart who had just signed a record deal with Don Kirschner, and they would come to my gigs and really dig what I was doing. They were very supportive of what I was doing and that I continue. And it impressed me so much. I was about 19 or 20, and because of that, it gave me some self-confidence. At the time I had no confidence, no self-esteem.

"I wish I had had more guidance as a child, learned how to read music and do basic theory things, some of which I had picked up over the years. There is a time in your life where you should learn that," she said.

Now enrolled at UMass, Willson got a chance to hang out backstage at a fantastic concert by Southside Johnny at the college's Fine Arts Center in 1978. "The whole thing was so intoxicating I knew I wanted to do it. But not rock because that involved a lot of screaming," she said.

But college life was not that satisfying. By New Year's 1979, she had dropped out.

"Ken (Harris) and I got married and started Animal Train, sort of like a Tower of Power funk band. We had two guitar players, five horns, bass, keyboards, drums. At the time, I'd hitch up with these great songwriters and we were working regularly, but I felt like I was awful. I'd listen to the tapes and I couldn't get up and over the band. I wanted to sing like Aretha Franklin, and I couldn't.

"My voice teachers told me that with a big voice, the voice doesn't mature until you are in your late-thirties. They said, 'Then you'll have the instrument that you've always been working for your whole life.'

"But now when I look back on it, my voice wasn't mature enough. But now I can sing like that," Willson said.

"So I always thought that I sucked. I was the most miserable creature on earth. I wanted it so badly but it wasn't going to happen.

"Now I'm at the point to where I'm grateful for that dissatisfaction because it led me to the point to where I am now (in 1998). But at the time, it was just awful. I was 35, I was getting divorced, my band broke up... I was really, really awful, and I decided to quit music. 'I'm old, I'm never going to go anywhere,' I thought.

"So I quit music and took a day job. But people used to give me some tapes to listen to and I finally started to listen to them because I had some free time," she said.

One of the people who gave her tapes was Pierre Beauregard, a founder of the Cambridge Harmonica Orchestra who had worked with Magic Dick of the J. Geils Band, on a line of harmonicas.

"People gave me tapes of Dinah Washington, Ruth Brown, Etta James and it was like a little light bulb that went off. Now I was interested. I didn't feel bad about whether people liked me or not or about getting famous. It was the music now, and it inspired me deeply," Willson said.

"And when I found out about these women's lives, I realized they had the same kind of problems I had. And they were black women in the 30s, 40s and 50s... and I had identified very strongly with what they had been through and how they were handling it.

"When I heard the music, it made me feel good again. And I hadn't felt good in a long time. This is in 1992 -- so I put together what I thought would be a one-night tribute to this music at the Tam, and I thought it would be fun.

"I decided on the songs, hired the musicians and had someone do the charts for me. And we rehearsed all summer long in Scott Shetler's attic. Then we went to the Tam in October, 1992.

"When I was in the bathroom changing up, I was so nervous because I had bought this 1950s kind of dress with zippers on the side. I was so nervous I forgot to unzip the zipper to get into the dress.

"So I'm wiggling into this dress figuring, 'Oh, my God, it doesn't fit any more. It fit this afternoon. What's happening. Oh no. Oh no.'

"But then I figured it out, got into the dress and when I walked out on stage, something happened in that split second. Everyone in the room, their heads swiveled around. I can picture it in slow motion. And they sat there with their mouths open for a half-hour.

"And when it was over they all came crowding up to me. 'Michelle, what have you done?' So I knew they were paying attention to me. And that felt pretty good," she said.

Boston's Blues

"A lot of people sing this music. But you have to have been through a certain amount of bullshit and really bad times and decide to come up out of it before you can really sing this music and have it mean anything to you. Until that time, it's all just a theory."

"I can tell when someone is singing this music and they haven't actually walked the walk. So suddenly to be singing these tunes, like 'Evil Gal Blues,' where she's sort of winking and laughing and saying, 'Yeah, I'm bad'... 'I feel good,'... 'I feel evil... 'I want you'... 'I don't want you'... It was empowering. It was like salvation, honestly," Willson said.

"I hated the blues because a lot of it was based on being a victim. If I wanted to feel miserable and feel like a victim, I can fuckin' live my own life. I don't need music to tell me how to do that. But this was a different kind of music that used humor and sex and it was very sophisticated musically but grounded in the roots music.

"For me, it's always been a little movie going on in my head, the story. And if it's not a movie that I want to watch or get behind and tell people about it, I don't want any part of it, no matter how good it is.

"So a lot of that music I listened to was the Dinah Washington early stuff with the Lionel Hampton Orchestra under Leonard Feathers. At that point, she had Quincy Jones, who was a teenager, doing arrangements for her, and Charlie Mingus playing bass. Heavy stuff.

"In early 1993, at Ryles after this thing at the Tam and everyone wanted to see us, especially the musicians. Of course if the musicians like you then, that's a sure sign you're not going to make any money," she said tongue-in-cheek.

Mark Ryder, then president of the Boston Blues Society, told Willson that her group should enter the battle of the blues bands competition at Harpers Ferry. She said Harpers owner Charlie Abel had already picked the bands for the battle later that summer, but Ryder convinced him to put me on, too.

"And so we did the thing, and I thought we'll get our names in the paper and get a couple of gigs out of it. So I talked the band into doing it," she said.

"During the scheduled finals, there was a big electrical storm over Allston that night, and Harpers didn't have electricity, so it got cancelled for a couple of weeks. By this time I'm thinking, 'Geez, can't we get this thing over with?'

"But no one was more shocked than me when we won. And it felt really good.

"And then I really had to talk the band into going down to Memphis. None of them wanted to go. And I said, 'If I can fly you down there, will you go?' and they said yes.

"So I started asking people for money to fly the band to Memphis and I did benefits for myself. And people were making fun of me saying, 'Hey Michelle, I think I'll do a benefit for myself, too.'

"Rick Russell and the House of Blues were very helpful, too. And that was the first time that I realized there was a Boston blues scene and that there were people involved who really cared about one another, such as Alan Muir and his wife Stephanie. I felt that I didn't belong and they weren't paying attention.

"I didn't raise enough to buy my own ticket, though. So the band flew down and I drove.

"And we won that, too. We were very good and I took everything very seriously. We walked out in our suits and I had this black dress. No one had ever seen anything like that and I think that all contributed to it.

"No one could believe we won.

"We also played at the King Biscuit Festival in Helena, Arkansas, in October and we went to the real recording studio owned by Sam Phillips. At King Biscuit Bob Vorel of Blues Revue magazine was one of our first fans. He dragged Marian Levy out of the meeting they were having and said, 'You've got to see this girl.' And I knew I wanted to be on Rounder Records. They were in Cambridge and they had a woman running the company. And I wanted a woman as a mentor. And when I saw Marian walking across the field, I knew she was going to sign me.

"So for me to play this music that I cared so much about and to play it for these people who had listened to this music when they were teenagers – that's the real test – they're hearing their own youth, all of them sitting there digging the music. It was like church. I had a whole new respect for the genre.

"I was beginning to figure out if you put yourself in a position and put yourself out there and you believe in what you're doing and you ask people for help -- this is a big deal for me -- so the concept that you would want something and ask for help and they would help you, was so foreign to me -- but there it was.

"I was assigned Ron Levy as a producer. And I was a big fan of his, his records always had a real groove. I'd be bopping down the highway listening and digging his music. One of the things I love about Ron's records -- I call it "deliberate naievete" is to capture the live sound. It's not by accident that bands sound like that. So I felt very lucky.

"Rosy (Rosenblatt) is a genuinely, nice, caring human being. He's used all of his talent and expertise to help out the people on his record label.

"I started writing tunes and I realized that it wasn't being better than Leonard Feather, it's about speaking in your own voice -- and nobody can do that better than you. And once I started doing it (and at the time I was involved in some bad relationships and some bad activities), you know if you manage to live through it, you've got some good song material.

"So I managed to crank out a couple of tunes… but I was still so paranoid that I thought the reason Rounder signed me was that they would turn the joke on me. And that's so stupid to think. But that's what I believed and that's what I thought would happen.

"So we went to the studio to make the second record, and at the time I was drinking pretty heavily and doing a lot of drugs, frankly. And I was thinking if I could get away with this record, I'll be lucky, because I'm not in the condition to be recording now. I'm not in the condition to be singing. I shouldn't be doing this -- it's a big mistake.

"Of course at the very same time, Ron and Marian were in the process of getting a divorce and it was pretty ugly. My producer and my boss… and they are bitter, mortal enemies.

"And there was a lot of weird game-playing going on between the two of them. But I don't hold any grudge for it because I've been on the other end of that type of thing.

"And Ron was drinking so heavily during the sessions. We'd start fine but three hours later he'd be out of his mind stomping around the studio yelling… and we'd be looking at each other, scared. For me this is a particular issue because that was a lot like my childhood. So I had a lot of buttons being pressed.

"Even though I was an adult, I was really scared of him. I know he must have been going through an enormously painful time because I know he's not the type of person who would do that to anybody.

"Now that's it's all over with -- I can look back on it and say 'Whew!!' Everyone came out of it fine.

"One day Ron Levy shows up two hours late and Ronnie Earl is sitting there, a perfect gentleman. And Ron is drunk out of his mind, blowing smoke in Ronnie's face… and he said, 'OK, let's go'… And you know what happened? That was "Long John Blues" and "You're So Mean to Me." I listen to those tunes now and they sound great.

"It just shows you that weird things can happen if you channel the energy correctly, it can make for some intense art.

"So out of a bad scene, good things happened and it gave me self-confidence and self-esteem, which I really didn't have up until that time. Right up until 1996, I was pretending, completely pretending all the time. As long as I was up on stage, everything was great. When I'm on stage, I would act like I'm really happy and know what's going on and be really evil and think that I'm the balls.

"But as soon as I'd walk off stage I'd start crying and I'd cry until it was time to go back on stage again. So to not feel that way any more, it was a great feeling.

"The real reason we're doing this is because the audience is gracious enough to give us their money and allow us to do it. They work for a living and we really don't. I'm so grateful to learn that lesson. Whatever else happens is all sort of gravy because I didn't learn anything about that side of life when I was growing up.

"I lived with my father because I couldn't afford an apartment. All the money was going into the band. No boyfriend. No friends. Nothing. Only work all the time.

"And to wake up one day to find that you only have casual acquaintances who wouldn't really miss you for two weeks, like you could be dead for two weeks in your apartment and no one would even notice; that's what made me start to think.

"Matt Woodburn and Cheryl Arena are perfect examples. I know they really care about me as a person, not just because I'm a good singer. I could stop singing tomorrow and they'd still care about me. They're both great people... I just got to say I'm happy to be alive.

"But not so long ago I couldn't conceive the idea that things could get better. It's definitely due to the support of people like Matt and Cheryl and the audiences. And yes, I'd like to hear that more people care about me.

"When you're an artist, it's very easy to get yourself all mixed up because you are someone else besides being an artist. But it's dangerous when you start living the myth. Sometimes I get very freaky and I can't leave the house because I'm outrageously shy."

"Other people have jobs, but they are also someone else when they don't do that job.

"There's one part of me that says, 'Who the hell do you think you are, Michelle? You're lucky to be doing this at all.' And there's another part of me that says, 'Look, if these people have faith in me and if they think I'm ready to do this and my internal thing isn't happy with what I'm doing any more, then maybe I should follow and try it.'"

"It's important to share and look at yourself in the mirror and be true to yourself," Willson said.

Web: harp.rounder.com

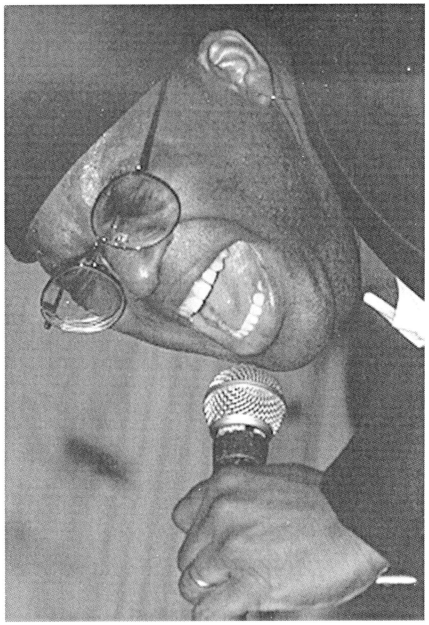

Barrence Whitfield

Boston's Blues

Barrence Whitfield: 'I was performing miracles everywhere'

"He's crazy."
"He's out of his mind doing that stuff."
"Do you believe what we just saw?"

Those were just typical reactions of people who have seen Barrence Whitfield in his Savages salad days when the talented vocalist turned the world upside down. On any night, he had people "smoking" as they left the Kenmore Square bars in Boston.

"People leaving the club would literally have smoke coming off their bodies because it would be so hot in there. People would say to each other, 'Man, you're smokin'. Look at you! You're smokin'.' And they'd tell others on the street to come inside. 'It's wild in there!' And they'd be exhausted at the end of the show," Whitfield said.

All of the wild histrionics had a purpose. Whitfield could read an audience's hot buttons and be in total command of himself, although sometimes it certainly did not appear that a sane person would do some of the things he did in the name of spontaneous showmanship.

"Throughout my career, I think it's all been spontaneous. If I saw the need to incite the crowd or get everybody excited, I'd do something to make that happen and not worry about the consequences -- even if I had to hang off a chandelier in a club or dive into a crowd of onlookers who were ready for something to happen. You know, you just do it. And that's what happened. And that was the creation of the Savage scene. People would go completely nuts."

Whitfield's road to center stage was built on the sweet soul and Motown sounds that came from Lloyd's Manor, a famous club that was two doors down the street from where Whitfield grew up in the Central Ward of Newark, N.J. "That was the area that bore the brunt of the 1967 riots," he said. "So I heard a lot of Motown, blues, Bobby Blue Bland, Little Junior Parker. An uncle was a promoter for all of the artists who played there like James Brown, Max Watts Revue, other Motown people. In fact, the first time I saw Bobby Blue Bland, I must have been about 10 or so, I saw a woman throw her bra up on stage. But my father covered my eyes, saying I wasn't ready to see this yet."

Radio station WNJR also played a lot of the black artists of the time, so Whitfield was surrounded by a lot of music. He said he and his stepbrother used to sing two-part harmony doo wop tunes.

271

Art Simas

In New Jersey, Whitfield hit it with a few rock-oriented bands that covered Led Zeppelin and Jimi Hendrix. But he was very far removed from the Barrence Whitfield who would bust onto the Boston scene in the 1980s.

He arrived in Beantown in late 1977 at Boston University, armed with a communications scholarship. "I got here just in nick of time for the Blizzard of '78," he said. "By the time I came here, I was pretty much out of the music end of it and more into the academics, until I took a job at Strawberries in Copley Square in 1981. There I met Carlos Santana, Grace Jones, John Belushi. That was my biggest influence as far as the music was concerned."

The academic life was short-lived at BU, and Whitfield eventually transferred to Emerson College and held down jobs in record stores. It was in these empty, spacious storerooms where the real Whitfield opened up. One day Des McDonald heard Whitfield singing in Nuggets, the discount record store in Kenmore Square.

Barrence said McDonald told him that Peter Greenberg, a guitar player with the Liars and DMZ, popular groups at the time, wanted to put together an R&B-type band on the side.

Curious, Whitfield went over and talked with Greenberg about this potential band. "He was telling me the type of music he wanted to do from Smiley Lewis to Jimmy Reed to all kinds of obscure rock and roll and R&B stuff. That was something I hadn't touched upon for a while.

"And so started the Savages in a little rehearsal room near Fenway Park. We stayed there for six months trying to get things down and by the fall we were ready," Whitfield said.

"The club scene was flourishing with The Rat, Jonathan Swifts, The Cantab, just to name a few, and so much happening. We were able to click into that scene. Once the word got out that Peter had a band with this singer -- me -- most of the clubs were shocked and dismayed at what they saw," Whitfield said.

"I always knew I could do it, it was just the fact of when I was going to do it. I think the time came was when I was working at the Harvard Coop. I was an in-store detective, I kept saying to myself, 'What am I doing? This isn't what I want to do.'"

Once he was determined to make music his life, there was no turning back. Looking at the opportunity to go with Greenberg, Whitfield said, "If I don't do it now, then I don't want to say to myself, What could have been? So I did it and look what happened almost 15 years later."

Boston's Blues

"And then things started to flourish. We were traveling up and down the East Coast down to DC and to New York. Word got out about this wild R&B crazy band that was slaying people, and the singer who was like Little Richard.

"Rounder Records signed us after an all-night crazy frat house party at Tufts University where there was beer up to your ankles," Whitfield said.

Recording followed and more and more gigs, and the reputation preceded the band wherever they played. Barrence Whitfield and the Savages then went international. Andy Kershaw, one of Britain's top DJs for the BBC was inoculated with Savages fever once he heard the group's calling card, "Bip, Bop, Bip."

As the story goes, Whitfield said, Kershaw, in London, heard the record from Dave Woodhead, who was the trumpet player with Billy Bragg. Once Kershaw got a little taste of what the band could do, he couldn't wait to see them live, so he booked a flight to Boston that Friday. "He was completely blown away," Whitfield said, "and he went back to England and he told everyone, 'I've seen Little Richard again and he is Barrence Whitfield.' He even filmed the band at Nightstage… and the legend lives on."

Posh gigs in London's finest upscale clubs with Robert Plant in the audience followed. Even Laval Wilson, the superintendent of schools in Boston, flew to England to see the band. "It was just amazing," Whitfield said. "We went on and played in France, Spain, Holland, just about every country over there. And the public treated us with a lot of respect. They know when they're seeing the real thing."

Whitfield was the main front man and vocalist for The Movers for about 18 months. He brought a lot of experience and professionalism to the band that had been in transition for a year after vocalist Danny Vitale left.

"The good thing about the Movers was the horn section and the way the whole band worked together," he said. "With that band, it was in the tradition of blues with a little swing and rock thrown in."

Whitfield left The Movers and went back to his Savage ways for about year (1998-99). Although he's not the ultimate savage of his younger days, Whitfield is happy where he is musically.

Whitfield said he is proud of his other musical accomplishments, especially in the field of country singing. He is a contributor to a Warner Brothers boxed set of black country music players called "From Where I Stand." Whitfield recorded a song called "Irma Jackson," written in 1966 by Merle Haggard about interracial love.

Art Simas

"In the early '90s, I was trying to do a country thing. I was doing research on blacks in country music and this (recording) came out of nowhere. From Al Green, Solomon Burke, Charley Pride, Deford Bailey, Ray Charles, for me it's a labor of love," to learn about these people, he said.

"So, I'm in their archives of Country Music Hall of Fame, and hopefully I can be the R&B and/or the Rock 'n' Roll Hall of Fame before it's all over," he said. "I've got some time left in me. Lots of time."

In 2000, Whitfield formed "Hillbilly Voodoo," an acoustic project that explores the roots of blues and country music with guitarist Michael Dinallo, formerly of the Radio Kings; Tim Taylor on harmonica; Steve Sadler on guitar, dobro and mandolin; and Paul Kochanski on bass.

Chapter 3:

Boston's blues DJs,
Mai Cramer and
Holly Harris

Teo Leyasmeyer and Mai Cramer

Mai Cramer: Boston's longtime voice of the blues

"Twenty years!!! My God!!!" exclaimed the undisputed queen of the blues on Boston radio when it finally sank in.

Generations have passed and Blues After Hours is still on the air.

Mai Cramer's show on WGBH 89.7 FM on Friday and Saturday evenings from 9 p.m. to 1 a.m. is a lesson in history and art -- history for its content of the indigenous American music, and art because of its presentation.

"One of the things that keeps me interested is evolving the art and taking the good things and trying to make them better," she said. "I get the pleasure of hanging things together for my show. Maybe it's because I'm doing it with other people's music, and the things that you do with it and how you construct it, how a set of music will flow and tell a story. It's those beautiful moments when you go from one song to the next and how it'll sometimes just hang there and flow. That's part of the art for me and in creating the mood with the music and communicating with the audience. It's really a performance, almost like a dance."

Mai says that although there's "a lot of me in my show," the DJ has to communicate with the audience. "You can't just be there for yourself."

Mai celebrated her 25th year in radio in 1999. She started at a small commercial station in Pittsfield, Mass., in 1975. After she finished getting a master's degree in film in England, she settled in the Berkshires and got to know some people who worked at WGRG. "They had acquired an FM license and they decided they wanted to have these specialty shows one night a week -- and on Monday they wanted to have a blues show," Mai said.

Since Mai had a collection of blues records that was unsurpassed, many gleaned from Times Square Records in the New York subway station, "My buddy at the station asked me to do a one-hour blues show. 'We'll call it the Blues Hour,' he said.

"Well, the first week my buddy did the engineering, but the second week, he said, 'OK, you do it.'

"The thing that was so interesting was that I had no idea that I'd be any good at it or that I had a nice voice or any of the things that developed over the years. I found that I did have a pretty good voice and the ability to put together a show," Mai said.

WGRG was eventually sold, most of her friends got fired and the new owners came in, changed formats and offered salaries barely above minimum wage, she said. After struggling for some months, she knew it was time to go -- to Boston.

"When I first came to Boston and got my first show 20 years ago the audience turned me on to stuff I didn't know. I was educated by them," she said.

Mai grew up in New York City and her mother was a professional classical pianist. But it was a friend in her honors high school math class that really turned her on to music, and the two of them would go to concerts at the Apollo Theater.

After that, there was no turning back.

"I'd listen to R&B on radio all the time and I loved it. I just went wild." During this initiation to the blues Mai began to acquire her record collection that now rivals the Library of Congress.

Mai is also an oils painter. But she admits that her drive for perfection was getting the best of her when she was trying to make it as a serious artist. "It was much more of a problem for me about being perfect. I was never able to make a living through painting. I don't know if it was partly because of luck or whatever, or partly because of this attachment to making it be perfect, which doesn't lead to happiness."

Yet realizing and accepting that imperfect quality "was one of the best revelations of my life because the joy is in the journey, in the discovery, of finding the things that work well and exploring them," she said.

Asked why Boston has such strong traditions for the blues, Mai said it's partly due to the popularity of Blues After Hours. She said there were some pretty lean times in the 1980s, especially during the recession years. Bars and live music venues were closing but the people still listened to the show. "It seems it's always been there. People will tune in during good times and bad times."

Holly Harris

Art Simas
Holly Harris: Super supporter of local musicians

Holly Harris, voice of WBOS 92.9 FM Blues on Sunday from 9 p.m. to midnight, was born into music and practically grew up on stage. She's been at WBOS for eight years now and has nurtured the careers of many local musicians.

"I got into this because I'm from a musical family. For example, my grandfather played trumpet and I had an uncle who played with Glenn Miller. Another relative was a trumpet player in New York. In all, I think there are about 10 musicians.

"My father went to Julliard and earned a doctorate in music education from Columbia University. He is a professional musician today. He still plays in some big bands and concert bands in New York. His main instrument is trumpet.

"My mom passed away a few years ago. She was an entrepreneur and founder of an Arts Council and was a tour director. My father retired from his job as chairman of a music department for a college in upstate New York. My mother and father were also music drama editors. So I come from a serious musical background.

"As a little girl my mother would bring me to many different musical events. I would be the little girl always going up on stage bringing flowers to the performers. So I was always involved.

"I tried a variety of instruments but I always knew that, to me, the rhythm and the spoken word held a message -- and that's where I was going to go. I was the voice at my high school during homeroom sessions. I won an essay contest and also won a couple of dance contests on TV.

"That was fun but I was never theatrical or a singer, though in my next life I'll come back as a background vocalist," she said. "I was more into dance and movement. I lived in Paris my freshman year. I graduated from Ithaca College as a literature major. All my undergraduate friends were radio/TV majors.

"In fact, one of my best friends now is a CEO and another one is a vice president of TNT. So they're doing all right.

"I started to listening to WMFO in the 1980s," Holly continued. "It had a wonderful blues program on Sunday morning with Nate Thayer."

Boston's Blues

Holly said she went to WMFO on Sundays to hang out and learn the ropes of radio. "I filled in one day when he (Thayer) left and was there for 10 years.

"I met Mai Cramer (Blues After Hours, 9 p.m. to 1 a.m. on WGBH-FM 89.7) in 1982, on jury duty in Boston. Then, my boyfriend at the time bought a house next door to Mai, and I knew we were destined to be friends; and we are best friends now. She's my daughter's (Brianna) godmother.

"I started filling in for Mai, and I've done that since 1984. I've also done some voice work, yoga and a lot of African dance, yeah, a lot of dancing. And traveling, all around the world every chance I got, from the time I was 16 to the time I was 30; from the minute school got out to the night before school started I'd travel everywhere!

"Yeah, it was really a good time to do it 'cause my life was different. And then CGY called and they were looking for someone to do a Sunday night rockin' blues show. I think it might have been '89 when I went to WCGY, which is now called the Eagle, out of Lawrence, Mass. I stood up the whole time I did the show. And it was a lot of fun.

"I did that for about a year and a half and then BOS called me and asked if I wanted to take over the existing blues show from Bill Smith and David O'Leary. They'd been on for a year and a half or two years. I started with BOS in '93.

"I'm really happy the name is already there -- BOS as in 'Blues On Sunday.' It goes with the name. And Bill and David were both very helpful to me.

"On the show itself I keep somewhat of a contemporary feel, but I'm very eclectic. I think radio can do that to you. My basic framework is I do a 10 o'clock new CD spotlight, and I like to use different (recording) labels each week. At 10:30, I do a local talent spotlight because I really think it's important to spotlight the local people, we have an incredible wealth of blues talent out there. I also always do blues birthday celebrations. I spotlight two or three blues artists' birthdays from that week.

"Sometimes, maybe once a month, I'll do an interview, such as Al Kooper or Bo Diddley, and I'll spotlight that person by playing some songs of theirs. I take a lot of requests and I'll try to personalize it for someone. If someone has a special gig, I will do my best to mention it, especially benefits.

"On Sunday night a lot of people are gearing down, but I have to gear up. I don't want to make it too upbeat but I also don't want to make it a drag so everyone goes to sleep. So I try and start things off with happy blues, party blues -- all different types of blues. I love to feature different instruments. And I often close out with soul blues.

"I had one caller who said he found a theme that ran through all my shows. He said, 'I'm going to call you Holly B. Harris because every song has wonderful bass lines.'

"Holly Bass Harris, Holly B. Harris. It's interesting because the one instrument I do play besides percussion is the bass. So I guess subconsciously I zero in on that groove, that bottom."

Holly has been the master of ceremonies for dozens of local blues festivals, including the City of Presidents Festival in Quincy, Mass., Newport, the Winter Island festival in Salem, Mass., and many others. Holly also served as a judge at many of the annual Harpers Ferry Battle of the Bands competitions in Allston, Mass.

In Holly's other life, she is a school adjustment counselor in a city school system. She says her daytime job is similar to her weekly DJ role.

"It's all about getting the message out, communicating and hooking up with people and furthering the good stuff, listening and instilling hope," she said.

"I love the music, I love the words and I love the sound of it and I just want other people to have access to it. We don't all get paid for things we can create but on the other hand, it does bring people together.

"Musicians have a hard life, but they love it. You just do it because you love it. The road life is the hard part.

"I went on the road a couple of times as a 'girlfriend.' I dated the bass player in Lou Reed's band and one time we went to Europe. I was very young. We were being driven around in a limo, and stayed in very fancy places. It was unreal. I saw the life, and it was exciting, but I knew that it wasn't what I wanted to do all the time. I needed more stability. I enjoy fun, but I also have a more serious side. I like home base.

"And I think the blues has a serious side, too. You get that from life's experiences. Life hasn't always been super easy, but I've been very fortunate. I've had a very, very, very good life. But, I think certain people feel the blues and

Boston's Blues

certain people don't. The more people I can expose blues to, or we can all expose blues to, there's likely to be someone in that group that's going to 'feeeeel' it.

"Now I know why I was born," Holly said. "I'm very happy when I'm in the blues world."

"Truly, there's plenty of room for everyone -- for musicians, for blues radio DJs, for good writers -- anyone who's interested in the blues."

Chapter 4:

a 10-year history of the Boston Blues Society

Art Simas

It was always the music. Then, and now, it is what binds us all in the blues community.

In 1988, there was a "vibrant" blues scene in Boston, according to one of the founders of the Boston Blues Society. Yet it was "pretty much scattered, and I guess our intention was to try and help focus it and create a stronger foundation," Karen Leipziger said.

Leipziger, now a national publicist with her own business, KL Productions of Nashville, was working for Newton-based Concerted Efforts, a booking agency for blues artists such as Luther "Guitar Jr." Johnson, Matt "Guitar" Murphy, Clarence "Gatemouth" Brown and Robert "Jr." Lockwood.

She was in charge of booking Nightstage in Cambridge, arguably one of the best venues to hear live music in the 1980s and early '90s. Since she was doing the publicity for the shows, Leipziger met many media people. One of those people was Holly Harris, host of Blues on Sunday on WBOS 92.9 from 9 p.m. to midnight.

Leipziger said, "Holly and I became friends. She was doing radio on WMFO (91.5 FM) and with me in the booking agency, I used to call her a lot. So it was the music that introduced us to each other. I can't really remember the exact thing that triggered it, but we said, 'Let's start a Blues Society' to support this pretty vibrant blues scene."

Clubs included Harpers Ferry in Allston, Johnny D's in Somerville, Ed Burke's and the Tam in Boston, The Yardrock in Quincy, Sit 'n Bull in Maynard, the 1369 in Cambridge and several others.

Harris had come to the same conclusion.

"There was a need for some sort of grouping of all the blues under an umbrella in the Boston area. And my friends, my compadres at the time, Karen, Rick Russell and Watermelon Slim (Bill Homans)... we got together a few times and we started to talk about that and then we decided to meet monthly," Harris said. "We set up a post office box and gave each other little assignments to do and we realized what an undertaking this was going to be. And we also decided that we really needed a newsletter. I said, simple task. I can write.

"Well, what happened was, Watermelon Slim left after a couple of meetings; Rick was busy playing and Karen eventually moved to Nashville and when I went to Memphis -- October 1988 -- sitting across from me in a club was Mark

Boston's Blues

Ryder and we started talking about blues and Boston. Mark had the energy and the time at that point to really help a lot. He was the major force in putting this together.

"Then we spoke to Charlie Abel who owned Harpers Ferry, and he was really interested in helping, so he wanted to come on board. A lot of people might say that there was a vested interest there with Charlie owning the club but he was genuinely interested in the music. So the Society just grew and grew. And we needed more people over time.

"We incorporated in December 1988, a couple of months after Mark and Charlie came on board. There was no way I could have done all this by myself. It was a lot of work. So that's how the baby was born," Harris said.

"It was really exciting, but I could envision a day when other people would come in with renewed energy and have new ideas. So other people came and went and we went through a lot of different stages. Bob Cohen; Donna Sweeney, a marvelous blues woman who moved between the Boston area and Virginia did a lot of writing; Frank-John Hadley and Bob Nelson were on board... and the quality went up. Ann Newman; Steve Bouchard, Flo Murdock from Johnny D's were a big help; writer and reviewer Deborah Nigro from the Cape; and photographer Tom Hazeltine was there right from the beginning," Harris said. "He used to ask me, 'Do you think you can get me backstage at the Chicago Blues Festival'? Now it's me asking him the same question."

Harris recalled, "We had some picnics and fund-raisers at Harpers a couple of years in a row and Ronnie Earl would play, Kat and the Hat (now the Woodburn-Arena Band), Paul Rishell and Annie Raines, so we had a lot of support.

"I was doing a lot of writing at the time (I was a literature major in college and then a psychology major in graduate school), but I had writer's block, so I figured this was a good way to get it out of me and extricate myself from that. So I did quite a few articles, such as "Blues in the 90s," an article on Bobby Blue Bland, a letter to the editor to the Boston Globe in response to an unfair column written about Barbeque Bob and the Rhythm Aces, winner of the Battle of the Blues Bands in 1992... and for years I did all the calendars and the jams.

"Mostly, I really wanted to be a voice for the community. That was a strong point for me. I'm good at coordinating things and getting the message out," she said. Holly's "voice" and her commitment to the music have graced many famous blues and jazz festivals. She has been master of ceremonies at the Newport Jazz Festival, The Boston Globe Jazz Festival, the City of Presidents Festival in

Quincy, the Winter Island Blues Festival in Salem, Blues 2000 and Beyond in New York, and, for 11 straight years, the Harpers' Battle of the Blues Bands, and many more.

"I really love the music. I find real pleasure in playing music and sharing it with others. I seem to be good at connecting people and having information," she said.

The ultimate musical honor came in 1995. Holly and Mai Cramer (host of Blues After Hours on WGBH 89.7 on Fridays and Saturdays, from 9 p.m. to i a.m.,) were given W.C. Handy Awards for Keeping the Blues Alive for both commercial radio and public broadcasting, respectively, at the gala ceremony in Memphis.

"I was in a couple of bands, but I knew that wasn't the life for me. I played a little bass (Music Master Fender bass) and played percussion in a band where we used to play on the Boston Common, and I was in the Hot Cottage Band and the Nightwalkers, which is part of Blue Heaven now, and was a vocalist in that band until I looked to the left of me and saw Gail Nixie, who could really sing, and I said, 'Ooooohhhh, this isn't for me.'"

In interviewing someone over the air, Holly usually asks the artist about his or her current musical situation; their influences; and the combination of experiences that led them to play blues.

"I also want to know if they are at peace with themselves." she said. "Do they like what they're doing? What do they see for themselves in the future, for the world? How did they start out? Who do they like to be with when touring? Is touring grueling? Is it harder for males or females?

"You've got to remember, that these people have gifts. Something happens to them when they get up on that stage. But still they're just people.

"I genuinely go from the heart. It's not really an interview but more like a conversation. For me that's my strong point. I really love people and love talking to people and I find it very interesting," Holly said.

For Holly, her greatest influence was hearing B.B. King and finally meeting him. But before that experience, it was her family where she drew her greatest support. Holly was born in Kalamazoo, Mich., and grew up in upstate New York. And one can truthfully say that music is in her. Her father is a professional musician who holds a Ph.D. in music from Columbia University and who, at 80, still plays in big bands; her mother was a former music and drama editor and arts council director; a great uncle played sax in the Glenn Miller Orchestra and her grandfather was Al Jolson's main man on trumpet.

She said that the first time she heard B.B. King, "it hit me like lightning. It was the music I had been waiting to hear."

Holly started listening to WMFO in Medford, in the early '80s because, she said, it had a wonderful blues program on Sunday morning. In 1982, she was behind the glass wall and producing the show, The Morning After Blues, which turned into a 10-year gig. "And it was wonderful. I loved WMFO. I really grew there and got all my radio experience."

In 1984, she met Mai Cramer on jury duty. Since that chance meeting in a courthouse, Holly and Mai have become best friends. They are even collaborating on a comic strip called "The Blues Girls," a story about "20-year blues women and their life and my little daughter, Brianna. We're working on it, it's still in progress," she said.

In 1991, Holly moved over to WCGY 93.7 in Lawrence and hosted the 10 p.m. to midnight Rockin' Blues show on Sundays. "I did that for about a year and a half and then BOS called me and asked if I wanted to take over the existing blues show on Sundays.

The other 1988 founding member of the BBS, Rick Russell, was busy hosting jams at Harpers Ferry and trying to make a new career playing blues instead of rock. A few years earlier, Russell had suffered a knee injury while he was working as an air conditioning technician in a local hospital.

"This was like God giving me the break. It was... here's the money (from workers' compensation), here's the time, here's the ball, run with it. So I got myself together, started getting back to it, and doing the jams that were around here, like at the 1369 started going there a lot.

Russell was able to link up with the first version of Boston Baked Blues, which evolved into another phase and became a very successful band in the late '80s and early '90s.

Russell said, "I had to let that go in 1990 and I decided that the next band was going to have my own name on it. So that's what I did from 1990 to the present. Once I made my commitment in 1986 I never looked back."

The Harpers connection between Leipziger and Russell is very important because a blues legacy was born from that association.

Russell said when Harpers first opened in the early 80s, it wanted to go with a country and western theme. Then in the mid-80s, they made a move toward blues and R&B. "There was a fellow named Mickey O'Halloran (one of the founders of the Boston Museum of Rock 'n' Roll on the Internet as www.dirtywater.com), a booking agent and entrepreneur and he was involved with Charlie Abel, owner of Harpers.

(O'Halloran died March 28, 2001 after a two-year battle with cancer.)

"When O'Halloran saw Boston Baked Blues consistently sell out shows at O'Brien's Pub, at the lower end of Harvard Avenue and Cambridge Street, about a half-mile from Harpers, he asked the band if they wanted to start a blues jam on Wednesday nights at Harpers. So the band went ahead and did that successfully for four or five years," Russell said.

When the House of Blues opened in 1992, Russell was ready to leave the Harpers blues jam scene. "It wasn't as much the fact that House of Blues came in but y'know, that's a high visibility place and you want to try and do what's right for yourself, too. I was actually hired as a consultant with George 'Leroy' Lewis when the House of Blues first came in here to help with their booking policy and help them get set up before Teo Leyasmeyer came in as music coordinator.

"George and I were involved from the beginning, and it's no secret that the folks from the House of Blues one of the first places they came to was my Wednesday night at Harpers Ferry. So, it's not like they were raiding or anything like that but y'know hey, that's sometimes how business is, you've got to try to do what's best for yourself.

"So when they approached me to come and bring things over there, things at Harpers weren't very good. We were sort of beating on a dead dog a little bit. So I said to Charlie, 'Hey, it's been good together but I feel bad about taking your money and not giving you a good night here because it hasn't been good. The opportunity's here for me to move.' So that was actually my band that opened the House of Blues to the public on Thanksgiving evening in 1992, after the week of parties," he said.

Since Leipziger was instrumental in bringing in national acts to Harpers through Concerted Efforts, she knew Russell, and he knew Leipziger's husband, Dennis Taylor, a very good sax player who toured regularly with Buckwheat Zydeco and

Boston's Blues

Duke Robillard. "I worked with Charlie (Abel) and I helped him set up his first blues festival," she said.

The monthlong festival in February remains a very successful feature at Harpers.

Russell said Karen Leipziger and Holly Harris knew that an early version of Boston Blues Society was formed in the 1970s, which petered out because of lack of organization. "But societies back then weren't nearly as organized as they are now," he said. "So before any of the folks up here went down to the International Blues Talent Competition in Memphis, Boston Baked Blues went there and I got to look around at what was going on nationally and I said to myself that 'we've (as a new society) got to get ourselves together.'

"So Holly and Karen and I, basically a shoestring budget, just decided to try to give it a shot and get it going. We got it up off its knees, and as time went by other folks got involved, and it is as you have it today," Russell said.

"Actually... we didn't want to have to have a president or a vice president or anything quite so delineated," he said. "It was more like, let's just work together for the music and not worry about the president and vice president business," Russell said.

After returning from the International Blues Talent Competition in October 1988, Russell said Mark Ryder (who later became BBS president for nearly eight years) wanted to get involved, as did Charlie Abel. "And then Karen and Dennis moved to Nashville in 1989, so it was kind of like the four of us for a while: Holly and myself, Mark Ryder and Charlie.

"And then my career got busier so I had to pull back and pull out of it a little bit. But there were a lot of nights of licking stamps, believe me," he said.

In 1992, Russell was one of the first local blues acts to cut an independent CD. "The CD ('Big Bad and Blue') came about because there were some people I wanted to work with in different situations and another friend of mine and I had worked on a bunch of original songs. We had a nice mix of covers and originals and then we just got the studio time. I had a small cassette that I had put out. You always got to have something to give people or show people when you're trying to promote yourself, get yourself out there.

"So we lined up the people that we wanted to work with and grabbed the bull by the horns and had a lot of fun with it... trying not to get too over-produced, trying to get that good old-time feeling with it. The big thing about that was the price. At first it was real expensive to put out a CD but now the cost of putting one out had dropped so significantly. I mean pretty soon you'll be able to get 1,000 CDs for $1,000," he said.

Looking back on 1988, Leipziger said there were a lot of great blues musicians here, including a lot of national acts, but there was nothing to connect everything. "We wanted to make people aware of the blues radio shows, and just to sort of become a central clearinghouse to help people together and make people aware of what everybody was doing," she said.

Chapter 5:

photographers of the blues

Hard-working blues photographers: Phil Monica, Jim Saley, J Place and Tom Hazeltine

"How was the show?" is most likely the first question you hear the day after a concert.

You can try to describe what you saw in words. But do your descriptions really capture the essence of the music?

Do you adequately describe the intensity of the guitarist's facial expressions when he or she hit and held that perfect note?

That's tough to do. But a photographer looks to capture that moment without juggling 1,000 words. As photographer **Phil Monica** said, "I'm on the prowl and I'm a hunter -- out to capture the energy."

Monica said he got his first camera when he was 8 years old.

He took a couple of courses in high school and pursued a science education, earning degrees in molecular science and biochemistry.

He became a professional photographer after pursuing a science career. Because of his years of scientific observation, Monica said, he learned to look for a concept, a story, a feeling, an idea.

"In anything everybody does, there's a story and I'm trying to tell it. I'm also looking for an emotional reaction... to see what this person is experiencing as they are performing. I try to get each member of a band as an individual and how they react to the music, rather than how they react to each other," he said.

Concentration is key to the profession, so, "When you're working like that you really don't get a chance to appreciate the performance," Monica said.

Although Monica shoots many live performers, he also does portrait, commercial and scientific/medical photography. But his specialty is in harnessing a live shot of a performer that is done in "available light" from the stage. The effect is dramatic, with images that focus on the facial expressions of the artist blended into waning shadows.

Boston's Blues

"While I was in school I did take some courses that dealt with stage craft and stage lighting. I like theatrical things, and I tend to look for lighting that is theatrical instead of a flat-out portrait effect. I really don't like flash, I think it bothers the performers and the audience too, I think the audience wants to see the performer's face as much as I do."

Some of his favorite subjects: Susan Tedeschi, Michelle Willson, Toni Lynn Washington, Steve Prisby ("does interesting things with the piano"), James Montgomery ("has photogenic sweat glands"); drummers (Tom Majors of Entrain, Tom Hambridge and Buddy Miles), and many of the side players.

****

Jim Saley got started in photography in high school, journeying into Harvard Square to shoot architecture. About 15 years ago, Saley went to the Newport Jazz Festival and that's where he really started to take the art seriously. He's been photographing artists -- mainly blues artists -- ever since including a cover shot of Ronnie Earl for the October 1997 issue of "Blues Revue" magazine.

Saley says he wants to capture the raw emotion of the performers. "Some are more subdued, yet some, like Luther Allison, wear their soul on their sleeve. I'm looking for what they're trying to bring out in their songs. You can tell when they're really into it -- and that's what I'm looking for."

He swears loyalty to his Nikon lenses. "The Nikon body, well that's a different story," he says. But with the lenses, he says he can draw out a more dramatic effect in natural light.

****

J. Place, who heads a band under his name, also didn't start out in a straight line into the photographic world.

"I was studying at Carleton College in Minnesota where I designed my own major -- film arts and English -- and part of the film arts curriculum was photography. However, I never got around to taking the courses and I ended up graduating without a diploma.

"Then I spent about five years in Denmark and when I came back in 1988, one of my priorities was to get my diploma. So I took a continuing education course in photography at the Museum of Fine Arts in Boston, where I got college credit. And I totally fell in love with the whole process, especially black and white photography. It seemed like a great medium. So in addition to my music I discovered I was quite visual," Place said.

"Primarily I shot live performances but also did dance and sports. A lot of what I'm about is capturing that quintessential moment when Albert Collins squeezes out a heavy note on the guitar," he said.

"I think my being a performer and knowing the genre helps a lot in terms of anticipation. I have a good educated guess on where things are going. Visually I like there to be some movement, sort of a lyrical sense of a photo. A lot of the stuff that I showcase tends to go for the more intense kind of moment instead of something that might be staid.

"It was my passion for my music and I think that passion shows up in my photography," Place said.

Place has worked for a number of publications, as have all of the photographers here, and showcased his work at two Blues Visions Galleries (Rockland, Mass., and at Harvard University), along with Jim Saley and Tom Hazeltine and Peter Rea. He also does a lot of promotional and cover CD work for other performers, such as the CD cover for Vykki Vox's "Woman's Touch."

"It's a very technical medium, but I'm not a very technical person. I just go for it, do it my way and shoot from the hip," Place said.

****

Tom Hazeltine began taking pictures in and around the Boston blues scene in 1978, after seeing Buddy Guy and Junior Wells at the Speakeasy.

"My father gave me a 35mm that he had used, and I began to tie the music and the photography together. Around 1985 or so, after realizing that I had taken a lot of different images over the years, I pored over them. I enlarged them and then set out to have them autographed by the artist. But I soon learned the image needed to be striking in order to capture the attention of the artist, as well I wanted to capture them in the right light," he said.

Hazeltine joined the Boston Blues Society in its first year in 1988 and attended various festivals across the country, most notably the Chicago Blues Festival, and has over 150 autographed pictures of blues performers.

Boston's Blues

"I grew up as a very shy person and asking the people who I considered the biggest stars in the blues to autograph pictures I took was somewhat difficult. However, most were very accommodating, especially Albert Collins, Little Milton Campbell and Charlie Musselwhite, who took time to talk to me about the photos and the show where they were taken.

"In 1991 I left for a tour of the country for six months. While in California, I went to a show in Arcata, featuring Albert Collins. I got there early enough to get a front row seat. Armed with my travel camera, I took quite a number of shots up close, as the stage was low and the lighting was bright. I developed them a short while later and was very pleased with the results. Unfortunately, I mailed the pictures back home because two months later, I saw Collins playing a one-armed bandit in Las Vegas. I spoke to him, telling him of the show and of the photos I took. He was friendly beyond my wildest dreams and told me to be certain I brought him a copy the next time he was in Boston.

"In May 1992, he played at Nightstage in Cambridge on a double bill with Lonnie Mack. Between sets, he remembered me and told everyone that I was a fan who traveled all over to see the blues. I'll never forget him holding up the picture and admiring it, telling me it was one of the best he's ever seen of himself. I doubt he really believed that, yet in that moment of time, I felt like I had won the lottery because a picture I took made Albert Collins happy," Hazeltine said. "Collins died later that year, but his kindness lives in me today."

So don't ask a photographer, "How was the show?" They won't be able to answer because they're working just as hard as the performer (without the photogenic sweat glands) to get that perfect shot that captures the night.

Art Simas

Chapter 6:

a blues short story:
A Night at the Highland Tap

A night at the Highland Tap

By Bob Margolin

Jimmy heard his apartment door open and sat straight up in bed. He realized he'd overslept and might be late for his gig. It had gotten dark while he had napped after getting home at 4:30 from his "day job" at the parking lot in South Boston. His wife walked in from her own job at the supermarket. They would have had a few minutes to catch up with each other, but now Jimmy had to get out the door as quickly as he could.

He found his band uniform in a pile on the chair, where he had thrown it at 3 a.m., when he got home from last night's gig. The polyester wouldn't wrinkle, but it sure did smell like Jimmy's sweat and beer and cigarettes. It had suffered three hot nights in bars since he had a chance to wash it.

Janie, his wife and sweetheart since junior high, was disappointed that they wouldn't at least get a chance to talk before he left. Her night would be long and lonely 'til Jimmy returned, and if she was up and he wasn't too tired, they might make love. That had been more frequent and exciting when they had been teen-agers and had to do it parking in Jimmy's dad's car. They were both only 22 now, but were their best years together behind them already?

Jimmy's B.S. degree in communications was unused as he parked cars during the day and played blues in bars at night. Janie watched Jimmy put on the uniform, so different from the jeans, tee-shirt and boots he had worn in his hippie blues-rock bands when he was in college, and it was a good show for her because Jimmy didn't wear underwear.

Still, once he got the uniform on, her arousal dissipated because he looked like a clown: the right sides of each pant leg were purple and the left sides were black. The purple shirt had puffed sleeves and eight-inch points on the collar. It was 1971, and that's how pimps and bands dressed in Roxbury, Mass., where Jimmy was going to play.

Jimmy apologized, grabbed his guitar, and ran down to his car, leaving Janie staring at the closed door, sighing. He drove to Cambridge to pick up Mark, the band's harp player. He rang the doorbell until Mark heard it between songs on the Sonny Boy Williamson LP he was listening to at high volume, blowing along with Sonny Boy. Mark was capturing Sonny Boy's percussive acoustic attack, phrasing, and lyrical expression, on the way to developing his own personal voice on the instrument. He had lost track of the time and didn't even realize that

Boston's Blues

Jimmy was late picking him up. Jimmy knew he'd be hearing a lot of Sonny Boy coming out of Mark's '59 Fender Bassman amp on the bandstand that night.

Jimmy and Mark crossed back into Boston over the Mass. Ave. bridge and continued a few more miles to Dudley Station in Roxbury. They parked behind The Highland Tap, a long, narrow nightclub near the elevated train station. They walked in the side door, near the stage, only 15 minutes before the band was supposed to hit.

The club hadn't filled up yet, and Luther "Snake" Johnson, the bandleader, had the other band members sitting and standing around him near the bar. He was telling them, "Rat'cheer gon' be da gig fo' three mo' weeks. We play Tuesday to Sunday, six 40-minute set a night wit' 20-minute breaks. Angelo d'Bartenda turn off da jukebox, we hit. Band don't hit, I be's fine' and you be's fire'. You got to wear yo' uny-fo'm. You play two insta-mentals and call me up. We through here, we do the same thang at Parker Street Lounge in Mission Hill, then Benn's Lounge in Field's Corner, Dorchester. Boys, we got reg'lar work. I pays you $80 a week. Oh, yeah -- there a three-set matinee Sunday afta-noons."

What Jimmy heard loudest was the "$80 a week." He would quit his job at the parking lot tomorrow. He was a full-time professional bluesman, starting tonight. The 39 sets a week would be tough, and his heavy Gibson Les Paul guitar was already making his left shoulder lower than his right, but he'd get his guitar chops together and learn Chicago blues from Luther.

Luther, who was about 40, had left Muddy Waters' band and moved to Boston, hiring local blues players for his band. Though many area clubs featured blues, from neighborhood taverns to college bars to jazz nightclubs, Luther was playing exclusively in a separate scene, in black neighborhoods for black clientele. Every night, though, musicians of all colors came to watch, sit in, and sometimes end up replacing a band member.

Time to hit. Jimmy picked "Hideaway" and Mark blew "Juke." Then, they started "Chicken Shack," broke it down in volume, and introduced Luther. Luther drained his Galliano and milk and picked up the orange Stratocaster that Mike the drummer had bought for him (but Luther hadn't yet paid him back).

Luther played a raw Chicago slow blues intro and went right into Muddy's "Long Distance Call." As soon as he sang the first line in his deep, lonesome voice -- "You said you LOVE me BAY-bee..." -- most of the women in the bar hollered.

Luther sang the first two verses and then gave everyone in the band (except for the drummer and bass player) two choruses of solos each. He had learned this format in Muddy's band and his own band was picking it up, like a minor-league Muddy Waters band. Like Muddy, Luther preached at the end of the song but before he delivered the last line, he ran out the side door and down the length of the building to the front door. Entering, he sang the last line, surprising his band and the mystified audience and driving them crazy.

On the third set, some neighborhood musicians sat in and Luther gave them the stage and his band while he went to the bar to drink and hit on women. A 30-ish very dark-skinned man named Sonny, wearing Levi jeans and jacket in contrast to the polyester all over the club, sang "Stand By Me" and the recently-departed Little Junior Parker's "Next Time You See Me."

Sonny was a brick mason by day and a Soul Man at night.

A sexy woman named Leola, wearing an overflowing halter top, a huge Afro and hot pants, breasted her way onstage and called off Aretha's "Dr. Feelgood." The band knew the modified blues changes of the song because six out of seven women sit-in singers had a go with Dr. F. Though she could have the crowd by her looks alone, Leola sang pretty well too. The band's eyes caressed her every movement as they backed her up. She enjoyed knowing that each was imagining being with her.

She had actually been watching Jimmy all night, and she gave him a guitar solo and answered his licks moaning "Feels GOOOD!" while she rubbed up against him as he played. Jimmy tried to be cool, but she felt both soft and firm, and smelled both sweet and funky, and seemed to be laying her sex on him. He sure wasn't thinking about Janie at home. Still, he was just worldly enough to know that if he tried to pursue the attraction off the bandstand, he'd likely be cut or shot by a husband or boyfriend or both. He might already be in trouble anyway.

On the last set, harmonica star James Cotton stormed into the club after playing a concert at Harvard, took the harp right out of Mark's hands and played a sped-up version of Muddy's "Blow Wind Blow" and his own high-energy instrumental, "The Creeper."

Jimmy knew the guitar parts to the songs from studying Cotton's guitar player, Matt "Guitar" Murphy (and before him, Luther Tucker) on the many occasions that he and Janie had gone to Cotton's shows as fans. He played the songs right, and Cotton turned to him and beamed. After the set, Cotton took Jimmy's phone number and said, "I'm always glad to meet a good git-tar player -- you never

Boston's Blues

know!" Jimmy avoided Leola, though a lower part of him didn't want to, and he drove Mark home, but all he could think of was that someday he might play in a major-league blues band with someone like Cotton.

When he got home, Janie was in bed, but not asleep. Jimmy stripped off the stinky clown uniform, which now had a subtle floral after-note of Leola's perfume, and threw it on the chair again. He showered quickly and crawled in with his wife, and excitedly told her what had happened with Cotton. After a long silence, Janie said what both of them realized: "You'd go on the road, and be away from home a lot..."

They lay apart together, wordless, until they fell asleep.

Art Simas

Chapter 7:

blues radio in New England

Connecticut

WPKN 89.5 FM, Bridgeport (203) 331-9756
Web site: www.wpkn.org/wpkn/
Antique Blues, Bill Nolan, Sunday 6-10 pm
In the Evening, Bob Shapiro, Thursday, 6:35 -10 pm and Amir Rashidd,
Wednesday
10 pm - 2 am.

WCCC 106.9 FM /1290 AM, Hartford (860) 525-WCCC (studio), 860-244-9677
Ext. 161 (voice).
Sunday Night Blues with Beef Stew 6 pm - midnight.

WFCS 107.7 FM, New Britain (860) 832-1883
Wednesday 10 am–noon Spyderman Blues Show
Thursday 10 am–noon RoadHog's Travelin' with the Blues with Domenic
Forcella

WHUS 91.7 FM, Storrs (203) 486-4007
Web site: http://w3.nai.net/~davecarp
Bluesline with Ramblin' Bert Rand, Saturday, 7-9 pm
The Blues Bus with Dave Carpenter, Saturday, 9 pm-midnight.

WWUH 91.3 FM, West Hartford (860) 768-4703
Contact: Peter Rost
e-mail: wwuh@uhavax.hartford.edu

WNHU 88.7 FM, West Haven (203) 934-9296
Blues Heaven with Doreen Richardson, Monday 8-11 pm

WECS 90.1 FM, Willimantic (860)465-5074
Tom Farrell Tuesday 8 - 11 pm and Wednesday 12-2 pm

Maine

WFNX 92.1 FM, Portland, Maine/Portsmouth, NH
"Backstage with the Blues" with James Montgomery, Sunday 1 pm

WERU 89.9 FM, East Orland (207)288-4166
Blues the Healer, Paula Greatorex, Sunday 1-3 pm

Boston's Blues

Mojo Boogie, Maureen Farr, Monday 8-10 pm
Blues Hangout, Royce Dixon, Thursday 10pm-1am
Extra Large Soul, Alan Sprague, Thurday 2-4pm

Maine Public Radio, (207) 874-6570
Blues Before Sunrise, Bob Caswell, Tuesday 10-11 pm

WMHB 90.5 FM, Waterville (207) 872-8037)
Fillet of Soul, Tom Gerenger, Sunday 10-midnight
Blues Off The Wall, D W Gill Thursday 3-6 pm

WXGL 95.5 FM, Bluezology, Friday, 6-9 pm with Rick Riley

WMPG 90.9-FM/ 104.1-AM, Portland (207) 780-4598
Evenin' Sun, Monday through Saturday 5-7 pm
Monday: Ed Murphy, Roots Blues
Tuesday: Blues Dr. "Bon Ton Roulet Edition"
Wednesday: Myron with "Finger Lickin' Good" Blues
Thursday: Ruby with Ladies Sing the Blues/Gonna Have Some Fun Tonight
Friday: Dan & Dee
Saturday: Liquid Al/Billy Boy Blue

Also on Monday, 7 - 9 a.m., "This Better Be Good" with Mike Cutting
Tuesday, 6:30 - 9 a.m., "Groove Yard Shift with Brother John
Saturday 6:30 - 9 a.m., "Rub Board Review" with Brian Rollins
Saturday 7 - 9 p.m., Soul Avenue
Monday through Thursday, 8:30- 10 pm, Down East Beat

WMDI 107.7 FM, Bar Harbor (207) 288-4166

WRBC 91.5 FM, Bates College, Lewiston (207) 777-7532

WMHB 90.5 FM, Colby College, Waterville (207) 872-8037

Massachusetts

WRSI 95.3 FM, Northampton and 100.7 FM, Wilmington, Vt. (simultaneously broadcast)
Diana Shonk with The Roadhouse, Saturday 6-9 pm

WFCR 88.5 FM, Amherst (413) 545-0100
Tom Reney e-mail: treney@admin.umass.edu

Art Simas

Wednesday 6:30-9 pm

WMUA 91.1 FM, Amherst (413) 545-2876
Web site: www.-unix.oit.umass.edu/~wmua
Monday - Friday 2:30-5 pm and Sunday 4-6 pm

WBOS 92.9 FM, Boston (617) 931-1111
Holly Harris, Blues on Sunday 9 pm-12 midnight

WERS 88.9 FM, Boston (617) 868-9171
Bluesology, Monday - Friday 11pm-1 am

WHRB 95.3 FM, Cambridge (617) 495-4818
Sunday 7-11 am

WMBR 88.1 FM, Cambridge (617) 253-8810
Dave Herwaldt, Out of the Blue on Saturday 12-2 pm

WRSI 95.3 FM, Greenfield (413) 774-2321
Jukebox John Hayman, Roadhouse on Saturday 8:30 pm to Sunday 12:30 am
Diana Shonk, The Roadhouse on Saturday 6-8 pm

WJUL 91.5, Lowell (978) 459-0579
John Guregian with Blues Deluxe, Saturdays and Sundays 3-6 pm

WATD, 95.9 FM, Marshfield
Peter Black's Wide World of Blues Monday - Thursday, 10 pm-2 am
and Friday, 10 pm to 6 am Saturday

WMFO, 91.5 FM, Medford (617) 625-0800
Blu Guilford with Morning After Blues, Sunday 12-3 pm

WSMU, 91.1 FM, Dartmouth (508) 999-8149
Russ Hart and Bob Malkoski with Cafe Blues, Sunday 5-8 pm; John Smyth and
Russ Hart with Blue Monday, Monday 6-8 am and Gloria Clark with Blues
Electric, Thursday 12-2 pm

WOMR 92.1 FM, Provincetown (508) 487-2619
Contact Bob Seay
Mulligan Stew, Sunday 4-6 pm

WMWM 91.7 FM, Salem (978) 745-9170

Boston's Blues

Blues Hideaway, Saturday 9 am-noon; The Juke Joint, Sunday 12-3 pm

WMHC 91.5 FM, South Hadley (413) 538-2044
Jazz and Blues, Monday through Saturday 2-4 pm; Sunday 5-6:30 pm

WGBH 89.7 FM, Boston (617) 868-9171
e-mail: mai_cramer@wgbh.org
Mai Cramer with Blues After Hours, Friday and Saturday, 9 pm-1 am

WMVY 92.7 FM, Vineyard Haven (508) 693-5000
Rock Bergeron with Blues at Eight, Monday - Friday, 8 pm

WBRS 100.1 FM, Waltham (781) 736-5377
Greg Sarni with True Blues Monday - Thursday, 10 am-noon; call-in show, Wednesday, 10 am-noon.

WCUW 91.3 FM, Worcester (508) 753-2284
Andy Salek or Mike Warren and Friends, Friday 5-8 pm
Gerry McManus, Saturday 6-9 pm

WICN 90.5 FM, Worcester
Blue Monday with Norm Rosen, 8–11 pm

WZLX 100.7 FM, Boston (617) 931-1007
Sunday Morning Blues with Carter Allen, 9–11 am

New Hampshire

WKNH 91.3 FM, Keene
Diana Shonk with Bluestime, Thursdays 3-5 pm.

WUNH 91.3 FM, Durham (603) 862-2222
Bruce Pingree, Sunday 5-8 pm

WFRD 99.3 FM, Hanover (603) 646-3313
Contact Bill House

WNEC 91.7 FM, Henniker (603) 428-6369
Contact C.B. Roy

WPCR 91.7 FM, Plymouth (603) 535-2242
Contact Laurie Van Valkenburgh

WHEB 100.3 FM, Portsmouth (603) 436-7300
Blues Power Hour, Sunday 9:30-10:30 am

MNWV 93.5 FM, Conway (603) 447-5166
Blues Summit with Roy Prescott, Sunday 6-9 pm

Rhode Island

99.3 Swing FM "Backstage with the Blues" with James Montgomery, Saturday
10 pm
1540 WADK "Backstage with the Blues" with James Montgomery, Saturday 4
pm

WRIU, 90.3 FM, Kingston, at URI
Paul Mania, Dan Shramek and Mark Crook with Shades of Blue, Sunday 11 am -
2 pm

Vermont

WKVT 1490 AM, Brattleboro (802) 254- 2342
e-mail: skvt@together.net
Contact Peter Case

WIZN 106.7 FM, Burlington (802) 860-2440
Contact Charlie Frazier

WWPV 88.7 FM, Colchester (802) 654-2334
e-mail: wwpv@smcvt.edu
Contact John Grimes

WEQX 102.7 FM, Manchester (802) 362-4800
Web site: www.weqx.com
Contact Martin Butler

WVMX 101.7 FM, Stowe (802) 253-4877
e-mail: deanwvmx@aol.com
Contact Dean Burnell

Chapter 8:

regional and major blues festivals

2001 Regional and Major Blues Festivals
By Debbie Simas

March
30- April 1 Tampa Bay Bluesfest,Vinoy Park, St. Petersburg, FL. (727) 824-6163
Web: tampabaybluesfest.com.

April
20-21 Dogwood Blues Festival, Charlottesville, VA. (804) 296-8548 Web: cvilledowntown.org/blues.
27- May 6 New Orleans Jazz & Heritage Festival, Raceway Fairgrounds, New Orleans, LA. (800) 488-5252.
Web: insideneworleans.com/partners/nojazzfest.

May
11-13 Catalina Island Blues Festival, Catalina Island, CA. (888) 25-EVENT. Web: catalinablues.com
19-20 Chesapeake Bay Blues Festival, Sandy Point State Park, MD. TicketMaster (800) 551-SEAT
Web: bayblues.org.
24-26 W.C. Handy Blues Awards, Memphis, TN. (901) 527-2583. Web: handyawards.com.
26-28 Brandywine River Blues Festival, Chadds Ford, PA. (610) 388-6221.

June
1-3 Western Maryland Blues Fest, City Park, Hagerstown, MD. (301) 739-8577 Ext. 116. Web: blues-fest.org.
2-3 Crawfish Fest, Waterloo Concert Field, Stanhope, NJ. (973) 347-0900. Web: crawfishfest.com.
7 Hartford Blues Festival, Bushnell Park Hartford, CT. 6 –11 pm. Free. (800) 278-7427.
7-10 Chicago Blues Festival, Grant Park, Chicago, IL. Free. (312) 744-3315. Web: cityofchicago.org/specialevents.
8-10 The Great Connecticut Cajun/Zydeco Music & Art Festival, Sunrise Resort, Moodus, CT. (800) 225-9033 or
(860) 873-8681. Web: sunriseresort.com.
8-16 Chattanooga Riverbend Festival, Chattanooga, TN. (423) 265-4112. Web: riverbendfestival.com.
16-17 Clearwater Great Hudson River Festival, Croton Point Park, Poughkeepsie, NY.
(800) 67-SLOOP or (845) 454-7673. Web: clearwater.org/festival.

Boston's Blues

28-8 Montreal International Jazz Festival, Montreal, Canada. (800) 361-4595. Web: montrealjazzfest.com.

July

6-15 Ottawa Cisco Systems Bluesfest, LeBreton Flats, Ottawa, Canada. (613) 233-8798. Web: ottawa-bluesfest.ca.

14 Fleet Empire State Blues Festival, Empire State Plaza, Albany, NY, Free. (518) 473-0559. Web: ogs.state.ny.us/plaza/festivals.

14-15 North Atlantic Blues Festival, Rockland, ME. (207) 236-7660. Web: midcoast.com/~bluesman.

19-21 Lehigh Valley Blues & Jazz Festival, Whitehall, PA. (610) 261-2888. Web: lvbluesfest.com.

20-22 New York State Rhythm and Blues Festival, Syracuse, NY. (315) 469-1723. Web: nysbluesfest.com.

22 New Bedford Whaling Blues Festival, Fort Taber Park, New Bedford, MA. (508) 990-1425.

21 Bucks County Blues Society R&B Picnic, Morrisville, PA. (215) 946-4794.

27-29 Lowell Folk Festival, Lowell, MA. (978) 970-5000. Web: lowellfolkfestival.org.

29 Red Hot and Blues Chili Cook-Off, East Hartford, CT. (800) 423-4933.

August

3-5 The 25th Annual Maine Festival, Thomas Point Beach, Brunswick, ME. (207) 772-9012 or (800) 639-4212. Web: mainearts.org.

4 Onset Blues Festival, Onset Harbor, Onset, MA. (508) 295-7072.

4-5 Pocono Blues Festival, Blakeslee, PA. (800) 468-2442. Web: big2resorts.com/blues.

5 Blues in the Vineyard Festival at Mellea Winery, Dudley, MA. 1-4 p.m. (508) 943-5166.

10-12 Bayfront Blues Festival, Bayfront Festival Park, Duluth, MN. (715) 394-6831 Ext. 101. Web: bayfrontblues.com.

18 Portsmouth Blues Festival, Strabery Banke, Portsmouth, NH. (603) 929-0654.

17-18 Chenango Blues Festival, Norwich, NY. (607) 336-2787. Web: 208.12.108.120/bluesfest.

19 North River Blues Festival, Marshfield Fairgrounds, Marshfield, MA. (781) 834-6629. Web: marshfieldfair.com.

26 Green Habor Rhythm & Blues Festival, Marshfield Fairgrounds, Marshfield, MA. (781) 834-6629.

31- Sept. 2 Rhythm & Roots Festival, Ninigret Park, Charlestown, RI. (888) 855-6940. Web: rhythmandroots.com.

31- Sept. 2 Dusk til Dawn Blues Festival, Rentiesville, OK. (918) 473-2411. Web: dcminnerblues.com.

September
8-9 4th Annual New England Blues Society-Wachusett Mountain Blues Festival. Wachusett Mountain Ski Area, Route 140, Princeton, MA. (978) 464-2300. Web: wachusett.com

12-16 Harvest Jazz and Blues Festival, Fredericton, New Brunswick, Canada. (888) 622-5837.
Web: harvestjazzblues.nb.ca.

14-16 Blues 2000 and 1 Festival, Nevele Grande Resort, Ellenville, NY. (845) 985-9407. Web: blues2000.com.

22-23 San Francisco Blues Festival, Great Meadow and Fort Mason, San Francisco, CA. (415) 979-5588.
Web: sfblues.com.

23 Indian Summer Blues Festival, Indian Ranch, Route 16, Webster, MA. (508) 943-3871.
Web: indianranch.com.

29 White Mountain Jazz and Blues Festival, North Conway, NH. (603) 356-5701. Web: jazzblues.com.

29-30 Charles River Boston Blues Festival, Hatch Shell, Storrow Drive, Boston, MA. Free.
(888) 733-2678. Web: bluestrust.com.

October
4-6 King Biscuit Blues Festival, Helena, AR. (870) 338-8798. Web: kingbiscuitfest.org.

November
3 Sarasota Blues Festival, Sarasota, FL. (941) 377-3279. Web: sarasotabluesfest.com.

About the Author

Art Simas, 47, has been covering blues artists in New England for more than seven years. While some of his articles have appeared in national blues publications such as Blues Revue and Experience Hendrix magazines, his main work has been on the local level in documenting and promoting New England-based artists. He served as editor of the Boston Blues Society bimonthly and The Blues Audience monthly newsletters for three years, and is editor of the Blues Spectrum, the quarterly magazine of the New England Blues Society, which was formed in 1998.

A relative newcomer to the blues, it was the raw, emotive sounds spilling from the musty doorways in New Orleans that caught his attention in 1992 – and wouldn't let go. He had to find out more.

He is the Special Sections Editor for the Worcester Telegram & Gazette newspaper in Worcester, Mass. In previous jobs he was the editorial manager at an environmental consulting firm; production manager and senior copy editor for a monthly computer magazine; a political reporter for a daily newspaper; and sports editor of a weekly newspaper.

E-mail: docblues6@aol.com.

Printed in the United States
6779